THE ISLAMIC
REVIVAL SINCE 1988

THE ISLAMIC REVIVAL SINCE 1988

A Critical Survey and Bibliography

**YVONNE YAZBECK HADDAD
and JOHN L. ESPOSITO
with Elizabeth Hiel
and Hibba Abugideiri**

Bibliographies and Indexes in Religious Studies,
Number 45
G. E. Gorman, Advisory Editor

Greenwood Press
Westport, Connecticut • London

Library of Congress Cataloging-in-Publication Data

Haddad, Yvonne Yazbeck, 1935–
    The Islamic revival since 1988 : a critical survey and
bibliography / Yvonne Yazbeck Haddad and John L. Esposito with
Elizabeth Hiel and Hibba Abugideiri.
        p.   cm.—(Bibliographies and indexes in religious studies,
ISSN 0742–6836 ; no. 45)
    Includes bibliographical references and indexes.
    ISBN 0–313–30480–7 (alk. paper)
    1. Islam—20th century—Bibliography.   I. Esposito, John L.
II. Title.   III. Series.
Z7835.M6H24   1997
[BP60]
016.297′09′045—dc21   97–2733

British Library Cataloguing in Publication Data is available.

Library of Congress Catalog Card Number: 97–2733
ISBN: 0–313–30480–7
ISSN: 0742–6836

First published in 1997

Greenwood Press, 88 Post Road West, Westport, CT 06881
An imprint of Greenwood Publishing Group, Inc.

Printed in the United States of America

The paper used in this book complies with the
Permanent Paper Standard issued by the National
Information Standards Organization (Z39.48–1984).

10 9 8 7 6 5 4 3 2 1

Contents

Foreword

Today the Muslim world population is estimated to have reached almost one billion, one fifth of humanity. Islam occupies the centre of the world. It stretches like a broad belt across the globe from the Atlantic to the Pacific, encircling both the "haves" of the consumer North and the "have-nots" of the disadvantaged South. It sits at the crossroads. . . .

-Gerhard Böwering

The power and vitality of contemporary Islamic revivalism is rooted in a broad-based phenomenon, the reassertion of Islam in Muslim personal and political life. While Islam remained a wide-spread presence in Muslims societies, in recent years it has proven to be a dynamic and vital socio-political force in Muslim societies.

-John L. Esposito

The Foreword to the first volume of *The Contemporary Islamic Revival: A Critical Survey and Bibliography* was written as we observed with fascination the Muslim world's reaction to Salman Rushdic and *The Satanic Verses*. Now, six or seven years later, we read of continuing success by the *Taliban* in Afghanistan, of political destablization fostered by *al-Gamaa al-Islamiya* in Egypt, of a devastating fire in Mecca during the annual *Haj*, of gender imbalance in Muslim families. While none of these may be as spectacular or, to Western eyes, as bizarre as the Rushdie incident, they all serve to remind us that Islam is growing, and doing so rapidly however we measure this: simple numbers of followers, strength of belief, social influence, political impact, economic power.

Accompanying this growing influence has been a gradual movement within Islam from the periphery to the centre; whereas a decade ago we commonly equated the Islamic revival with extremism in one form or other, today we are much more aware that this revival is ". . .a broad-based religio-social movement, part of mainstream Muslim society."[1] Of course the radical fringe elements persist, but these have become less influential as an institutionalized Islam takes hold in many societies.

While many commentators have highlighted this institutionalization, one must never forget that we are dealing with many varieties of Islam, and with different perceptions among Muslims. In many Islamic countries, for example, there is a significant rift between the apparent secularism of the entrepreneurial and professional Muslim elite and the generally traditional worldview of the masses. Equally, in some countries the political elites seem to hold power as if by divine right and with little reference to their Muslim heritage, whereas their ruling counterparts in other countries regularly rely on Islamic rhetoric and traditional Islamic views to mobilize the masses by presenting a somewhat mythic view of the Islamic resurgence and threats to the faith from nonbelievers.

These common trends combined with individual manifestations within Islam are characterized by John Renard as "unity within diversity." He makes the telling point that the continuum between Islamization and indigenization has resulted in culturally contextualized varieties of Islam that are both similar to and different from one another (he cites the example of Morocco and Indonesia).[2] That is, while Islam interacts uniquely with each cultural matrix in which it finds itself, there remains an underlying cohesiveness and identity that allows Muslims around the world to recognize themselves as members of the same faith.

Thus we remain aware that the Islamic world has a strong sense of unity arising from its common heritage -- a heritage overriding economic, political, social and ethnic differences. While other religions in the semitic tradition also share this trait of solidarity, there is a uniquely Muslim call to rebel against the existing order when it departs from the salvific norms established by Allah and articulated by the Prophet. When one's salvation is at risk because of an imperfect social order, traditional Islamic teaching maintains that religious ideology and military power must combine to overthrow imperfection and recreate a more ideal religious state. Beneath the surface, then, there remains something of a reforming zeal in Islam, and it is perhaps this that makes it such an intriguing religio-political phenomenon.

---

[1] John L. Esposito, "The Threat of Islam: Myth or Reality?" *Concilium* 3 (1994): 41.

[2] John Renard, "Islam, The One and the Many: Unity and Diversity in a Global Tradition," *Concilium* 3 (1994): 31-38.

Islam and its resurgence are thus complex topics, and it is perhaps this complexity that has been attracting scholars in recent years. Certainly the production of high quality scholarly literature has continued unabated since the appearance in 1991 of *The Contemporary Islamic Revival: A Critical Survey and Bibliography*. In view of this factor, and the success enjoyed by that compilation, my colleagues at Greenwood Press were very pleased when Professors Haddad (Georgetown University) and Esposito (Georgetown University) suggested a supplementary edition of their guide, devoted specifically to the period 1989-1994. Their intention in this new compilation is to present an annotated record of recent scholarship on Islam as an aid to further study. In this regard they, and their associates, have proven themselves once again to be assiduous and meticulous researchers, collecting, evaluating and annotating more than 1200 new items.

My perception of present-day Islam, and of the literature about it, is that it affects us most profoundly in two respects: as a focal point for diverse political movements, and as a way of life with significant impact on the world's social fabric. Like Darrow and a host of other commentators, one recognizes that ". . .it is in terms of Islam and/or in Islamic terms that political and social issues are addressed by most inhabitants of the contemporary Islamic world. Islam is a major component of the framework in which these issues are discussed. This is because Islam has always addressed all aspects of a believer's life. . . ."[3] These political and social foci are reflected in the bibliography, which is replete with references to the scholarly literature on democracy, elections, education, welfare, gender issues, law -- indeed, all aspects of Islam that have exercised the minds of scholars both Eastern and Western.

Yvonne Haddad, John Esposito and their associates present in *The Islamic Revival Since 1988: A Critical Survey and Bibliography* a valuable complement to their earlier work. Their two volumes form a comprehensive scholarly guide to the literature on Islam's revival in the last two-and-a-half decades. It provides a wide range of specialists - Islamicists, social scientists, scholars of religion and political studies, philosophers and historians - with a valuable compendium that will serve as the major resource on late twentieth century Islam for some time. Beyond doubt the themes and issues recorded here will continue to evolve in the coming years, and *The Islamic Revival Since 1988: A Critical Survey and Bibliography* will help us understand this evolution. If, as Böwering suggests, "Islam is. . .at the crossroads, destined to play a world role in politics and to become the most prominent world religion in the next century," then the insights afforded by this volume and its

---

[3] William R. Darrow, "Marxism and Religion: Islam." In *Movements and Issues in World Religions. A Sourcebook and Analysis of Developments since 1945: Religion, Ideology and Politics*, eds. Charles Wei-bsun Fu and Gerhard E. Spiegler (Westport, CT: Greenwood Press, 1987), p. 394.

predecessor will be invaluable.[4] Therefore, we are pleased to include this work in Bibliographies and Indexes in Religious Studies, and hope that we may have the pleasure of a further update on Islam's continuing revival in the near future.

Dr. G. E. Gorman
Advisory Editor
Charles Sturt University–Riverina
July 1997

---

[4] Gerhard Böwering, "Christianity -- Challenged by Islam," *Concilium* 3 (1994): 114.

Preface

The need to provide an update to the bibliography on Islamic resurgence became evident even as *The Contemporary Islamic Revival: A Critical Survey and Bibliography*[1] went to press. During the five years since its publication, coverage of Islamic revivalism, in particular political Islam or Islamic fundamentalism, has proliferated at a remarkable rate. This reflects both its continued religious and political relevance as well as its marketability.

As is to be expected, there are many new studies that reflect the changing contexts in Muslim societies and in relations between the Muslim world and the West. The landscape of the Muslim world has witnessed the emergence of new Islamic republics in Iran and Sudan, and the consolidation of power by Islamist groups in Afghanistan (in addition to Saudi Arabia's self-described Islamic state and the Islamic Republic of Pakistan). At the same time, the fall of the Soviet Union resulted in the emergence of Central Asian Muslim republics. Despite a continued emphasis on the Middle East and on Iran in particular, North Africa (especially Algeria), Sudan, the Central Asian republics, and Turkey have received greater attention.

The post-Cold War and post-Gulf War periods have witnessed a sharper focus and debate in the literature on several topics (political liberalization and democratization, the Arab-Israeli peace process, the clash of civilizations or Islamic threat, and Islam in the West) as well as continued strong interest in many others, in particular gender issues and women in Muslim societies.

---

[1] Yvonne Yazbeck Haddad, John Obert Voll and John L. Esposito (with Kathleen Moore and David Sawan) *The Contemporary Islamic Revival: A Critical Survey and Bibliography* (New York: Greenwood Press, 1991).

While there remains a propensity to focus on Islamic radicalism, recent scholarship has increasingly demonstrated the diversity of the contemporary Muslim experience and of political Islam both in terms of government implementation of Islam and the nature of Islamic movements. If analyses of Islamic movements in the 1980s focussed primarily on Iran and its export of revolutionary Islam as well as the activities of clandestine radical groups, in the 1990s one finds a significant increase of coverage of the "quiet revolution," the emergence of Islam as a major political and social force within the institutions of society. From Egypt to Indonesia, Islamic activists have become part of mainstream society not just its radical periphery. They are major actors in the development of religiously inspired and oriented social and political organizations, institutions, and parties from educational institutions and social welfare agencies to Islamic banks and publishing houses, from political parties to parliamentarians and prime ministers.

Islamic social and political movements have mobilized diverse and disparate sectors of society in response to the political, economic, and sociocultural failures of regimes and/or their discredited nationalist and socialist policies. In countries like Egypt and Algeria, the presence and effectiveness of Islamist social services have often been seen as an implicit, if not explicit, critique of the inability of the state to deliver adequate social services. The critique has been exacerbated by issues of high unemployment, poverty, maldistribution of wealth, and corruption.

However, the most contentious development in the late 1980s and early 1990s was the electoral performance of Islamist candidates and parties. Economic failures at the end of the '80s and the international democratization wave that accompanied the fall of the Soviet Union and liberation of Eastern Europe brought elections in many Muslim countries and a lively debate over issues of political participation, democracy, and civil society. If many governments in the Muslim world and the West in the 1980s had believed that Islamists were an unrepresentative minority that would be defeated in elections, such elections in Tunisia, Egypt, Jordan, Algeria, and subsequently in Turkey, Yemen, and Kuwait revealed the strength of political Islam. Tunisia's Islamic Tendency Movement (later renamed Hizb al-Nahda or Renaissance Party), and the Muslim Brotherhoods of Egypt and Jordan emerged as the leading opposition blocks in their respective parliaments. In Jordan, Islamists not only won 32 of 80 seats but held five cabinet portfolios as well as that of Speaker of the assembly.

Algeria, however, sent shock waves throughout the region and the world. Having swept municipal elections, the Islamic Salvation Front then subsequently swept the first round of parliamentary elections and seemed poised to do the same in the second round and thus to come to power through the electoral system. The visage of Islamists coming to power through ballots rather than bullets and its potential catalytic effect on other countries became a matter of grave concern. The Algerian military intervened, seized power in the name of preventing the hijacking of democracy, raising the question, "Who hijacked democracy?" The ability of Turkey's Refah (Welfare) Party to sweep municipal elections and subsequently elect Turkey's first Islamist Prime Minister has contributed to the issue of Islam's relationship, particularly that of Islamic organizations, to democracy.

The emergence of political Islam as a force in mainstream society and its relationship to electoral politics has generated a substantial number of case studies of individual countries (Egypt, Tunisia, Algeria, Yemen, Kuwait, Pakistan, Jordan) as well as broader regional and thematic analyses, addressing such questions as: Are Islam and democracy compatible?; Are Islamists, who participate in electoral politics, prepared to play by the rules of the game? What is the relationship of Islam to civil society? As a result a host of studies have appeared ranging from analyses of the relationship of Islamic sources (the Qur'an, traditions of the Prophet, law) to democracy to the writings of contemporary Muslim intellectuals and activists.

The literature on Islam and democracy reflects a lively debate. Muslim authors are deeply divided, ranging from secularists and accommodationists to rejectionists. At issue is the nature of religion, the relationship of divine sovereignty to popular sovereignty, revelation and reason, tradition and change. While some Muslim intellectuals argue the inherent secular democratic need to separate religion from politics, others have engaged in a wide-ranging process to formulate legitimate "authentic," indigenous, Islamically acceptable forms of democratization. Traditional concepts and institutions of consultation (shura), community consensus (ijma), and reinterpretation (ijtihad) to support parliamentary forms of government. At the same time, other Muslims argue that modern notions of democracy are antithetical to Islamic belief and tradition. These "rejectionists" represent diverse constituencies ranging from King Fahd of Saudi Arabia to radical revolutionary Islamic organizations and governments.

The question of whether Islam and democracy are compatible or incompatible is often linked by some to the peace process, support for Israel, and to Western access to oil. Thus, academic or intellectual discussions are often tied to foreign policy issues regarding the promotion of self determination and democratization in the Middle East. Despite broad support for the American-brokered Palestinian-Israeli peace process, there is a vocal and at times militant minority (in the Arab world as in Israel) both secular and religious, who are vehemently opposed to it. Strong Islamic activist opposition may be found both within Palestine and the broader Muslim world. HAMAS (the Palestinian Islamist movement) and Islamic Jihad have been both vocal and militant. Many Islamic movements outside the territories have been persistent in their rejection of what they regard as a process of pacification rather than an equitable solution. Many of the new studies reflect the diversity and conflicts that surround the peace process from significant publications on HAMAS and Islamic Jihad to the nature and tactics of Islamist responses in the broader Muslim world as well as authors who argue whether the promotion of democracy in the Middle East will undermine the peace process, threaten the stability of Arab governments and Israel, and thus endanger Western access to oil.

While some studies still continue to portray political Islam or "Islamic fundamentalism" as a monolithic, non-democratic threat to both Muslim societies and to the West, others argue the need to see Islamist groups in their diversity and to judge them individually. The former emphasize the experiences of Iran and Sudan, often identified as "rogue" or terrorist states, while the latter look more globally at Islamist participation in electoral politics. What continues to stand out on this issue as well as on all coverage of contemporary Islamic revivalism is its Middle East orientation. Indeed, the extent to which Iran continues to dominate perceptions of the Middle East and Islamic activism is reflected in the sheer number of studies that focus on Iran's domestic and foreign policy. Although coverage is global, studies of African and Asian experiences still remain underrepresented, reflecting the geostrategic orientation of interest in and coverage of political Islam.

The relationship of Islam to democracy, the peace process, and the West has often crystallized around particular themes such as the clash of civilizations or Islamic threat. The tendency of some to look for a post Cold war global ideological and political threat and to identify a potential clash between Islamic and Western civilization has been exacerbated by the specter of a political Islam that might come to power through ballots not just bullets, through electoral politics not just violent revolution or guerilla warfare. Thus, we find a significant increase in articles which deal with issues of Islam and modernity, Islam and change, Islam and pluralism, Islam and human rights. Some place the discussion within the broader context of the relationship of Islam and the West raising the question of whether Islam is a political, cultural, and demographic threat. The awareness that Islam is now the second or third largest religion in Europe and America and events like the World Trade Center bombing have generated concerns about the export of Islamic radicalism to the West and also politicized the assimilation or integration of Muslims in Europe and America. In recent years, there has been a significant proliferation of studies of Islam in the West or the Muslims of the West. Issues of assimilation, integration and multiculturalism have become more prominent in countries like Britain, France, and the United States.

While gender and Islam have received significant coverage for some time, the growth of literature in this genre reflects the continued relevance of the topic as well as an increase in the number of interested scholars. Studies reflect both common themes and concerns counterbalanced by a diversity of experiences and issues. There is a noticeable increase in case studies that demonstrate the religious and cultural diversity of the Muslim world and its differing impact on the status and roles of women. Prominent themes or issues are the impact of "fundamentalism" and the implementation of Islamic law on women, women in Islamic law, family law, Islamic dress and the veiling (hijab), gender and national identity, legal and educational reforms, feminism, employment, violence and rape. Among the most prominent case studies of the effect of Islamization on women are those of Iran, Algeria, Sudan, Pakistan, and Egypt.

In 1997, the realities of the Muslim world and of global politics continue to indicate the ongoing significance of Islam in Muslim politics and society. Many governments continue to struggle with issues of legitimacy, authoritarianism, stability, and security in a world of shrinking economic resources. While some governments appeal to Islam, others contend with oppositional politics (legitimate and illegitimate) conducted in the name of religion. While a "crackdown" against Islamists has proven effective in some contexts, in others it has led to further radicalization and violence and to a polarization in society in which the majority are caught between the actions and vested interests of a minority, whether it be that of governing elites or Islamists. Western countries remain conflicted over how to respond to Islam in power or Islamists in electoral politics. If many Muslim countries waged successful wars of national independence, they now face a second battle over cultural identity. The burgeoning Muslim minority populations of the world face new issues of faith and identity.

At the dawn of the twenty-first century, Islam and Muslim communities are part and parcel of a global religious resurgence, one that will influence many political and social debates for decades to come.

This bibliography is designed to provide a useful reference tool on contemporary Islamic revival published in English between 1989 and 1994. It concentrates on academic studies rather than the popular press which can be located through other databases. All the entries have been annotated in order to facilitate locating important information on the variety of topics discussed.

Most of the entries are classified according to geographical areas with subdivisions for specific countries where appropriate, determined in large part by the availability of relevant literature on the topic. The general outline of the material follows that of the earlier volume. A new section on democracy was added since it has become the center of discourse and has generated a significant corpus of literature on the subject. Subsections on the revivalist movements in North Africa, Sudan, the Gulf States, Jordan and Palestine were included reflecting the growth in scholarship production on those nations.

The compilation and annotation of the bibliography has been done primarily by Elizabeth Hiel and Hibba Abugideiri under the supervision of the editors. Many of the authors whose work has been cited helped in locating information about their publications. Funding for the project was provided by the Center for Muslim Christian Understanding at Georgetown University. For all these contributions we express our appreciation and thanks.

Abbreviations

AA	*African Affairs*
AR	*African Report*
AFS	*African Studies*
AAA	*American Arab Affairs*
AE	*American Ethnologist*
AJCL	*American Journal of Comparative Law*
AJISS	*American Journal of Islamic Social Sciences*
AJIS	*American Journal of Islamic Studies*
APSR	*American Political Science Review*
AAAPSS	*Annals of the American Academy of Political and Social Sciences*
ALQ	*Arab Law Quarterly*
ASJ	*Arab Studies Journal*
ASQ	*Arab Studies Quarterly*
ArOr	*Archiv Orientalni*
AAS	*Asian and African Studies*
AS	*Asian Survey*
AM	*The Atlantic Monthly*
AWA	*Australia and World Affairs*
BJMES	*British Journal of Middle East Studies*
BJFA	*Brown Journal of Foreign Affairs*
BSOAS	*Bulletin School of Oriental and African Studies*
Com	*Commentary*
CR	*Contemporary Review*
CSA	*Contemporary Southeast Asia*

CT	*Contention*
C	*Critique*
CH	*Current History*
DA	*Daedalus*
DWDS	*Die Welt Des Islam*
DR	*The Drama Review*
E	*Ethos*
EJS	*European Journal of Sociology*
FI	*Feminist Issues*
FR	*Feminist Review*
FS	*Feminist Studies*
FFWA	*Fletchu Forum of World Affairs*
FA	*Foreign Affairs*
FP	*Foreign Policy*
GO	*Government and Opposition*
HI	*Hamdard Islamicus*
HT	*History Today*
IM	*The India Magazine*
INQ	*India Quarterly*
IJ	*International Journal*
IJICI	*International Journal of Intelligence and Counter-Intelligence*
IJIAS	*International Journal of Islamic and Arab Studies*
IJMES	*International Journal of Middle East Studies*
IJSL	*International Journal of the Sociology of Law*
IPSR	*International Political Science Review*
InS	*International Spectator*
IJIA	*Iranian Journal of International Affairs*
IrSt	*Iranian Studies*
ICMR	*Islam and Christian Muslim Relations*
IMA	*Islam and the Modern Age*
IC	*Islamic Culture*
IP	*Islamic Perspectives*
IQ	*Islamic Quarterly*
IS	*Islamic Studies*
JIMEE	*Japanese Institute of Middle Eastern Economies*
JQ	*Jerusalem Quarterly*
JAA	*Journal of Arab Affairs*
JAAS	*Journal of Asian and African Studies*
JAS	*Journal of Asian Studies*
JCCP	*Journal of Commonwealth and Comparative Politics*
JCFS	*Journal of Comparative Family Studies*
JCA	*Journal of Contemporary Asia*

JOD	*Journal of Democracy*
JDA	*Journal of Developing Areas*
Journal IKIM	*Journal IKIM*
JIMMA	*Journal Institute of Muslim Minority Affairs*
JIA	*Journal of International Affairs*
JIS	*Journal of Islamic Studies*
JPHS	*Journal of the Pakistan Historical Society*
JPS	*Journal of Palestine Studies*
JRA	*Journal of Religion in Africa*
JSAM	*Journal of South Asian and Middle Eastern Studies*
MQ	*Mediterranean Quarterly*
MEAJ	*Middle East Affairs Journal*
MEI	*Middle East Insight*
MEJ	*Middle East Journal*
MEP	*Middle East Policy*
MEQ	*Middle East Quarterly*
MES	*Middle East Studies*
MESAB	*Middle East Studies Association Bulletin*
MS	*Midstream*
MR	*Monthly Review*
MW	*Muslim World*
NR	*National Review*
Orbis	*Orbis*
Orient	*Orient*
PA	*Pacific Affairs*
PDR	*Pakistan Development Review*
PIJ	*Palestine-Israel Journal*
PM	*Peuples Méditerráneens*
POC	*Problems of Communism*
RC	*Race and Class*
ROAPE	*Review of African Political Economy*
RA	*Reviews in Anthropology*
SAIS	*SAIS Review*
S	*Signs*
SC	*Social Compass*
SF	*Sociological Forum*
SAB	*South Asia Bulletin*
SS	*Strategic Studies*
SCT	*Studies in Conflict and Terrorism*
TWQ	*Third World Quarterly*
UR	*Utne Reader*
Views	*Views*

WQ	*Washington Quarterly*
W&P	*Women and Politics*
WD	*World Development*
WPJ	*World Policy Journal*
WT	*The World Today*

THE BIBLIOGRAPHY

I. GENERAL STUDIES

A. Interpretive Studies

0001 "Eric Rouleau Talks About the Peace Process and Political Islam." *JPS* 22, no. 4 (June 1993): 45-61.

The *Journal of Palestine Studies* interviews Eric Rouleau, former chief Middle East editorialist for *Le Monde*, former French Ambassador to Tunisia and Turkey, and French President Mitterand's special envoy and advisor on the Middle East. He discusses his views and opinions on the Middle East peace process and Islamic groups in Algeria, West Bank, Gaza Strip, and Turkey.

0002 ABRAHAM, A. J. and GEORGE HADDAD. *The Warriors of God and Jihad (Holy War) and the Fundamentalists of Islam.* Bristol, IN: Wyndham Hall Press, 1990.

Seeks to better define the term Islamic fundamentalism and the concept of *jihad* (holy war) in Islam to demonstrate that not all Muslims are "fanatics." Seven chapters look at various interpretations and different aspects of holy war including its doctrine, the rules concerning the spoils of war, and the treatment of non-Muslim subjects.

0003 ABUKHALIL, AS'AD. "The Incoherence of Islamic Fundamentalism: Arab Islamic Thought at the End of the 20th Century." *MEJ* 48, no. 4 (1994): 677-694.

Drawing upon Arabic sources, this article offers a critique of the Islamic fundamentalist movement. The work examines various fundamentalist concepts and asserts that "Islamic fundamentalist programs--if one can call them that--suffer from ambiguity."

0004   ABULJOBAIN, AHMAD. "Has the West Replaced 'Commun' with Islam as the New 'ism' ?" *MEAJ* 1, no. 1 (June 1992): 37-44.
Describes the misperceptions that the Western media often portrays about Islamic movements.

0005   _____. "Media Polemics and Islamism." *ASJ* 1, no. 2 (September 1993): 10-14.
Examines the misconceptions of Islamism among some Western media organizations that has led to Islamic activists being unfairly demonized.

0006   _____. *Radical Islamic Terrorism or Political Islam?* Annandale, VA: United Association for Studies and Research, 1993.
The author argues that the Islamic religion has been vilified in the Western media. To elucidate his point, the author cites excerpts from both written and broadcast media in the period following the 1993 World Trade Center bombing.

0007   _____. "The Western Pen: A Sword in Disguise?" *The Politics of Islamic Resurgence: Through Western Eyes*, 8-21. Eds. Ahmed Bin Yousef, and Ahmad AbulJobain. Springfield, VA: United Association for Studies and Research, Inc., 1992.
Examines the motives of the Western media and intelligentsia who write about Islam and the Islamic revival.

0008   ABU-RABI, IBRAHIM M. "Discourse, Power and Ideology in Modern Islamic Revivalist Thought: The Case of Sayyid Qutb." *IC* 65, no. 2-3 (April 1991): 84-102.
Examines various aspects of Sayyid Qutb's thought within the context of Egyptian society and polity, concluding with an assessment of his impact on modern Islamic thought.

0009   _____. "Is Liberalism in the Muslim Middle East Viable? A Critical Essay on Leonard Binder's *Islamic Liberalism: A Critique of Development Ideologies.*" *HI* 12, no. 4 (December 1989): 15-30.
Offers a critique of Leonard Binder's book presenting Islamic Liberalism as a viable philosophy that the Muslim world should adopt.

0010   _____, ed. *Islamic Resurgence: Challenges, Directions and Future Perspectives: A Round Table with Khurshid Ahmad*, Tampa, Florida: The World and Islam Studies Enterprise, 1994.
This edited volume is the proceedings of a conference at the University of South Florida in 1993 entitled the "Round Table with Professor Khurshid Ahmad." Through conversations and debate between American scholars and the Muslim thinker Khurshid Ahmad, the pertinent issues raised by the modern

Islamic revival are highlighted. The first chapter offers an article that includes information about the life and economic theories of Khurshid Ahmad. The second chapter is a record of the opening remarks of the conference. The third chapter, written by Dr. Ahmad, provides his views on Islamic revivalism. Chapters four, five, and six are general discussions between Dr. Ahmad and other participants about the following topics; "Islamic Conception of Economic Development and Modernization," "Islamic Movements," and "Muslim Minorities in the Western World." The final chapter offers concluding remarks by Dr. John Voll.

0011 _____. "Reflections on the Islamic Renaissance in the Modern Arab World: Some Methodological Questions." *IC* 63, no. 3 (July 1989): 42-59.
Addresses the subject of the renaissance in modern Arab/Islamic thought with particular focus on Egypt.

0012 _____. "Secularization, Islam, and the Future of the Arab World: A Derivative Discourse!" *PM* 60 (1992): 177-191.
Explores the role that the Arab intelligentsia has played in reaching a rapproachment between the Islamic tradition and the needs of contemporary society.

0013 EL AFFENDI, ABDELWAHAB. *Who Needs an Islamic State?* London: Grey Seal Books, 1991.
Divided into five small chapters and a conclusion, this work explores the issue of how Muslims should govern themselves. The first chapter attempts to identify the problem and compares the idea of the nation-state from Ibn Khaldun to Karl Marx with modern Islamic discourse on an Islamic state. The second chapter provides an overview of the notion of political authority in the Islamic tradition. The third chapter deals with the contemporary discourse on the Islamic state. This section touches on the ideas of Mustapha Kemal, 'Ali 'Abd al-Raziq and his opponents, Hasan al-Banna, Abul A'la al-Mawdudi and aspects of the Iranian Revolution. The next section deals with the reasons behind Western fears of the rise of Islamic militancy and the rights of non-Muslims in an Islamic state. The fifth chapter offers suggestions to rethink Islamic political activism and appeals for freedom and dignity for all Muslims. The conclusion summarizes the author's vision of an Islamic state.

0014 AHADY, ANWAR-UL-HAQ. "The Decline of Islamic Fundamentalism." *JAAS* 27, no. 3-4 (July 1992): 229-243.
This article argues that since the mid-1980's, Islamic fundamentalism has either declined or stagnated. The author examines elections in the 1970s and 1980s in Indonesia, Malaysia, Pakistan, and Turkey and surveys Muslim students to illustrate this decline.

0015   AHMAD, KHURSHID. "Islam and the New World Order." *MEAJ* 1, no. 3 (March 1993): 2-13.
Examines Islamic resurgence and the new world order as defined by Western foreign policy makers.

0016   _____. "Islamic Resurgence: Challenges, Directions, and Future Prospects." *Islamic Resurgence: Challenges, Directions and Future Perspectives: A Round Table with Khurshid Ahmad*, 49-65. Ed. Ibrahim M. Abu-Rabi'. Tampa, Florida: The World and Islam Studies Enterprise, 1994.
A reproduced speech delivered at the University of South Florida in 1993 entitled the "Round Table with Professor Khurshid Ahmad." Provides insight into how a Muslim scholar perceives Islamic revivalism.

0017   AHMED, AKBAR S. "Islam: The Roots of Misperception." *HT* 41 (April 1991): 29-37.
This article promotes the theory that the study of Islam and misconceptions about it are embedded in previous historical encounters between the West and the Muslim world.

0018   _____. *Postmodernism and Islam: Predicament and Promise.* London: Routledge, 1992.
Provides insight into why East and West are different and how we can understand each other. Also helps the reader to comprehend Islam and Muslims in contemporary society.

0019   _____. "Postmodernist Perceptions of Islam: Observing the Observer." *AS* 31, no. 3 (March 1991): 213-231.
This article seeks to study different variables that shape postmodernist perceptions of Islam. The author's methodology consists of using over 120 reviews and comments of his book *Discovering Islam: Making Sense of Muslim History and Society* as a way to define intellectual responses.

0020   _____. "A Third Encounter of the Close Kind." *HT* 39 (November 1989): 4-9.
This commentary looks at Western misperceptions of Muslims through a historical survey of two previous encounters between Islamic and Western civilizations--from the rise of Islam, the Crusades, and the expansion of the Ottoman empire to the gates of Vienna and the subsequent era of Western colonialism.

0021   AHSAN, M. M. "Human Rights in Islam: Personal Dimensions." *HI* 13, no. 3 (1990): 3-14.
Asserts that the Qur'an offers a complete blueprint for human rights.

0022 AHSAN, M. M. and A. R. KIDAWI, eds. *Sacrilege Versus Civility: Muslim Perspectives on the Satanic Verses*, U.K.: The Islamic Foundation, 1993.

An enlarged second edition of the 1991 work which seeks to provide the Muslim perspective of the Salman Rushdie affair. Divided into five chapters, the first contains selections from *Satanic Versus*, a survey of the Muslim response to the Iranian edict against Rushdie, and the author's conversion to Islam. Chapter two offers selections of Rushdie's thought on the creation of *Satanic Verses*. Chapters three and four contain excerpts from Western articles and are entitled "In Defence of Sacrilege," and "Voices of Civility." Chapter five offers the wide ranging Muslim perspective to Rushdie's work. Appended to this work are several documents and an annotated bibliography of this affair.

0023 AJAMI, FOUAD. "The Summoning." *FA* (September 1993): 2-9.

A critique of Samuel Huntington's essay, "The Clash of Civilizations." Citing examples from the contemporary Middle East, the author argues that Huntington's theory is flawed and that civilizations are not as cohesive as Huntington portrays them to be.

0024 AKHAVI, SHAHROUGH. "The Clergy's Concept of Rule in Egypt and Iran." *AAAPSS* 524 (November 1992): 92-102.

This article focuses on the contemporary cycle of Islamic resurgence and the question of rule by examining Islamic writers in Iran and Egypt. The author finds that the writers have various interpretations on the subjects of the role of secular leaders, *jihad*, rebellion, and the power of the *ulama*. However, all the clerics agree that Islam is both religion and politics and that the *shari'ah* must be applied in both public and private matters.

0025 _____. "Sayyid Qutb: The 'Poverty of Philosophy' and the Vindication of Islamic Tradition." *Cultural Transitions in the Middle East*, 130-152. Ed. Serif Mardin. Leiden: E.J. Brill, 1994.

Through a critique of Sayyid Qutb's work, this chapter asserts that Sayyid Qutb utilizes Western discourse in his writings "to champion Islamic tradition."

0026 AL 'ALWANI, TAHA JABIR. "Toward an Islamic Alternative in Thought and Knowledge." *AJISS* 6, no. 1 (1989): 1-12.

Begins with a brief overview of the current state of Islamic thought and knowledge as well as educational and cultural systems in the Muslim world. Seeks to outline an Islamic alternative for the contemporary Islamic community.

0027 ALI, SHAUKAT. *Islam and Politics: A Short Essay and Comprehensive Bibliography*. Lahore, Pakistan: Aziz Publishers, 1990.

This essay briefly highlights some of the characteristics of the Islamic revival and provides a short analysis of its impact upon Muslim states and international relations. This work also contains a bibliographical reference on the Islamic revival.

0028   AMIN, SAYED HASSAN. *Islamic Law and Its Implications for the Modern World*. Worcester, Great Britain: Billing & Sons Ltd, 1989.

This work examines the new stage of development in Islamic law due to the rise in popularity of Islamic movements and the implications for the present-day on a regional and international level. The book, divided into six sections, explores different aspects of Islamic law in the Muslim world. Part one contains two chapters, the first looks at constitutional law and offers Sunni and Shi'i as well as Zaidi, Isma'ili, Ibadi, Druze, and 'Alawi interpretations. The second chapter deals with crime, punishment, and human rights in Islam and looks at human rights in Syria, the Gulf States, Turkey, and Iraq. This chapter also examines Islamic environmental law. Part two explores private law and offers chapters on family law and Islamic financing and banking. Part three explores the basic principles of Islamic international law. Part four attempts to categorize the legal systems of Muslim countries according to their doctrinal and theological basis as well as their political and economic policies. Part five offers a comparative analysis of Islamic and common law. Part six is the author's conclusions which provide a discussion of what is necessary to create an Islamic federation among Muslim states.

0029   AMUZEGAR, JAHANGIR. "The Truth and Illusion of Islamic Fundamentalism." *SAIS* 13, no. 2 (June 1993): 127-139.

The author argues that both the alarmist view of Islamic fundamentalism as a threat and the view that it is compatible with democracy and Western interests are simplistic. Asserts that the U.S. must recognize Islam's diversity and craft its policy accordingly.

0030   ANDERSON, NORMAN. *Islam in the Modern World*. Leicester, England: Apollos, 1990.

Seeking to enhance mutual understanding between Muslims and Christians, this work by an Islamic scholar explores various aspects of modern-day Islam. The first four chapters examine Islamic theology and law, mysticism, and fundamentalism in their modern manifestations. The material is placed alongside Christian ideology.

0031   ANSARI, A. A. "Iqbal, Islam and the West." *IC* 65, no. 2-3 (1991): 1-14.

Explores Mohammad Iqbal's contradictory relationship with the West and shows how his experience with the West influenced his ideology.

0032 ANSARI, ABDUL HAQ. "Islamic Ethics: Concept and Prospect." *AJISS* 6, no. 1 (1989): 81-91.

Outlines the issues, explores the problems, and attempts to define the concept of Islamic ethics.

0033 ANVAR, IRAJ and PETER J. CHELKOWSKI. *God Is Beautiful and He Loves Beauty*, 111-129. Eds. Alma Giese, and J. Christoph Bürgel. Bern: Peter Lang, 1992.

Beginning with a brief description of an Iranian *ta'ziyeh* play entitled "Moses and the Wandering Dervish" a prologue to the main play such as the *Martyrdom of Imam Hussein*, this article offers an English translation of the Persian text as performed at a Trinity College drama festival in Hartford, CT.

0034 ARJOMAND, SAID AMIR. "The Emergence of Islamic Political Ideologies." *The Changing Face of Religion*, 109-123. Eds. James A. Beckford, and Thomas Luckmann. Sage Publications, 1989.

Explores the interaction between religion and politics and focuses on the development of Islamic political ideologies defined as "a total unified socio-political system and a total way of life based on the full unity of doctrine and practice."

0035 ARKOUN, MOHAMMED. "The Concept of Authority in Islamic Thought: *La hukma illa lillah*." *The Islamic World: From Classical to Modern Times*, 31-54. Eds. C. E. Bosworth, Charles Issawi, Roger Savory, and A.L.Udovitch. Princeton, NJ: The Darwin Press, Inc., 1989.

Asserting that the Orientalist and traditional or revolutionary Islamic approaches to understanding the concept of authority in Islamic thought are inadequate, this chapter seeks to provide an alternative critique. The article argues that what is needed is fresh intellectual articulations to fully understand Islamic authority.

0036 _____. *Rethinking Islam: Common Questions, Uncommon Answers*. Boulder, CO: Westview Press, 1994.

Written by an Algerian Islamic scholar, this work provides the author's response to twenty-four basic questions about Islam. For example, "Can one speak of a specific understanding of Islam in the West or must one rather talk about the Western way of imagining Islam?" "What do the words 'Muslim' and 'Islam' mean." "Are there dogmas in Islam? If so, what are they?" "What is the status of women according to the Qur'an and according to the wider tradition as interpreted by various orthodoxies." The questions and answers, geared toward the beginning student of Islam, illustrate the author's perspective of how Islam must be rethought if Muslims are to reconcile with themselves and with the outside world.

0037   AL-AWA, MOHAMMAD SALIM. "Political Pluralism: An Islamic Perspective." *Power-Sharing Islam?*, 65-76. Ed. Azzam Tamimi. London: Liberty for Muslim World Publications, 1993.

Provides an Islamic view of political pluralism that the author contends is a necessity in an Islamic society.

0038   AYUBI, NAZIH N. *Political Islam: Religion and Politics in the Arab World.* London: Routledge, 1991.

Applying a deconstructionist approach, *Political Islam* examines the theory that Islam is by nature a political religion. The author contends, in an overview of early Islamic history that original Islamic sources such as the Qur'an and Hadith contain very little information about the specific form of government that an Islamic state should take. Thus Ayubi asserts that "political Islam is a new invention - it does not represent a 'going back' to any situation that existed in the past or to any theory that was formulated in the past."' (p. 3) Though an analysis of the utopian reconstruction of the past and historical reality, he ascertains that it was the state which appropriated Islam and not the reverse. He then moves on to explore the "variety of modern Islam,"' which is followed by an examination of Islamic movements in Egypt, Syria, Jordan, Saudi Arabia, Sudan and Tunisia. In addition, the author offers information on the intellectual sources and socio-economic bases of political Islam, Islamic banks, companies and services. The work concludes with a chapter on Islamic liberals and the future of political Islam.

0039   _____. "State Islam and Communal Plurality." *AAAPSS* 524 (November 1992): 79-91.

Looks at the historical role of Sunni Islam in an Islamic state and its relations with sects and non-Muslim groups. It examines the distinctions between Sunni and Shi'i political thought. Concludes by looking at the prospects for the territorial state since the author believes that the modern state ignores the perennial problems of minorities and sects.

0040   AL-AZM, SADIK J. "The Importance of Being Earnest About Salman Rushdie." *DWDI* 31, no. 1 (1991): 1-49.

Through a comparison of some of the statements made by Rabelais, Voltaire, and Joyce in their time to that of Salman Rushdie, this article provides a defense of the work *Satanic Verses*.

0041   AL AZMEH, AZIZ. *Islams and Modernities*. London and New York: Verso, 1993.

This work is a compilation of previously published articles contending that there are many different forms of Islam. Chapters deal with various strains of Islamic revivalism and the relationship between Islamic fundamentalism and other ideologies such as enlightenment universalism and Arab nationalism.

0042 AZZAM, MAHA. "Islamist Attitudes to the Current World Order." *ICMR* 4, no. 2 (1993): 247-256.

Explores Islamic movements' perceptions of various issues including democracy, economic division, and the perceived threat from the West.

0043 BABEAIR, ABDULWAHAB SALEH. "Contemporary Islamic Revivalism: A Movement or Moment?" *JAA* 9, no. 2 (September 1990): 122-46.

Asserting that there are two strains of Islamic revivalism--one positive and the other negative--he critiques both of them.

0044 _____. "Intellectual Currents in Contemporary Islam." *MW* 81, no. 3-4 (1991): 231-244.

This article examines four intellectual currents in contemporary Islam: orientalism, traditionalism, modernism, and Islamic revivalism. The author investigates the impact of the first three currents upon the last.

0045 _____. "The Role of the 'Ulama' in Modern Islamic Society: An Historical Perspective." *IQ* 37, no. 2 (1993): 80-94.

Examines how the modernists and neo-fundamentalists view the role of the ulama in the Muslim world.

0046 BADR, GAMAL. "The Middle East Peace Process: An Islamic Perspective." *AAA* 30 (September 1989): 81-83.

Written by a legal advisor to the State of Qatar's Mission to the United Nations, this article argues that Islam is a peaceful religion and can co-exist peacefully with Christianity and Judaism.

0047 BARAKAT, HALIM. "Religion in Society." *The Arab World: Society, Culture, and State*, 119-147. Berkeley: University of California Press, 1993.

From a sociological perspective, this chapter contends that an understanding of society is necessary before one can understand religion in the Middle East. The author examines the social beginnings of religion; the relationship between popular and official Islam; the differences between religion and sects; and the various functions of religion--"as mechanisms of control, instigation, and reconciliation."

0048 BARAZANGI, NIMAT HAFEZ. "Arab Muslim Identity Transmission: Parents and Youth." *ASQ* 11, no. 2&3 (March 1989): 65-82.

Using a small group of Arab-Muslim children aged 14-22 and their parents as a case study, this article seeks to discover how these people view their religion and how these beliefs impinge on their practice.

0049   BILL, JAMES A. "Populist Islam and US Foreign Policy." *SAIS* 9, no. 1
(December 1989): 125-139.
Reviewing the contents of "populist Islam" and the movement's broad
characteristics, the author contends that the U.S. has to try to understand
Islam's relationship to societies and politics. Argues that the U.S. had to make
more balanced approaches to the Iran-Iraq war and the Palestinian-Israeli
conflict.

0050   BIN YOUSEF, AHMED. "Islamists and the West: From Confrontation to
Cooperation." *The Politics of Islamic Resurgence: Through Western Eyes*,
22-44. Eds. Ahmed Bin Yousef, and Ahmad AbulJobain. Springfield, VA:
United Association for Studies and Research, Inc., 1992.
Through an examination of Western perceptions of Islam and the Islamic
revival, this article seeks to provide a methodological approach to further this
study.

0051   BOULARES, HABIB. *Islam: The Fear and the Hope*. London and Atlantic
Highlands, NJ: Zed Books, 1990.
Written by a former Tunisian Minister of Culture, this work concerning the
political, social and intellectual history of Islam, attempts to provide insights
into the world of Islam. The writer seeks to challenge common stereotypes of
Islam, often emanating from the West, in addition to offering advice on how to
adapt Islam to modernity. He provides a list of the political and social factors
which facilitated the rise of Islamic activism. The author is critical of Islamists
such as Abu al-A'la al-Mawdudi, Sayyid Qutb and the Ayatollah Khomeini
because he believes that they place too much emphasis on the role of the ulama
in Muslim societies. Taking a liberal-humanist approach, he asserts that the
reductive learning methods of the ulama is not conducive to the strengthening
of Islamic societies and bringing Muslims into the modern age. The best way
for Muslims to attain this goal is to free themselves from old traditions and
customs and adopt the universal aspects of Islam which he believes are
advocated by the peaceful Islamic mainstream.

0052   BOWEN, JOHN R. "On Scriptural Essentialism and Ritual Variation: Muslim
Sacrifice in Sumatra and Morocco." *AE* 19, no. 4 (1992): 656-671.
A comparative analysis of the way in which Sumatran Muslims and
Moroccan Muslims observe the Feast of Sacrifice.

0053   BUTTERWORTH, CHARLES. "Political Islam: The Origins." *AAAPSS* 524
(November 1992): 26-37.
Inquires why Islamists favor non-democratic and non-liberal political rule
found in revelation-based politics. Begins with a historical overview of key
Islamic figures from the Prophet Muhammad to twentieth century thinkers. The

author asserts that contemporary thinkers continue to call for non-democratic politics and his conclusion questions the views of Western analyses and critiques of political Islam.

0054 CHOUDHURY, MASUDUL ALAM. "A Critique of Modernist Synthesis in Islamic Thought: Special Reference to Political Economy." *AJISS* 7, no. 4 (1994): 475-503.
Analyzes the influence of the modernist methodology found today in much of Islamic thought.

0055 _____. "Islamic Futures After the Desert Storm." *HI* 14, no. 4 (December 1991): 5-21.
Evaluates theories applied to the problems facing the Muslim community as well as future Islamic options in light of the consequences of the Gulf war.

0056 _____. "Muslims, Islam and the West Today." *HI* 17, no. 1 (March 1994): 19-34.
Depicts the reality of the confrontation between Islam and the West in modern times.

0057 CHOUEIRI, YOUSSEF M. *Islamic Fundamentalism*. Boston, MA: Twayne Publishers, 1990.
A scholarly historical analysis on the topic of Islamic activism which is identified as a socio-political reaction to the forces of change. Revivalism, reformism and radicalism are identified as the three basic ideologically reactionary political movements. The author writes that revivalism emerged in the 18th and 19th centuries among tribally organized political groups. It was followed by reformism which arose in the mid-19th century among the urban educated middle class. Radicalism, he asserts, arose in the 20th century among the great socio-political changes such as the breakup of the Ottoman empire and the rise of Western political, social and economic encroachment. In order to understand the world view of the radicals, the author analyzes the writings of Sayyid Qutb and Abu al-'A'la al-Mawdudi as the intellectual basis of Islamic radical thought. The Iranian revolution is analyzed as a case study to determine the social bases of the radicals' appeal.

0058 DECTER, MOSHE. "Arab Rage, Islamic Fury and the Culture of Violence." *MS* 36, no. 8 (1990): 4-7.
Asserts that the 'rage' of the Arab nation is rooted in the religion of Islam which the author states "was a militant faith of military conquest."

0059 DUNN, MICHAEL COLLINS. "Islamic Activists in the West: A New Issue Produces Backlash." *MEP* 3, no. 1 (1994): 137-145.

Addresses the impact of Islamic activism displayed by Muslims living in the West. Assesses various situations in the United States, France, Germany and Britain.

0060   EHSAN, MANSOOR. "Nationalism, Islamic Revival and the Need for a New Political Discourse in the Middle East: A Response for Hisham Sharabi." *CT* 2, no. 1 (1992): 139-147.

A response to Hisham Sharabi's article entitled "Modernity and Islamic Revival: The Critical Task of Arab Intellectuals." Through an examination of the current political ideologies of Arab nationalism and Islamic fundamentalism, this essay advocates the need to create a new political discourse in the Middle East.

0061   EICKELMAN, DALE F. "Mass Higher Education and the Religious Imagination in Contemporary Arab Societies." *AE* 19, no. 4 (November 1992): 643-655.

This essay examines the interplay between mass higher education and religious activism in the Arab Muslim world, particularly in Oman and North Africa as well as the implications of the "objectification" of religious imagination that may be encouraged by modern education.

0062   EICKELMAN, DALE F. and JAMES PISCATORI, eds. *Muslim Travellers: Pilgrimage, Migration and the Religious Immigration,* Berkeley: The University of California Press, 1990.

This edited volume focuses on travel in different Muslim countries from early Islamic times to the present and looks at the role that religion plays in motivating travel. Demonstrates that other forms of travel, aside from pilgrimage, such as migration, visits to shrines, and travel as a learning experience all add to the religious experience of Muslims. The contributors examine the significance of various forms of travel on the local and transnational level. Describes how these travels increase a Muslim's awareness of "being Muslim."

0063   EICKELMAN, DALE F. and JAMES PISCATORI. "Social Theory in the Study of Muslim Societies." *Muslim Travellers: Pilgrimage, Migration and the Religious Imagination,* 1-28. Ed. Dale F. Eickelman, and James Piscatori. London; Berkeley and Los Angeles: Routledge; The University of California Press, 1990.

Lays out the social theory the author's employ in their study of Muslim religious traditions and Muslim incentives to travel.

0064   EILTS, HERMANN FREDRICK. "Islamic Fundamentalism: A Quest for a New Order." *MQ* 1, no. 4 (September 1990): 27-36.

Former U.S. Ambassador to Egypt and Saudi Arabia writes about the primary characteristics of Islamic fundamentalism as well as the misperceptions of Americans about political Islam.

0065 ELGINDY, KHALED. "Sovereignty and Natural Law in Islamic Constitutional Theory: A Contemporary Analysis." *ASJ* 1, no. 2 (September 1993): 22-25.
Examines the debate over the source of authority and sovereignty among contemporary Islamic theorists.

0066 ELHAQ ALI, HASSAN. "The New World Order and the Islamic World." *AJISS* 8, no. 3 (December 1991): 461-472.
Looks at premises of the "new world order," to discern to what extent it may reflect interests of the "South" in general and Islam in particular as well as the implication for these regions. Argues that economic and social issues are of concern to the South but the North controls the new global agenda.

0067 ENDE, WERNER. "Sunni Polemical Writings on the Shi'a and the Iranian Revolution." *The Iranian Revolution and the Muslim World*, 219-232. Ed. David Menashri. Boulder, CO: Westview Press, 1990.
Examines the main religious issues between the Sunnis and Shi'a in the contemporary era and how these issues have been dealt with by Sunni polemicists recently.

0068 ENGINEER, ASGHAR ALI. "Religion, Ideology and Liberation Theology--An Islamic Point of View." *IP* 5 (1989): 134-148.
Looks at how Muslim societies can be transformed to create a socially just society.

0069 ESPOSITO, JOHN L. "The Gulf War, Islamic Movements and the New World Order." *IJIA* (March 1991):
Discusses the impact of the Gulf war on the Islamic movements as well as their place in the "new world order."

0070 _____. *Islam and Politics*. Syracuse, NY: Syracuse University Press, 1991.
The third and revised edition of the study of the relationship between Islam and politics begins with a historical perspective of the role that religion has played in the early Islamic era. The primary focus of this work is on the contemporary Islamic revival. Drawing upon examples of country case studies from Pakistan to Sudan, the work addresses issues such as modernity, Islamic law, women's rights, non-Muslim minority rights, nationalism, Islamization, and education.

0071 _____. *The Islamic Threat: Myth or Reality?* New York: Oxford University Press, 1992.

This work addresses Western misperceptions of Islam and contends that a monolithic view of Islam and Muslims by the West and of 'the West' by Muslims only hampers our understanding of each other. Divided into six chapters, the first chapter examines the dynamics of the Islamic revival. Chapter two looks at the evolution of the conflict between the West and Islam. The third chapter explores the impact of Western colonialism on Muslim society. Chapter four looks at the interplay between Islam and the state. The fifth chapter surveys the various Islamic organizations and the final chapter assesses Western perceptions of Islam and Islamic revivalism.

0072 _____. "Political Islam and U.S. Foreign Policy." *BJFA* (December 1993): 63-82.

Examines whether Islam and the West are bound to collide and offers perspectives on what U.S. foreign policy should be toward political Islam. Also looks at issues of political liberalization and democratization in the Muslim world.

0073 _____. "Political Islam: Beyond the Green Menace." *CH* 93, no. 579 (January 1994): 19-24.

A challenge of the widely-held theory that political Islam is a threat to the West. The author describes the great diversity of Islamic movements and asserts that treating Islam and Islamic movements as a monolithic whole may have detrimental effects on U.S. policy.

0074 _____. "Revival and Reform in Contemporary Islam." *Fundamentalism in the Modern World*, 31-46. Ed. William M. Shea. Lanham, MD: University Press of America, 1989.

Originally presented to the annual convention of the College Theology Society in 1989, this article explores the factors which led to the development of an Islamic revival and recent manifestations in the Middle East.

0075 _____. "The Study of Islam: Challenges and Prospects. Presidential Address." *MESAB* 24, no. 1 (July 1990): 1-11.

This article addresses the scholarly inadequacies of the study of Islam, particularly the political dimension of Islam.

0076 _____ "Trailblazers of the Islamic Resurgence." *The Contemporary Islamic Revival*, 37-56. Ed. Yvonne Yazbeck Haddad, John Obert Voll, John L. Esposito, Kathleen Moore, and David Sawan. New York: Greenwood Press, 1991.

Traces the Islamists and Islamic movements of the Islamic revival and illustrates their diversity.

0077 ESPOSITO, JOHN L. and JOHN OBERT VOLL. "Khurshid Ahmad: Muslim Activist-Economist." *MW* 80, no. 1 (January 1990): 24-36.
Explores the life of Khurshid Ahmad, a prominent figure in contemporary Islamic revivalism, his relationship with the Jama'at-i-Islami, and his theories of Islamic economics.

0078 FAKSH, MAHMUD A. "The Prospects of Islamic Fundamentalism in the Post-Gulf War Period." *IJ* 49, no. 2 (1994): 183-218.
Explores the fate of Islamic movements given the wide range of responses of different states to the rise of these movements.

0079 FANDY, MAMOUN. "Tribe Vs. Islam." *MEP* 3, no. 2 (1994): 40-51.
This article demonstrates through the results of the Jordanian and Yemeni elections how tribal loyalties supersede Islamic ideology. The second portion assesses the importance of the tribe in the Middle East and its impact on the democratic process in light of Islamic resurgence.

0080 FARHAN, ISHAQ. "Islamization of the Discipline of Education." *AJISS* 6, no. 2 (1989): 307-318.
Discusses some of the major weaknesses of the Western educational system and argues the need for Islamization of education.

0081 FISCHER, MICHAEL M. J. and MEHDI ABEDI. *Debating Muslims: Cultural Dialogues in Postmodernity and Tradition.* Madison: University of Wisconsin Press, 1990.
A collection of seven essays by two anthropologists about Islam in general and Shi'ism in particular using recent scholarship on Islamic societies. In order to bring verbal articulations of Muslims to the reader, the authors have drawn on insights from feminism, post-structuralism, Marxism, and post-modernism to deconstruct stereotypical Orientalist ideas. In the essays the anthropologists acquaint the reader with Islamic argumentation, an intercultural dialogue between Shi'ism, Baha'ism and Zoroastrianism, the varying traditions of Qur'anic exegesis, and the contemporary Islamist ideology of Khomeini and his followers. In addition the work seeks to locate Shi'ism territorially to allow the readers to hear the voices of those who are politically marginalized in Iran and the United States.

0082 GAFFNEY, PATRICK D. "Popular Islam." *AAAPSS* 524 (November 1992): 38-51.

Traces the roots of popular Islam and points out that in the past Sufism paralleled the clerical elite. The author states that overall structures of popular Islam have survived the changes of the last two centuries and concludes that popular Islam persists to this day but has taken two directions: one towards the elite leadership and the other towards the masses.

0083   GANNOUCHI, RACHID. "Islam and the West: Realities and Potentialities." *ThePolitics of Islamic Resurgence: Through Western Eyes*, 45-54. Eds. Ahmed Bin Yousef, and Ahmad AbulJobain. Springfield, VA: United Association for Studies and Research, Inc., 1992.

Written by the Islamist leader of the Tunisian Islamic movement, this article evaluates the relationship between Islam and the West.

0084   GHANNOUCHI, RASHID. "The Participation of Islamists in a Non-Islamic Government." *Power-Sharing Islam?*, 51-63. Ed. Azzam Tamimi. London: Liberty for Muslim World Publications, 1993.

Participation in a non-Islamic government is justified. The author contends that it is not the Muslim community but the regimes in power that need convincing to join in the political order.

0085   GELLNER, ERNEST. "Marxism and Islam: Failure and Success." *Power-Sharing Islam?*, 33-42. Ed. Azzam Tamimi. London: Liberty for Muslim World Publications, 1993.

Through a sociological analysis, this chapter examines the failure of Marxism in the twentieth century and compares this to the variables that have contributed to the survival of Islamic revivalism.

0086   GOBEL, KARL-HEINRICH. "Imamate." *Expectations of the Millennium: Shi'ism in History*, 3-6. Eds. Seyyed Hossein Nasr, Hamid Dabashi, and Seyyed Vali Reza Nasr. Albany, NY: State University of New York Press, 1989.

Author interprets the Shi'i thinker Muhammad Mughniyah's work on the Imamate in which he draws important distinctions between Sunni and Shi'i theories.

0087   GODDARD, HUGH. "Some Reflections on Christian and Islamic Political Thought." *ICMR* 1, no. 1 (1990): 25-43.

Disagrees with the assertion that Christianity is only interested in spiritual matters, while Islam is interested in both the political and religious. Concludes that Christianity is concerned with politics and that the Islamic religion considers the state to be a religious institution.

0088   HADAR, LEON T. "What Green Peril?" *FA* 72, no. 2 (March 1993): 27-42.

Debates the theory that Islam is a threat to the West.

0089　HADDAD, YVONNE YAZBECK. "Muhammad Abduh: Pioneer of Islamic Reform." *Pioneers of Islamic Revival*, 30-63. Ed. Ali Rahnema. London: Zed Press, 1994.

Through an examination of the Islamic modernist Muhammad Abduh's political vision, this chapter examines his ideology, the political circumstances that shaped it, and his legacy for the Islamic world.

0090　_____. "The Authority of the Past: Current Paradigms for an Islamic Future." *The Authority of the Past*. Ed. Tony Siebers. Ann Arbor: Institute for the Humanities, University of Michigan, 1993.

Assesses the way in which the cherishing of the past was adopted as a means of preserving Islam from deviance, innovation, and error and the way it has played a unique role in justifying change. The paper also deals with issues of westernization, secularization, the role of Israel, intellectual crisis, authenticity, and renewal.

0091　_____. "Islamists and the 'Problem of Israel': The 1967 Awakening." *MEJ* 46, no. 2 (March 1992): 266-285.

Drawing upon Islamist literature, this article analyzes the Islamist response to the 1967 war. Illustrates how Islamic revivalism grew out of the policies of the U.S. and Israel following the defeat of the Arabs.

0092　_____. "The 'New Enemy'? Islam and Islamists After the Cold War." *Altered States: A Reader in the New World Order*, 83-94. Eds. Phyllis Bennis, and Michel Moushabeck. New York: Olive Branch Press, 1993.

Surveys the Islamist understanding of the 'new world order' as they see it imposed upon the Middle East.

0093　_____. "Operation Desert Shield/Desert Storm: The Islamist Perspective." *Beyond the Storm: A Gulf Crisis Reader*, 248-260. Ed. Phillys Bennis. New York: Interlink Books, 1991.

Provides the Islamist perspective on the causes behind Operation Desert Shield/Storm and the destruction that ensued.

0094　_____. "Presidential Address 1990 'Middle East Area Studies: Current Concern and Future Directions.'" *MEAB* 25, no. 1 (September 1991): 1-14.

Urges those who study the Middle East and Islam to ensure that current happenings are placed in their proper historical context and notes the importance of the role that Islam plays in the Middle East.

0095 _____. "The Revivalist Literature and the Literature on Revival: An Introduction." *The Contemporary Islamic Revival*, 3-22. Ed. Yvonne Yazbeck Haddad, John Obert Voll, John L. Esposito, Kathleen Moore, and David Sawan. New York: Greenwood Press, 1991.

Discusses the Islamic revivalist literature to show how Muslims perceive themselves, their society, and relations with the West. Also analyzes the trends found in the Western writings on the Islamic revival.

0096 HADDAD, BASSAM SA. "Islamic Liberals and Secularism." *ASJ* 1, no. 2 (September 1993): 26-31.

Recounts some of the arguments concerning the relationship between Islam and politics made by Islamic liberals in the Arab world in general and Egypt in particular.

0097 HAMDANI, ABBAS. "Islamic Fundamentalism." *MQ* 41, no. 4 (September 1993): 38-47.

This article poses the argument that Islamic fundamentalism is not a monolithic whole and points to misconceptions about Muslim fundamentalism.

0098 HAYNES, JEFF. "The Political Resurgence of Islam in the Third World." *Religion in Third World Politics*, 64-94. Ed. Boulder, CO: Lynne Rienner Publishers, 1994.

Explores how the Islamic card is played in different ways by both opposition groups and the regimes of the Muslim world.

0099 HELMS, CHRISTINE M. *Arabism and Islam: Stateless Nations and Nationless States*. Washington, D.C.: The Institute for National Strategic Studies, 1990.

Provides insight into the often conflicting relationship between Islamic activism and Arabism. Illustrates why both are so popular in the Arab world.

0100 AL HILLI, ALLAMAH. "Jihad." *Expectations of the Millennium: Shi'ism in History*, 61-64. Eds. Sayyed Hossein Nasr, Hamid Dabashi, and Seyyed Vali Reza Nasr. Albany, NY: State University of New York Press, 1989.

A discussion of the classical Shi'i concept of jihad in a social and legal context.

0101 HIRO, DILIP. *Holy Wars: The Rise of Islamic Fundamentalism*. New York: Routledge, 1989.

Examines different aspects of Islamic fundamentalism, which the author uses as a term for those who have defined and adhere to the fundamental principles of their religious belief system. The work gives an overview of the Prophet's life, his role as the messenger, military commander, administrator and judge, and the divisions which occurred in the Islamic community following his death. The book then moves on to discuss orthodox Islam, Sufism and Islam in the modern era. He presents six case studies of Islamic fundamentalism in Egypt, Afghanistan, Syria, Libya, Saudi Arabia and Iran. The work ends with a conclusion which summarizes the book and adds an epilogue about conditions in Egypt, Iran and Afghanistan.

0102 HOFMANN, MURAD. *Islam: The Alternative*. Reading, England: Garnet Publishing, 1993.

Written by a former German diplomat who converted to Islam, this work covers a multitude of topics to provide Europeans with a greater understanding of the issues concerning Islam. Chapters discuss topics such as Islam's view of Christianity, Islamic fundamentalism, the Islamic political system, Islamic economics, human rights, and legal issues.

0103 HOROWITZ, DONALD L. "The Qur'an and the Common Law: Islamic Law Reform and the Theory of Legal Change (Part 2)." *AJCL* 42, no. 3 (June 1994): 543-580.

Second in a two-part series, this study weighs the impact of common law methods on the process of re-formulating old Islamic legal statutes and in the formation of new laws. Argues for "legal acculturation" in which two legal norms are merged together without losing the identity of either side.

0104 H.R.H. THE PRINCE OF WALES. "Islam and the West." *ALQ* 9, no. 2 (1994): 135-143.

A reproduction of a speech delivered at the Oxford Centre for Islamic Studies. This article discusses the relationship between the West and the Islamic world. The author argues for a better understanding of each other to improve the often strained relations.

0105 HUNTINGTON, SAMUEL P. "The Clash of Civilizations." *FA* 72, no. 3 (June 1993): 22-49.

In this widely publicized article, the author argues that new sources of international conflicts will be cultural, particularly along the Western-Muslim "fault line." Argues that the U.S. should forge alliances with similar cultures and spread its values wherever possible. States that the U.S. should be accommodating if possible and confrontational if necessary with "alien civilizations."

0106 HUSSAIN, SHOWKAT SHEIKH. "Status of Non-Muslims in an Islamic State." *HI* 16, no. 1 (March 1993): 67-79.

Assesses what the legal status of non-Muslims might be in an Islamic state.

0107 HUSTED, WAYNE R. "Karbala' Made Immediate: The Martyr as Model in Imami Shi'ism." *MW* 83, no. 3-4 (July 1993): 263-278.

Examines various categories of martyrs in *jihad*. The article asserts that Imam Husayn in the battle of Karbala is the archetype of martyrs. The essay assesses the types of 'enumerated martyrs' and the role the city of Karbala plays in Shi'a Islam.

0108 IMAM, YAHYA OYEWOLE. "Heredity Succession in Islamic Polity." *IQ* 37, no. 2 (1993): 143-155.

A discussion of the principles of heredity succession and its effect on the Islamic polity. The author gives examples from the Sokoto Caliphate to assert his claim that heredity succession is not an Islamic principle but was introduced from outside.

0109 ISRAELI, RAPHAEL. *Fundamentalist Islam and Israel: Essay in Interpretation.* Lanham, New York and London: University Press of America, 1993.

This volume is a collection of essays and lectures previously published or delivered. They were written under the auspices of the Harry S. Truman Research Institute for the Advancement of Peace. Divided into three parts, the first focuses on the nature of Islamic fundamentalism in general as well as its political and socio-economic impact on the countries of the Middle East. The second section deals with Muslim attitudes toward Jews, Israelis, and Zionism and includes the Charter of Hamas as translated, annotated and interpreted by the author. The third part provides brief case studies of the experience of Muslim minorities in China, Israel, Cyprus and Sweden. The work ends with a postscript of the implications of Islamic revivalism for Israel and the West.

0110 ABD AL-JABBAR, FALIH. "The Gulf War and Ideology: The Double-edged Sword of Islam." *The Gulf War and the New World Order*, 211-218. Eds. Haim Bresheeth, and Nira Yuval-Davis. London and Atlantic Highlands, New Jersey: Zed Books Ltd., 1991.

Points out that the Gulf war has brought to the fore a new kind of popular Muslim fundamentalism that is more closely associated with Arab nationalism than Iranian or Saudi Islamism. Far from a pan-Arab movement, this new fundamentalism is characterized by a variety of Islamism, of the kind adopted by Saddam Hussein during the period leading up to the war.

0111 JANSEN, JOHANNES J. G. "Hasan al-Banna's Earliest Pamphlet." *DWDI* 32, no. 2 (1992): 254-258.

Provides an analysis of the importance of a pamphlet published in 1929 which the author contends may be one of the first activities of the Muslim Brotherhood.

0112   JAWAD, HAIFAA. "Pan-Islamism in the Middle East: Prospects and Future." *IQ* 37, no. 3 (1993): 207-222.

    Traces the evolution of the pan-Islamic ideology in the Middle East in order to gain better insight into contemporary happenings. Also examines the successes and failures of the movement and implications for the Middle East region.

0113   KAMALI, MOHAMMAD HASHIM. "Freedom of Expression in Islam: An Analysis of *Fitnah*." *AJISS* 10, no. 2 (1993): 178-200.

    Based on previously unconsolidated material from the Shari'ah, this article explains the concept of sedition and its impact on the freedom of expression for Muslims.

0114   _____. "Fundamental Rights of the Individual: An Analysis of Haqq (Right) in Islamic Law." *AJISS* 10, no. 3 (September 1993): 340-366.

    Seeks to define the term *haqq* (right) in Islamic law. Asserts that Islamic law seems to place less emphasis on rights and more on obligations.

0115   _____. "Shari'a and the Challenge of Modernity." *Journal IKIM* 2, no. 1 (January 1994): 1-24.

    The author examines complex issues such as the importance of the *Shari'ah* as a religious law and the extent to which Islamic law should be adapted for modern society.

0116   _____. "Siyasah Shar'iyah or the Policies of Islamic Government." *AJISS* 6, no. 1 (1989): 59-80.

    Analysis of the delineation of the legitimate and non-legitimate uses of power in the *shari'ah*.

0117   _____. "Source of Nature and Objectives of Shari'ah." *IQ* 33, no. 4 (1989): 215-235.

    Through a detailed analysis of Islamic law, the author argues that *ijtihad* must continue at all times in order to keep abreast of worldly change.

0118   KAPLAN, LAWRENCE ed. *Fundamentalism in Comparative Perspective*. Amherst: The University of Massachusetts Press, 1992.

    This collection of essays examines the interplay of religion and politics on an international level. Articles which cover Islamic political activism include Emmanuel Sivan's article about civil society and Islamic revivalism, Valentine Moghadam's chapter concerning the impact of Islamic fundamentalism on women in Afghanistan and Ervand Abrahamian's essay on the Ayatollah Khomeini. Martin E. Marty also brings a comparative approach to the question of how one analyzes fundamentalists and fundamentalisms on a global level.

0119 KARAMAN, M. LUTFULLAH. "Aspects of a Framework for Inter-national Law and Relations in Islam: Some Notes From a Theoretical and Historical Perspective." *JPHS* 42, no. 1 (January 1994): 67-91.
Develops a theory of Islamic international law dealing with such issues as equality, mutual assistance, freedom, justice, peace and tolerance. The author focuses on the Muslim law of war and treaties.

0120 KARAWAN, IBRAHIM A. "Reislamization Movement According to Kepel: On Striking Back and Striking Out." *CT* 2, no. 1 (1992): 161-179.
A response to Giles Kepels article entitled "God Strikes Back!: Reislamization Movements in Contemporary History." Contends that in order to understand the phenomenon of Islamic revivalism a new conceptual framework is needed.

0121 KARBAL, MOHAMED. "Western Scholarship and Islamic Resurgence in the Arab World." *AJISS* 10, no. 1 (1993): 49-59.
Provides an analytical critique of Western scholarship's approach to Islamic revival in the Arab world.

0122 KATTANI, SULAYMAN. "Ruler and Society." *Expectations of the Millennium: Shi'ism in History*, 82-91. Eds. Seyyed Hossein Nasr, Hamid Dabashi, and Seyyed Vali Reza Nasr. Albany, NY: State University of New York Press, 1989.
An interpretation of Ali's view of leadership and the relation between ruler and ruled.

0123 KEANE, JOHN. "Power-Sharing Islam?" *Power-Sharing Islam?*, 15-31. Ed. Azzam Tamimi. London: Liberty for Muslim World Publications, 1993.
Discusses the misperceptions about Islam by the West and contends that they have led to an often hostile relationship between the two. Also notes that the lack of flexibility displayed by some Islamists hinders critical debate within the Islamic community.

0124 KEDDIE, NIKKI R. "Sayyid Jamal al-Din al-Afghani." *Pioneers of Islamic Revival*, 11-29. Ed. Ali Rahnema. London: Zed Press, 1994.
This chapter first provides a biography of the Islamic modernist Jamal al-Din al-Afghani and then assesses the influence of al-Afghani's teachings on the Islamic revivalist movement.

0125 KELSAY, JOHN. "Islam and Distinction between Combatants and Noncombatants." *Cross, Crescent, and Sword: The Justification and*

Limitation of War in Western and Islamic Tradition, 197-220. Eds. Turner James Johnson, and John Kelsay. Westport, CT: Greenwood Press, 1990.

Draws upon classical Sunni perspectives of combat to define a just or non-just war.

0126 KELSAY, JOHN and JAMES TURNER JOHNSON, eds. *Just War and Jihad: Historical Perspectives and Theoretical Perspectives on War and Peace in Western and Islamic Traditions.* New York: Greenwood Press, 1991.

This edited volume of essays provides a comprehensive analysis of Islamic and Christian perspectives on morality, law, and war. Based on historical and theoretical analyses, the authors examine differing ideologies on these topics. Commenting on Islamic tradition, the authors point out that previous studies on this issue have neglected the influence of Muslim religion and culture.

0127 KEPEL, GILLES. "God Strikes Back! Reislamization Movements in Contemporary History." *CT* 2, no. 1 (1992): 150-160.

Examines the factors that led to the rise of Islamic movements in the Muslim world.

0128 KEPEL, GILLES. *The Revenge of God: The Resurgence of Islam, Christianity and Judaism in the Modern World.* University Park, PA: Pennsylvania State University Press, 1994.

An analysis of the contemporary resurgence of commitment to religious faith in Judaism, Christianity (both Catholic and Protestant in Europe and the United States) and Islam. Kepel argues that the resurgence is a reaction to the failure of modernity to provide comfort which has turned adherents to their respective sacred scriptures to find relevance and meaning. Their quest for guidance for personal living and political life is modern which makes it appealing to those who are unhappy with secular society.

0129 KHALIDI, TARIF. "Religion and Citizenship in Islam." *Religion and Citizenship in the Arab World and Europe*, 25-30. Ed. Jorgen S. Nielsen. England: Grey Seal Books, 1992.

Explores the concept of the division, or lack thereof, of religion and state in Islam.

0130 KHURI, FUAD. *Imams and Emirs: State, Religion and Sects in Islam.* London: Saqi Books, 1990.

A comparative study of Islamic sects in the Arab world and an examination of the relations between sects and the state. The book focuses on the Sunni, Shi'a, Druze, 'Alawis, Yazidis, 'Ibadis, Zaidis, and the Maronites. The author explores the sovereignty of the sects over their religious communities despite state control over the law and public order. Divided into three sections, the first section examines the history, structure, and dogma of various sects in an attempt to differentiate sects from religious minorities. In the second section, the author explores the principle of sovereignty among the various sects and explains why allegiance to the sects is stronger than allegiance to the state. The author contends that while Sunni ideology is adapted to the sovereignty of the state, the ideology of sects is adapted to the sovereignty of the community. The last section examines the organization of sects and looks at the source of authority of both the ulama and sultans.

0131   KIMBALL, CHARLES A. *Religion, Politics, and Oil: The Volatile Mix in the Middle East*. Nashville, TN: Abingdon Press, 1992.

Written primarily for the Christian churches in the West to create a framework of better understanding, this work seeks to explain the interrelatedness of religion, politics, and oil in the Middle East following the Gulf war.

0132   KOSUGI, YASUSHI. "Restructuring Islamic Political Theories: Basic Concepts in a Contemporary Framework." *Nature of the Islamic Community*, 37-70. Eds. Toshio Kuroda, and Richard I. Lawless. Tokyo: Keiso Shobo Publishing Co., 1993.

Seeks to introduce a framework for interpreting modern Islamic political theories and analyzes elements that are common among these theories.

0133   KRAMER, GÜDRUN. "Islamist Notions of Democracy." *MERIP* 183 (July 1993): 2-14.

Challenging the assumption that there is one political Islamic doctrine, this article utilizes Arabic sources written by Islamic intellectuals and analyzes the debate on the compatibility of Islam and democracy.

0134   KUCUKCAN, TALIP. "The Nature of Islamic Resurgence in Near and Middle Eastern Muslim Societies." *HI* 14, no. 2 (June 1990): 65-104.

This study explores the evolution of contemporary religious revivalist movements through an examination of Jewish and Christian revivalism, the origins of earlier contemporary Islamic movements as well as through an identification of the causes of the Islamic revival in the Middle East.

0135   _____. "Some Reflections on the Wahhabiya and the Sanusiya Movements: A Comparative Approach." *IQ* 37, no. 4 (1993): 237-251.

Compares and contrasts the ideology and organization structures of the Wahhabiya and Sanusiya movements.

0136 KURODA, TOSHIO. "On the Nature of Community in the Arab-Muslim World." *Nature of the Islamic Community*, 3-35. Eds. Toshio Kuroda, and Richard I. Lawless. Tokyo: Keiso Shobo Publishing Co., 1993.

Examines the structure and organization of Islamic societies and discusses values that are common to all Muslims.

0137 KURODA, TOSHIO and RICHARD LAWLESS, eds. *Nature of the Islamic Community*, Tokyo: Keiso Shobo Publishing Co., 1993.

A collection of papers presented at two international symposiums in Japan: State, Community, and Regional Politics in the Middle East and Community and Inter-State Relations: Islamic and Middle Eastern Dimensions. This work examines the fundamental aspects of community formation in the Islamic world.

0138 LAMBTON, ANN K. and SAID AMIR ARJOMAND. "Political Theory and Practice." *Expectations of the Millennium: Shi'ism in History*, 93-114. Eds. Seyyed Hossein, Hamid Dabashi, and Seyyed Vali Reza Nasr. Albany, NY: State University of New York Press, 1989.

This essay explores Shi'i political theory and analyzes its implementation during various periods in history.

0139 LANDAU, JACOB M. *The Politics of Pan-Islam: Ideology and Organizations*. Oxford, UK: Clarendon Press, 1990.

This work explores the literature on the movement for Islamic political and economic unity from Morocco to Turkey to India in the modern era. It utilizes archival sources from Washington, Paris, Bonn, and London and secondary sources in Arabic, Russian and Turkish. The opening chapter focuses on the reign of Sultan 'Abd al-Hamid II in which Jamal al-Din al-Afghani and the Sultan are central to the author's analysis. The work then moves on to the Young Turk movement and pan-Islamic ideology during World War I. Chapters three and four explore Tsarist Russia and the Soviet Union and India and illustrate the centrality of political faith and nationalism to a wide range of people with diverse pan-Islamic ideas. The next section focuses on the years between the two World Wars which are deemed as irrelevant for pan-Islamic ideas. Chapter six deals with the changes in the Muslim world as various nations attained independence and were able to formulate their own ideas on Islamic unions. The conclusion of this work compares Pan-Islamic ideology to other transnational ideologies and movements and declares that the religious character of Pan-Islamic ideology differentiates it from others.

0140 LAPIDUS, IRA M. "The Political Concepts of Islam." *AAAPSS* 524 (November 1992): 13-25.

The author examines the role of Islam in Middle East politics and considers it to be a reconstruction of historical paradigms. From the golden age of Islam the author traces two paradigms; integrated Islam and pre-Islamic Middle Eastern structures. He notes that in the contemporary era, historical paradigms have lost much of their influence thus the modern Islamic states appeal to a new conception of an Islamic nation-state.

0141 LAWRENCE, BRUCE B. "Fundamentalists in Pursuit of an Islamic State." *Defenders of God: The Fundamentalist Revolt against the Modern Age*, 189-226. Bruce B. Lawrence. New York: Harper and Row, 1989.

Divided into four sections, this chapter offers an examination of Islamic revival after the Iranian Revolution, the polarity between the speeches of Islamists and the reality of politics, Islamic revival in Indonesia, Pakistan, and Egypt, and the Shi'i brand of fundamentalism practiced in Iran.

0142 LEACH, HUGH. "Observing Islam from Within and Without." *AA* 21, no. 1 (February 1990): 3-19.

This article discusses how Muslims perceive their religion, what they believe to be the Western perceptions of their religion, and examines new discourses in Islamic political thought.

0143 LEWIS, BERNARD. "Islam and Liberal Democracy." *AM* (February 1993): 89-98.

Examines the relationship between Islam and liberal democracy. Seeks to illustrate that from a political perspective Islam and liberal democracy are incompatible.

0144 _____. "Legal and Historical Reflections on the Position of Muslim Populations Under Non-Muslim Rule." *JIMMA* 13, no. 1 (January 1992): 1-16.

Provides historical and legal background of the Muslim view of law and authority.

0145 _____. "The Roots of Muslim Rage." *AM* (September 1990): 47-55.

Discusses the reasons behind the Islamic world's mistrust of the West.

0146 MAHDI, AKBAR. "Islam, the Middle East, and the New World Order." *Islam, Iran, and World Stability*, 75-96. Ed. Hamid Zangeneh. New York: St. Martin's Press, 1994.

Examines the role of Islam in the new world order, asserting that Islamic revival is not a reaction against the western world, but a reaction against undemocratic governments. The author suggests that the West should encourage participation by Muslims in their governments.

0147   MALIK, IBRAHIM. "Jihad -- Its Development and Relevance." *PIJ* 2 (1994): 26-33.

Examines the multiple meanings of jihad in Islamic thought, the religious meaning and the historical and political interpretation.

0148   MALTI-DOUGLAS, FEDWA. "A Literature of Islamic Revival?: The Autobiography of Shaykh Kishk." *Cultural Transitions in the Middle East*, 116-129. Ed. Serif Mardin. Leiden: E.J. Brill, 1994.

Through a critique of the Muslim activist's autobiography, this chapter seeks to discover the relationship between "Islam and modern literature."

0149   MARR, PHEBE. "The Islamic Revival: Security Issues." *MQ* 3, no. 4 (1992): 37-50.

Assesses the impact of the Islamic revival on the Middle East's regional stability as well as how the U.S. and Western interests will be affected.

0150   MARTY, MARTIN E. and R. SCOTT APPLEBY, eds. *Accounting for Fundamentalisms: The Dynamic Character of Movements*, Chicago and London: The University of Chicago Press, 1994.

This fourth edited volume is part of the series the Fundamentalism Project sponsored by the American Academy of Arts and Sciences examining religious reaction to secularism in modern times. It explores the conditions under which a religious fundamentalist group modifies its ideology, world view and actions as a result of internal developments or outside influences. Divided into four sections, the first three sections examine movements or organizations according to a religious tradition; Christianity, Judaism, Islam. The fourth section is organized around South Asia. Section three comprises articles on the Islamic movements of Egypt, Algeria, northern Nigeria, Iraq, Palestine as well as articles on Soviet Islam and the similar characteristics of Islamic movements. The fourth section contains essays on the Jama'at-i-Islami and the Tablighi Jama'at in South Asia.

0151   _____, eds. *Fundamentalisms and Society: Reclaiming the Sciences, the Family, and Education*, Chicago and London: The University of Chicago Press, 1991.

Fundamentalisms and Society is the second edited volume of the Fundamentalist Project sponsored by the American Academy of Arts and Sciences. It discusses different fundamentalist perceptions of their own society. Divided into three sections, the first part offers an analysis of various fundamentalist world views and attitudes towards scientific inquiry and technology. This section offers three case studies of which two deal with Sunni Arab world views and the Iranian Shi'i perceptions on this topic. In part two, the impact of fundamentalism on women, the family and interpersonal relations is explored. Within this context the section includes chapters on women in Iran and Pakistan and personal relations in Egypt. The third section explores the influence of fundamentalism on educational institutions and the media including an article on Iran.

0152 _____, eds. *Fundamentalisms and the State: Remaking Polities, Economies, and Militance*, Chicago and London: The University of Chicago Press, 1991.

This work is the third volume of a collection of essays sponsored by the American Academy of Arts and Sciences. It seeks to explore the impact of religious fundamentalism on politics, economics and militancy. Divided into three sections, the first deals with the theme of religion and politics and those who believe that religion and politics are inseparable. Studies on Islamic movements include topics such as: Shi'i Jurisprudence in Iran, the impact of Islamic political activists on law, politics, and the constitutions of Iran, Pakistan and the Sudan, the Muslim Brethren and Takfir groups in Egypt, the Nigerian Islamic movement and the Naqshabandi Sufi order in Turkey. Part two explores the subject of those fundamentalist movements which desire to restructure their economies according to religious regulations. A chapter is devoted to the characteristics of an Islamic economic system. The third and final section analyzes militancy of fundamentalist movements. Three articles deal with Islamic movements in Iran, Afghanistan, and Lebanon.

0153 _____, eds. *Fundamentalisms Observed*, Chicago and London: The University of Chicago Press, 1991.

The first edited volume of the Fundamentalist Project is a study sponsored by the American Academy of Arts and Sciences. These essays explore different forms of religious fundamentalism around the globe including the Americas, Middle East, South and Far East Asia. Each author seeks to answer a set of questions concerning reasons for the evolution of fundamentalist movements, the discovery of their specific political, socio-economic and religious aims and how each individual organization seeks to realize these goals. The work pays special attention to the religious nature of each movement. This volume offers essays on Sunni Fundamentalism in the Sudan and Egypt, Shi'i political activism in Lebanon, Iran and Iraq, the Jama'at-i-Islami and Tablighi Jama'at in South Asia and Islamic Revivalism in Indonesia and Malaysia.

0154 Masud, Muhammad Khalid. "The Obligation to Migrate: The Doctrine of *hijra* in Islamic Law." *Muslim Travellers: Pilgrimage, Migration and the Religious Immigration*, eds. Dale F. Eickelman, and James Piscatori. London; Berkeley and Los Angeles: Routledge; The University of California Press, 1990.

Explores the issue of emigration and its development. Analyzes two periods of civil war in Muslim history and then discusses recent developments in India, Pakistan, and Nigeria.

0155 Matsumoto, Akiro. "A Survey on the Concept 'Velayat' of Velayat-e Faqih." *Nature of the Islamic Community*, 143-165. Eds. Toshio Kuroda, and Richard I. Lawless. Tokyo: Keiso Shobo Publishing Co., 1993.

Asserts that the concept of *velayat-e faqih* (guardianship of the jurisconsult) has been misinterpreted by scholars. States that the root of this misunderstanding is the translation of the word velayat--a word that had many interpretations.

0156 Mayer, Ann Elizabeth. *Islam and Human Rights: Tradition and Politics.* Boulder, CO: Westview Press, Inc., 1991.

Studies the notions of Islam and human rights as compared to universal norms on the character of human rights principles set forth in international law. The author's analysis focuses on a set of five Islamic documents concerning human rights--a commentary on the Universal Declaration of Human Rights by Sultan Tabandeh, the 1981 Universal Islamic Declaration of Human Rights sponsored by the Islamic Council in London, a pamphlet by Abu'l-A'la Mawdudi, the "Draft of the Islamic Constitution" issued by scholars affiliated with al-Azhar, and the 1979 Iranian Constitution. Two chapters explore the subject of equality, the rights of women and non-Muslims in an Islamic Society. In addition the author provides a comparative legal study of the process of Islamization in Iran, Pakistan, and the Sudan and its impact on human rights.

0157 _____. "The Shari'ah: A Methodology or a Body of Substantive Rules." *Islamic Law and Jurisprudence*, 177-198. Ed. Nicholas Heer. Seattle and London: University of Washington Press, 1990.

This chapter discusses the implications raised by the current Islamization process and assesses the significance of the codification of the Shari'ah movement and how it relates to traditional ideas of the Shari'ah and Islamic law.

0158 MAZRUI, ALI A. "Islam at War and Communism in Retreat: What is the Connection?" *The Gulf War and the New World Order*, 502-520. Eds. Tareq Y. Ismael and Jacqueline S. Ismael. Gainesville: University of Florida Press, 1994.

Looking through a Muslim-Christian dichotomy that is rooted in the Crusades, this chapter examines the rise of Islam and the decline of communism and the connection between the two.

0159 _____. "Satanic Versus or a Satanic Novel? Moral Dilemmas of the Rushdie Affair." *TWQ* 12, no. 1 (June 1990): 116-139.

This article examines the 'mutual incomprehension' between the Muslim and Western worlds over the Rushdie Affair.

0160   MERARI, ARIEL. "The Readiness to Kill and Die: Suicidal Terrorism in the Middle East." *Origins of Terrorism: Psychologies, Ideologies, Theologies, States of Mind*, 192-207. Ed. Walter Reich. Cambridge: Cambridge University Press, 1990.

Offers an examination of the sources, reasons, and scope of suicidal terrorism and an overview and discussion of such incidents in the Middle East.

0161   MILLER, JUDITH. "The Challenge of Radical Islam." *FA* 72, no. 2 (March 1993): 43-56.

Offers a profile of various leaders of contemporary Islamic movements to determine whether they are a threat to the interests of the United States.

0162   _____. "Faces of Fundamentalism: Hassan al-Turabi and Muhammed Fadlallah." *FA* 73, no. 6 (1994): 123-142.

Written by a journalist and based on interviews conducted with two Islamic leaders, this essay offers a comparison of al-Turabi's and Fadlallah's ideology and movements.

0163   MOADDEL, MANSOOR. "The Egyptian and Iranian Ulama at the Threshold of Modern Social Change: What Does and What Does Not Account for the Difference?" *ASQ* 15, no. 3 (June 1993): 21-46.

Using a historical framework, this article contrasts the reasons behind the influential role of the Iranian ulama with the declining role of the Egyptian ulama.

0164   MOIN, BAQER. "Khomeini's Search for Perfection: Theory and Reality." *Pioneers of Islamic Revival*, 64-97. Ed. Ali Rahnema. London: Zed Press, 1994.

This chapter traces the life of the Ayatollah Khomeini and provides insight into the important circumstances that affected and shaped his political Islamic discourse.

0165   MONSHIPOURI, MAHMOOD. "New Islamic Thinking and the Internationalization of Human Rights." *MW* 84, no. 3-4 (July 1994): 217-239.

Identifies Islamic norms and standards of human rights and compares the international norm against the Islamic standard.

0166   MOORE, ALVIN JR. "The Sword of Islam (Sayf Al-Islam)." *HI* 14, no. 1 (March 1991): 15-19.

Examines the various meanings of the concept of the sword in Islam.

0167   MOUSSALLI, AHMAD S. "Two Tendencies in Modern Islamic Political Thought: Modernism and Fundamentalism." *HI* 16, no. 2 (June 1993): 51-79.

Compares Islamic modernism as advocated by Jamal al-Din al-Afghani, Mohammed Abduh, Muhammad Iqbal and Ali Shari'ati with Islamic fundamentalism as advocated by Abu'l-A'la al-Mawdudi, Hasan al-Banna, Sayyid Qutb, and the Ayatollah al-Khomeini.

0168 _____. "Hasan al-Banna's Islamist Discourse on Constitutional Rule and Islamic State." *JIS* 4, no. 2 (1993): 161-174.
Provides a framework based upon Hasan al-Banna's concept of what constitutes an Islamic state.

0169 _____. *Radical Islamic Fundamentalism: The Ideological and Political Discourse of Sayyid Qutb*. Beirut, Lebanon: The American University of Beirut, 1992.
Asserts that Islamic fundamentalism is both an intellectual and political movement; that it is progressive and provides for modern reform, and that the movement understands more clearly the impact of science and technology on society. To illustrate these assertions, the author lays out Sayyid Qutb's discourse and then compares this ideology with other fundamentalist thought. Divided into three chapters, the first is a biography of Sayyid Qutb's life. The second chapter centers on the theoretical foundation of Islamic fundamentalism. Chapter three compares political Islamic ideology with Western political thought. The conclusion is a critical summation of Qutb's political discourse.

0170 _____. "Sayyid Qutb's View of Knowledge." *AJISS* 7, no. 3 (1990): 315-334.
Through an examination of the work of the revivalist theoretician Sayyid Qutb, this article assesses his view of knowledge.

0171 _____. "The Views of Islamic Fundamentalism on Epistemology and Political Philosophy." *IQ* 37, no. 3 (1993): 175-189.
Provides the core political ideology of Islamic movements through a synthesis of some of the most important Islamic ideologues such as al-Mawdudi, Hasan al-Banna, Sayyid Qutb, and the Ayatollah Khomeini.

0172 MUSSALLAM, ADNAN A. "Sayyid Qutb and Social Justice, 1945-1948." *JIS* 4, no. 1 (1993): 52-70.
Traces the political, social, and economic period in the region to discover why Sayyid Qutb chose to write his landmark work "Social Justice."

0173 NASR, SEYYED VALI REZA. "Reflections on the Myth and Reality of Islamic Modernism." *HI* 13, no. 1 (March 1990): 67-82.
Asserts that Islamic modernism evolved as a way to bridge the gap between the Western and Eastern worlds.

0174 _____. "Religious Modernism in the Arab World, India and Iran: The Perils and Prospects of a Discourse." *MW* 83, no. 1 (January 1993): 20-47.

Investigates the possibility of a synthesis between modernism and Islam. The article examines this process in the structure of modern discourses, Shi'i modernism, the socio-political foundations of Islamic modernism, the causal linkages between modernization and revolution, and modernism and structures of religious thought in Islam.

0175 NEUMANN, ROBERT G. "The Next Disorderly Half Century: Some Proposed Remedies." *WQ* (December 1993): 33-49.

Discusses the problems facing the world in general and weak states in particular: "the frailty of new democracies, nationalism and ethnic strife and religious radicalism, especially Islamic." Offers a critical analysis of political Islam asserting that it is a destabilizing force.

0176 PAPPE, ILAN. "Moderation in Islam: Religion in the Test of Reality." *PIJ* 2 (1994): 11-25.

Seeks to determine who the Islamic moderates are in the Arab world and assesses their strengths vis-a-vis the Islamic fundamentalists.

0177 PARIS, JONATHAN A. S. "When to Worry in the Middle East." *Orbis* 37, no. 4 (September 1993): 553-565.

This essay argues that due to the 'Islamic fundamentalist threat,' it is not always in America's best interest to promote democracy in the Middle East.

0178 PELLETREAU, ROBERT H., Jr., DANIEL PIPES, and JOHN L. ESPOSITO. "Resurgent Islam in the Middle East." *MEP* 3, no. 2 (1994): 1-21.

This is an edited version of a symposium convened by the Middle East Policy Council in May 1994. Includes opinions about political Islam of Robert Pelletreau, Assistant Secretary of State for Near Eastern Affairs; Daniel Pipes, Editor of Middle East Quarterly; and John Esposito, Director of the Center for Muslim-Christian Understanding, Georgetown University.

0179 PETERS, RUDOLPH. "The Islamization of Criminal Law: A Comparative Analysis." *DWDI* 34, no. 2 (November 1994): 246-274.

Compares the criminal laws which have been promulgated in the last twenty years to better comply with Islamic injunctions and classical provisions.

0180 PIPES, DANIEL. "The Muslims are Coming! The Muslims are Coming!" *NR* 19, no. 22 (19 November 1990): 28-31.

This article assesses the notion that Muslims and Islam are a threat to the West. Contends that "it is better to exaggerate the danger" because "the fear of Islam has some basis in reality."

0181 _____. *The Rushdie Affair: The Novel, the Ayatollah, and the West.* New York: Birch Lane Press, 1990.

Seeks to explain the causes behind the international fury caused by the book "Satanic Verses." Also examines the impact of the incident on both the West and the Muslim world. Focuses much of the work's attention on the Muslim interpretation of the book as well as the Soviet reaction to the controversy. Also looks at the significance of this uproar for Muslim minorities living in Europe and North America.

0182 PISCATORI, JAMES. "Accounting for Islamic Fundamentalisms." *Accounting for Fundamentalisms: The Dynamic Character of Movements*, 361-373. Eds. Martin E. Marty, and R. Scott Appleby. Chicago and London: The University of Chicago Press, 1994.

Outlines the similar characteristics that arise from empirical studies on differing Islamic fundamentalist movements, whether Shi'i, Sunni, Central Asian, Arab, or African. These patterns help the reader understand the origins and evolution of the movements and how they influence their societies.

0183 _____. "Religion and Realpolitik: Islamic Responses to the Gulf War." *Islamic Fundamentalisms and the Gulf Crisis*, 1-27. Ed. James Piscatori. United States of America: The American Academy of Arts and Sciences, 1991.

Describes how Iraqi President Saddam Hussein was able to play upon certain Islamic themes to gather support throughout the Islamic world. Also outlines the dilemma that the leadership of most Islamic movements faced during the Gulf war with a pro-Saddam constituency. Also notes the fact that the Gulf states often helped considerably in financing Islamist organizations.

0184 _____. "The Rushdie Affair and the Politics of Ambiguity." *IJ* 66, no. 4 (1990): 767-789.

Examining the multiple Muslim reactions to the Rushdie affair, the author finds that the idea of an Islamic force in international relations is highly simplistic.

0185 PISCATORI, JAMES, ed. *Islamic Fundamentalisms and the Gulf Crisis.* United States of America: The American Academy of Social Sciences, 1991.

An edited volume of a collection of essays that addresses the impact of the Gulf War on Islamic movements from South Asia to North Africa. The work draws upon the information of different scholars with in-depth knowledge of the Islamic movements in question. Contains excellent articles on the Iraqi, Iranian, Palestinian, Jordanian, Egyptian, Algerian and Pakistani Islamic movements. In addition, this book provides an overview of Islamic responses to the Gulf War and the impact of the Gulf War on Islamic fundamentalism and democracy. The authors in this edited volume offer information on the organizational and political structures, political ideologies and their responses to the Gulf crisis as well as a post-war update on these Islamic movements.

0186 POSTON, LARRY A. *Islamic Da'wah in the West: Muslim Missionary Activity and Dynamics of Conversion to Islam*. New York: Oxford University Press, 1992.

Provides a discussion of Muslim missionary activity in classical times as well as the effort to convert the West to Islam. The author discusses the writings of Hasan al-Banna, Abu al-A'la al-Mawdudi, and Khurram Murad; the institutionalization of the Da'wah in Western societies; and the dynamics of conversion to Islam.

0187 QURESHI, SALEEM. "The Muslim Family: The Scriptural Framework." *Muslim Families in North America*, 32-67. Eds. Earle H. Waugh, Sharon McIrvin Abu-Laban, and Regula Burckhardt Qureshi. Edmonton, Alberta: The University of Alberta Press, 1991.

Examines the scriptural framework of the Muslim family including issues such as family and marriage, modesty, temporary marriage, dowry, polygamy, adultery, and inheritance.

0188 RAHNEMA, ALI. "Ali Shariati: Teacher, Preacher, Rebel." *Pioneers of Islamic Revival*, 208-250. Ed. Ali Rahnema. London: Zed Press, 1994.

This chapter examines the formative periods in the life of Ali Shari'ati and demonstrates how his milieu was instrumental in the development of his new Islamic discourse.

0189 _____, ed. *Pioneers of Islamic Revival*, London: Zed Press, 1994.

This informative collection of works examines the lives, ideology, and legacy of some of the most important pioneers of Islamic revival in the nineteenth and twentieth centuries in the Islamic world. The edited volume contains chapters on Sayyid Jamal al-Din al-Afghani, Muhammad Abduh, the Ayatollah Khomeini, Mawlana Mawdudi, Hassan al-Banna, Sayyid Qutb, Musa al-Sadr, Ali Shari'ati, and Muhammad Baqir as-Sadr. Exploring the lives and events that shaped their visions is a central point of each article. In addition, these studies also relay the importance that their ideology has had on their followers and successive generations.

0190 RAPOPORT, DAVID C. "Sacred Terror: A Contemporary Example From Islam." *Origins of Terrorism: Psychologies, Ideologies, Theologies, States of Mind*, 103-130. Ed. Walter Reich. Cambridge: Cambridge University Press, 1990.

Focusing on the al-Jihad group that assassinated Egyptian President Anwar Sadat, this essay seeks to differentiate between the characteristics of holy terror and secular or political violence.

0191 RAZI, HOSSEIN G. "Legitimacy, Religion, and Nationalism in the Middle East." *APSR* 84, no. 1 (March 1990): 69-91.

Assesses the importance of the relationship between religion and nationalism in the Arab world.

0192 ROY, OLIVIER. *The Failure of Political Islam.* Cambridge: Harvard University Press, 1994.

This book analyzes Islamic radicalism maintaining that this phenomenon is essentially anti-clerical and eventually leads to political oppression. Also argues that proponents of political Islam lack a clear political and economic agenda.

0193 SACHEDINA, ABDULAZIZ A., and HAMID ENAYAT. "Martyrdom." *Expectations of the Millennium: Shi'ism in History*, 45-57. Eds. Seyyed Hossein Nasr, Hamid Dabashi, and Seyyed Vali Reza Nasr. Albany, NY: State University of New York Press, 1989.

An examination of the political and religious significance of the concept of martyrdom in Shi'i ideology. Sachedina discusses the role that martyrdom has played in Shi'i ideology while Enayat explores the transformation of the image of Imam Hussein in modern Shi'i political thought.

0194 SAFI, LOUAY M. "The Islamic State: A Conceptual Framework." *AJISS* 8, no. 2 (1991): 221-234.

Defines the primary components found in the concept of an Islamic state and provides an analysis of the political legitimacy of the ruler and the scope of an Islamic state's power.

0195 SAID, ABDUL AZIZ. "Islamic Fundamentalism and the West." *MQ* 3, no. 4 (September 1992): 21-36.

Defines the term Islamic fundamentalism and examines the relationship between Islam and the West.

0196 SAIF, WALID. "Human Rights and Islamic Revivalism." *ICMR* 5, no. 1 (1994): 57-65.

Identifies the various trends among Islamic movements. Argues that the use of human rights issues to attack Islamic movements may only serve the interests of "state oppression in the Muslim world."

0197 SALAME, GHASSAN. "Islam and the West." *FP* 90 (1993): 22-37.

Provides a synopsis of the Islamist world view in order to gage how powerful the Islamic movement is and to determine whether Western policies have encouraged its rise.

0198 SALEM, PAUL. "Islamic Fundamentalism." *Ideology and Politics in the Arab World*, 89-146. Paul Salem. Syracuse, NY: Syracuse University Press, 1994.

This chapter surveys the historical roots of Islamic revivalism and provides a brief background on the Islamic movements in Egypt, Syria, Iraq, and Lebanon. The study also examines the ideology of Sunni and Shi'i Islamic discourse and ends with a short synopsis of the appeal and legacy of Islamic fundamentalism.

0199 SHARABI, HISHAM. "Modernity and Islamic Revival: The Critical Task of Arab Intellectuals." *CT* 2, no. 1 (1992): 127-138.

From an Arab intellectual perspective, contends that Islamic revivalism is incompatible with modernity.

0200 SHARON, MOSHE. "The Islamic Factor in Middle East Politics." *MS* 40, no. 1 (January 1994): 7-10.

Briefly describes the reasons for the rise of Islamic political activism.

0201 SHEPARD, WILLIAM E. "Islam as a System in the Later Writing of Sayyid Qutb." *MES* 25, no. 1 (1989): 31-50.

Through Sayyid Qutb's writings, this article explores the degree to which Qutb considers Islam a system. Also looks at why his writings have such a popular appeal.

0202 SHEPHARD, WILLIAM. "The Development of the Thought of Sayyid Qutb as Reflected in the Earlier and Later Editions of 'Social Justice in Islam.'" *DWDI* 32, no. 2 (1992): 196-236.

Through an analysis of Sayyid Qutb's work, this article seeks to understand the reasoning behind the changes in Qutb's thinking.

0203 SHITU-AGBETOLA, ADE. "Theory of Al-Khalifah in the Religio-Political View of Sayyid Qutb." *HI* 14, no. 2 (June 1991): 25-34.

Assesses Sayyid Qutb's theory of the Caliphate.

0204 SIDDIQUI, DILNAWAZ A. "Mass Media Analysis: Formulating an Islamic Perspective." *AJISS* 8, no. 3 (1991): 473-499.

Analyzes Western mass media principles and compares them to fourteen Qur'anic principles identified by Mawdudi.

0205 SIVAN, EMMANUEL. "Islamic Radicalism: Sunni and Shi'ite." *Religious Radicalism & Politics in the Middle East*, 39-75. Eds. Emmanuel Sivan, and Menachem Freidman. Albany: State University of New York Press, 1990.

This chapter examines the phenomenon of Sunni and Shi'ite Islamic radicalism and illustrates, that while there was not much interaction between Sunni radicals and their Shi'i counterparts, there exists striking similarities in their philosophical outlook.

0206 _____. "The Islamic Resurgence: Civil Society Strikes Back." *Fundamentalism in Comparative Perspective*, 96-108. Ed. Lawrence Kaplan. Amherst: The University of Massachusetts Press, 1992.

Discusses how since the independence of Arab nations, civil society has increasingly come under the control of the state. Traces how the state's weakening led to an Islamic resurgence that sought to reshape the borders between state and society.

0207 _____. "Sunni Radicalism in the Middle East and the Iranian Revolution." *IJMES* 21 (1989): 1-30.

Surveys the four primary areas of contention between Sunni and Shi'i ideology as well as their influence on revolutionary thought in order to ascertain the degree of similarity.

0208 SMITH, CHARLES D. "The Intellectual, Islam, and Modernization: Haykal and Shari'ati." *Comparing Muslim Societies: Knowledge and the State in a World Civilization*, 163-192. Ed. Juan R. I. Cole. Michigan: The University of Michigan Press, 1992.

Through an examination of Egypt and Muhammad Husayn Haykal (1888-1956) and Ali Shari'ati of Iran, the author addresses the assumption that Western-oriented intellectuals are predisposed to Western-style changes. The author shows how both intellectuals rejected Western forms of modernization and concludes that both sought to preserve or restore a community where social harmony is protected against Western precepts that cause social friction.

0209 SONN, TAMARA. *Between Qur'an and Crown: The Challenges of Political Legitimacy in the Arab World*. Boulder, CO: Westview Press, 1990.

An insightful examination of the conflict between secularism and Islam that is apparent in many Middle Eastern countries. The author compares the development of western secular government to the contemporary Middle East. The work contends that colonialism in the Middle East interrupted the development of secular states in the region. The nature of colonialism, the author argues, led to a renunciation of everything western, including secular government. Provides a detailed introduction to twentieth century Arab history focusing on the emergence of Arab nationalism.

0210   _____. "The Islamic Alternative: Cause or Effect?" *IJ* 46, no. 2 (1991): 291-325.
   Discusses Islamic fundamentalism as a result of regional domestic dynamics and not the cause of regional instability.

0211   STAV, ARYE. "The Muslim Threat to the Western World." *MS* 39, no. 1 (1993): 2-6.
   Briefly argues that "the Islamic ethos *ennobles* the Jihad (i.e. war on unbelievers) and therefore the countries of the Arab world "with their nuclear, chemical, and biological weapons" are a threat to the "civilized world."

0212   TAMADONFAR, MEHRAN. *The Islamic Polity and Political Leadership: Fundamentalism, Sectarianism and Pragmatism*. Boulder, CO: Westview Press, 1989.
   Contending that Western social science ideologies for the study of the developing world are inadequate, this work offers a theoretical framework in which to examine the phenomenon of Islamic revivalism and specifically Islamic political leadership. Divided into four chapters, the first presents a theoretical framework for the study of Islamic leadership. The second chapter examines political and theological issues surrounding the Islamic polity and the Islamic state by Muslim scholars. Chapter three is allocated to the study of the origins of Islamic political schisms over what constitutes political authority in Islam as well as the impact of the schisms on the Muslim community. The final chapters compare and contrast Sunni and Shi'i theories of Islamic political leadership.

0213   TIBI, BASSAM. "International Relations and the Universality of Human Rights As a Background for Islam's Predicament With the Western Concept of Human Rights." *ICMR* 3, no. 1 (1992): 58-68.
   Contends that the concept of human rights is a Western concept. Presses for the need to establish "cross-cultural foundations of human rights" between Muslims and Christians.

0214   _____. *Islam and the Cultural Accommodation of Social Change*. Boulder, CO: Westview Press, 1990.
   Drawing upon Clifford Geertz's anthropological approach to religion, particularly that "religions represent cultural systems," this work examines Islam as a cultural system and its relationship to social change. Divided into five parts, the first section explores the main thesis. Part two examines whether culture is a vehicle for change and the role of Islam in cultural patterns. The third part discusses social change and the resistance to this change within the Islamic socio-cultural system. Part four analyzes Islamic revivalism and the

"politicization of the Islamic cultural system." Part five provides a summation of the author's findings as well as prospects for the future.

0215 _____. "Major Themes in the Arabic Political Literature of Islamic Revivalism, 1970-1985: The Islamic System of Government (*al-nizam al-Islami*), *shura* Democracy and the Implementation of the *sharia* as Opposed to Secularism (*ilmaniyya*)." *ICMR* 3, no. 2 (1992): 183-210.

First in a two part series, this article surveys and analyzes literature of Islamic revivalism contending that "political Islam is a burden for modern Islam and an obstacle to the accommodation of the needs of Muslim people to the modern age."

0216 _____. "Major Themes in the Arabic Political Literature of Islamic Revivalism, 1970-1985: The Islamic System of Government (*al-nizam al-Islami*), *shura* Democracy and the Implementation of the *sharia* as Opposed to Secularism (*ilmaniyya*)." *ICMR* 4, no. 1 (1993): 83-99.

Second in a two-part series, this article analyzes the two integral parts of the Islamic political system, the legal system and the consultative council as the authentic Islamic pattern of parliamentarianism.

0217 _____. "The Worldview of Sunni Arab Fundamentalists: Attitudes Toward Modern Science and Technology." *Fundamentalisms and Society: Reclaiming the Science, the Family, and Education*, 73-102. Eds. Martin E. Marty, and R. Scott Appleby. Chicago and London: The University of Chicago Press, 1991.

Analyzes Sunni Arab fundamentalist ideological attitudes toward modern science and technology which the author believes to be one of the core issues facing them. Discusses the challenge faced by fundamentalist thinkers that Western science possesses a universal status as well as the impact of the modern globalization process on Islamic culture.

0218 TRIPP, CHARLES. "Sayyid Qutb: The Political Vision." *Pioneers of Islamic Revival*, 154-183. Ed. Ali Rahnema. London: Zed Press, 1994.

This chapter examines the life and political vision of Sayyid Qutb. In exploring his ideology, the author looks at the tensions within his writings and discusses some of the problems they cause for his followers.

0219 VOLL, JOHN OBERT. "Conservative and Traditional Brotherhoods." *AAAPSS* (November 1992): 66-78.

Examines the historical role of Sufi brotherhoods and their impact on the development of political Islam. The author asserts that the brotherhoods played a conservative role while preserving a sense of Islamic identity under colonial rule. In the post-independence period, the Sufis acted as conservative forces in contemporary activist Islamic groups. States that political Islam today reflects the influence of traditional and conservative Sufi brotherhoods in creating the strong sense of community in public life.

0220 _____. *Islam: Continuity and Change in the Modern World*. Syracuse, NY: Syracuse University Press, 1994.

This revised second edition of a volume first published in 1982, offers an examination of the important historical events that have shaped the Islamic world. Beginning with a historical survey of the Prophet Mohammed and the rise of Islam, the work defines the central issues that faced the Muslim community following the death of the Prophet Mohammed. The second chapter explores the dominant issues during the eighteenth century and discusses topics such as the Ottoman empire, the Wahhabi movement, Islam in the Indian region and in Africa, and the emergence of Shi'ism in Iran. The third chapter deals with the Islamic response to Western colonialism. The fourth chapter explores the challenges that face the dominant majorities in the Middle East and North Africa in the twentieth century. The fifth chapter looks at the Muslim experience in the Indian subcontinent and Southeast Asia and Muslim minorities in Africa in the twentieth century. The sixth and seventh chapters, which have been totally rewritten, discuss significant aspects of Islamic revival in the 1980s and 1990s.

0221 _____. "Islamic Fundamentalism and Regional Dynamics." *The Gulf War: Regional and International Dimensions*, 32-41. Eds. Hanns W. Maull, and Otto Pick. London: Pinter, 1989.

Discusses the nature and status of Islamic fundamentalism in order to illustrate the role that Islamic fundamentalism plays in the regional sphere.

0222 _____. "The Revivalist Heritage." *The Contemporary Islamic Revival*, 23-36. Ed. Yvonne Yazbeck Haddad, John Obert Voll, John L. Esposito, Kathleen Moore, and David Sawan. New York: Greenwood Press, 1991.

Provides an analysis of how the Islamic heritage affects the Islamic revivalist movement today.

0223 VOLL, JOHN OBERT and JOHN L. ESPOSITO. "Islam's Democratic Essence." *MEQ* 1, no. 3 (September 1994): 3-11.

Examines Islamic heritage in order to illustrate that many elements of Islam are compatible with democracy.

0224 VOLL, JOHN OBERT and FRED R. VON DER MEHDEN. "Religious Resurgence and Revolution: Islam." *Revolution & Political Change in the Third World*, 99-116. Eds. Barry M. Schultz, and Robert O. Slater. Boulder and London: Lynne Reinner Publishers and Adamantine Press Limited, 1990.

Offers an analysis that seeks to classify the characteristics of Islamic resurgence and define those facets which may be deemed revolutionary.

0225 WATT, WILLIAM MONTGOMERY. "A Western Response." *HT* 39 (December 1989): 5-8.

This commentary is a response to Dr Akbar Ahmed's essay on Western misperception of Muslims in the November 1989 issue of *History Today*. The author also discusses the role that the *ulama* (religious leaders) have played in Arab politics.

0226 WILL, JAMES E. "The Politics of Religion in the Middle East Peace Process: Manipulated Ideology or Genuine Religion?" *AAA* 30 (September 1989): 77-80.

Argues for a greater understanding among Americans for the Muslim set of beliefs and the role it plays in the Middle East peace process.

0227 ZAKZOUK, MAHMOUD. "Cultural Relations between the West and the World of Islam: Meeting Points and Possibilities of Co-operation on the Academic Level." *ICMR* 3, no. 1 (1992): 69-82.

In order to facilitate cooperation between the West and Islam, the author encourages academics to research Islam in the most impartial way possible.

0228 ZEBIRI, KATE. *Mahmud Shaltut and Islamic Modernism.* Oxford, UK: Clarendon Press, 1993.

Through an examination of Mahmoud Shaltut's--the Shaykh al-Azhar--life and work, this study seeks to shed greater light on what Islamic revivalism actually means for Muslim societies. The opening two chapters introduce his work and the "social realities in Egypt and the Muslim world generally." Chapter three depicts Shaltut's interpretation of an Islamic worldview. The fourth chapter examines the attempt of Islamic scholars to address the obstacles and challenges that face Muslims today. Chapters five and six center on his interpretation of Islamic law and the next two chapters look at Shaltut's contribution to *tafsir*.

0229 _____. "The Fatwas of Mahmud Shaltut (1893-1963)." *MR* 16, no. 1-2 (1991): 109-124.

Analyzes the *fatwas* of the Egyptian religious scholar, Mahmud Shaltut, who held the position of Shaykh al-Azhar from 1958-1963. Weighs their importance and the ways in which they were implemented.

0230 ZIRING, LAWRENCE. "Constitutionalism and the Qur'an in the Final Decades of the 20th Century." *HI* 13, no. 3 (1990): 15-21.

Examines the compatibility between the precepts of the Qur'an and the elements of constitutionalism.

0231 ZIRKER, HANS. "Revelation in History and Claims to Finality: Assumptions Underlying Fundamentalism in Christianity and Islam." *ICMR* 3, no. 2 (December 1992): 211-235.
    The author argues that Christianity and Islam have competing claims to finality and universality which leads both to "historical disappointments, theoretical irritations, communication difficulties and identity problems." Community life as well as theological reflection in both faiths are an attempt to overcome this disappointment which has precipitated the current fundamentalist trends in both religions.

0232 ZUBAIDA, SAMI and RICHARD TAPPER, eds. *Culinary Cultures of the Middle East,* London: I. B. Tauris, 1994.
    Surveys the growing field of studies of the cultural and social aspects of food and cookery in the Middle East. Underlying this study is the belief that in the present century, this varied heritage is being overlaid and transformed by the global processes of world markets and the revolution in transport and communications.

0233 ZUBAIDA, SAMI. *Islam, the People and the State: Political Ideas and Movements in the Middle East.* London: I.B. Tauris, 1993.
    A discussion of the quest for an Islamic government in Egypt and Iran. The author writes on the political actors in the Iranian revolution, class and community in urban politics, components of popular culture as well as the nation state in the Middle East.

B.   Economics

0234 AHMAD, ZIAUDDIN. *Islam, Poverty and Income Distribution.* Leicester, England: The Islamic Foundation, 1991.
    This work examines how poverty may be eradicated by utilizing the Islamic concept of distributive justice. Divided into three chapters, the first chapter outlines Imam Shatib's Islamic framework of basic needs. Chapter two addresses Islamic policy issues such as tithing, inheritance, the abolition of interest, and the establishment of a profit-sharing system in its place. Chapter three offers a comparative study of contemporary economic approaches to resource allocation.

0235 AKHTAR, M. RAMZAN. "An Islamic Framework for Employer-Employee Relationships." *AJISS* 9, no. 2 (1992): 202-218.

Using the Islamic principles of brotherhood, justice, and benevolence as its basis, this article explores employer-employee relations in an Islamic economy.

0236 ALI, S. NAZIM and NASEEM N. Ali. *Information Sources on Islamic Banking and Economics*. London: Keagan Paul International, 1994.

Islamic banking has been a growing phenomenon in the world of finance over the past decade. This book discusses how to access information on Islamic finance from sources such as on-line services and electronic databases.

0237 AMUZEGAR, JAHANGIR. "The Iranian Economy Before and After the Revolution." *MEJ* 46, no. 3 (June 1992): 413-425.

Assesses the Iranian economic experience through a comparison of the pre-and post-revolutionary state of the economy.

0238 AZIZ, ABDUL. "Firm Level Decisions and Human Resource Development in an Islamic Economy." *AJISS* 10, no. 2 (1993): 201-216.

Offers a Muslim perspective on how human resource development will bring about economic development in an Islamic society.

0239 EL-BADAWI, MOHAMED H. and SULTAN M. AL-SULTAN. "Net Working Capital Versus Net Owner's Equity Approaches to Computing Zakatable Amount: A Conceptual Comparison and Application." *AJISS* 9, no. 1 (1992): 69-85.

Divided into five parts, this article explores whether using accounting principles and the net equity approach to define the percentage of zakat from trade assets is a viable option.

0240 BADR, GAMAL M. "Interest on Capital in Islamic Law." *AAA* , no. 29 (June 1989): 86-95.

Examines the position of Islamic law on interest as practiced in contemporary society. Offers an analysis of the manner in which the Qur'anic verses on *riba* (usury) were defined and applied by Muslim jurists in the classical Islamic era.

0241 BASHA, ZAKARIA A. "The Development of Islamic Banking and the Money Multiplier process." *Orient* 31, no. 3 (September 1990): 389-401.

An examination of the primary features of the Islamic banking system and the importance of the money multiplier process.

0242 CHAPRA, M. UMER. *Islam and Economic Development*. Islamabad: International Institute of Islamic Thought, 1993.

Number fourteen in the series of books on Islamization of Knowledge, the work affirms that it is impossible to have "national development with justice" without moral development. Asserts that a Muslim society is under a collective obligation to ensure proper training and optimal employment. Economic development strategies borrowed from the West have failed to realize Islamic goals because of their secular grounding. The author elaborates an Islamic strategy for economic development and shows why it has the potential for success in promoting development with justice and political stability.

0243 _____. *Islam and the Economic Challenge*. Leicester, UK and Herndon, VA: The Islamic Foundation and the International Institute of Islamic Thought, 1992.

Written by an economist, this work attempts to answer whether "reconstruction of the economies of Muslim countries in the light of Islamic teachings can be helpful." Divided into two sections, the first looks at the failure of socialism and capitalism to provide an example worth emulating by Muslim countries in their quest to realize their social and economic goals. The second part provides the Islamic response. Chapters discuss the Islamic worldview, five suggested policies for Muslim countries to adopt in light of Islamic injunctions, and a summation of the analysis of the work.

0244 _____. "The Role of Islamic Banks in non-Muslim Countries." *JIMMA* 13, no. 2 (July 1992): 295-297.

Discusses the role that Islamic banks can play in the development of small- and medium-sized business of Muslims in non-Muslim countries.

0245 CHOUDHURY, MASUDUL ALAM. *The Principles of Islamic Political Economy*. New York, NY: St. Martin's Press, 1992.

Provides an empirical study of an Islamic approach to political economy. Seeking to "develop the substantive and methodological foundations of the Islamic political economy," this work spells out five major points which are elaborated in the book. Divided into two parts, the first section establishes the theoretical grounding of the elements of Islamic political economics while the second applies these theories. The first chapter examines the role of a consultative counsel and an Islamic economy as a means of developing an "Islamic theory of value." The second chapter explores the "ethico-economic social welfare function" of an Islamic economic system. Drawing upon ideas of other Islamic economic theories, the third chapter develops a cost-benefit analysis. The fourth chapter offers an analysis of an Islamic profit-sharing system. Chapter five spells out the author's Islamic economic methodology. Part two provides the applied portion of the work and chapter six examines topics such as the integration of "Islamic economic principles and instruments to the capital market." The last two chapters analyze the Islamic economic experiment of Malaysia.

0246 _____. "Social Choice in an Islamic Economic Framework." *AJISS* 8, no. 2 (1991): 259-274.

Explores how the consultative component (*shura*) of an Islamic political system will help formulate the social welfare function in an Islamic political and economic state.

0247 EBRAHIM, MUHAMMED SHAHID. "Mortgage Financing for Muslim Americans." *AJISS* 10, no. 1 (1993): 72-87.

Examines the problems facing American Muslims concerning mortgage financing due to the Islamic injunction against interest.

0248 HAQUE, ZIAD. "Islamization of Economy in Pakistan (1977-1988): An Essay on the Relationship Between Religion and Economics." *PDR* 30, no. 4 (December 1990): 1105-1118.

Using the example of Pakistan, this article explores the relationship between religion and economics in general and economics and Islam in particular.

0249 HARDIE, ALEXANDRA R. and M. RABOOY. "Risk, Piety, and the Islamic Investor." *BJMES* 18, no. 1 (1991): 52-66.

Explores the ethical aspects of investment for the Muslim investor. Describes the basic Islamic principles involved for the investor and investigates whether Islamic banks uphold these principles.

0250 KAMEL, SALEH ABDULLAH. "Islamic Banking in Practice: The Albaraka Group in Muslim Minority Countries." *JIMMA* 13, no. 2 (July 1992): 325-336.

Looks at the goals of the Albaraka Group to create an Islamic banking system that meets the requirements of an Islamic economy.

0251 KURAN, TIMUR. "The Economic Impact of Islamic Fundamentalism." *Fundamentalisms and the State: Remaking Polities, Economies, and Militance*, 302-341. Eds. E. Martin Marty, and R. Scott Appleby. Chicago and London: The University of Chicago Press, 1991.

Provides an analysis of the varying interpretations of Islamic economics including finance and banking and *zakat* (an annual tax on wealth)--voluntary and obligatory, and the response of conventional banks.

0252 MALAMI, HUSSAINI USMAN. "Prospects of Islamic Banking in the Muslim Minority Communities." *JIMMA* 13, no. 2 (July 1992): 308-316.

Surveys the prospects of setting up an Islamic banking system in countries where Muslims are the minority.

0253 MEENAI, S. A. *The Islamic Development Bank: A Case Study of Islamic Co-operation*. London and New York: Kegan Paul International, 1989.

Written by a former Vice President of the Islamic Development Bank, this book traces the historical development of the bank which seeks to conform to the dictates of the *shari'ah*. Through a look at its rise to become the leading economic institution of the Islamic world, the author shows how much power the institution wields. In addition, the work offers a critical analysis of the bank's past performance and proscriptions for the future.

0254   MIKA'ILU, A. S. "A Note on the Implications for Capital Budgeting Decisions." *HI* 14, no. 3 (1991): 71-75.
Explores the implications on capital budgeting by using an Islamic profit-sharing system.

0255   _____. "On the Prohibition of *Riba* (Interest) and the Implications for Optimum Economic Performance." *HI* 12, no. 1 (March 1989): 57-65.
From an Islamic perspective, this article explores the concept of interest in an economic system.

0256   AL MUTAIRI, H. "An Islamic Perspective Towards Development." *HI* 16, no. 4 (1993): 27-50.
Proposes an Islamic alternative toward development in the Muslim world. Contends that underdevelopment in many parts of the Muslim world is not due to Islamic beliefs and practices.

0257   NASR, SEYYED VALI REZA. "Islamic Economics: Novel Perspectives on Change." *MES* 25, no. 4 (1989): 516-531.
Explores the basic principles which are the foundation for Islamic economics.

0258   _____. "Towards a Philosophy of Islamic Economics." *HI* 12, no. 4 (December 1989): 45-60.
Explores the topics concerning the development of a "philosophy of Islamic economics."

0259   PAL, IZZUD-DIN. "Pakistan and the Question of Riba." *MES* 30, no. 1 (January 1994): 64-78.
Surveys four different theories of interest in Pakistan to illustrate that interest found in a capitalist society is not "incompatible with Islamic justice."

0260   PERVEZ, IMTIAZ A. "Islamic Finance." *ALQ* 5, no. 4 (1990): 259-281.
Explores the Islamic ideology upon which the principles of Islamic finance is drawn.

0261 QUAZI, NASEEM. "Economic Morality in Islam." *HI* 16, no. 4 (1993): 89-102.

Examines the Islamic concepts of *zakat* (tithing) and *riba* to determine how to create a more equitable Muslim society.

0262 RAHMATULLAH. "Islamic Banking in India." *JIMMA* 13, no. 2 (July 1992): 317-324.

Examines the system of Islamic banking as it is conducted in India.

0263 ROY, DELIVIN A. "Islamic Banking." *MES* 27, no. 3 (1991): 427-456.

Provides historical background on Islamic banking and an explanation of the workings of Islamic financing.

0264 SALEH, NABIL. "Arab International Corporations: The Impact of the Shari'a." *ALQ* 8, no. 3 (1993): 179-183.

Examines several Arab international corporations: The Arab Monetary Fund, the Arab International Bank, and the Arab Organization for Industrialisation in order to determine the impact that Islamic law has on their functions.

0265 SPIESSBACH, MICHAEL F. "Principles of Islamic Investment: A Primer for Western Businessmen." *AAA* 27, no. 40 (Winter): 88-89.

This article explains the fundamentals of the Islamic business and investment restrictions for Western business entrepreneurs.

0266 VALIBEIGI, MEHRDAD. "Banking and Credit Rationing Under the Islamic Republic of Iran." *IrSt* 25, no. 3-4 (1991): 51-65.

Traces the changes in the Iranian banking system following the revolution and the new trends that have emerged.

0267 WILSON, RODNEY. "Islamic Financial Instruments." *ALQ* 6, no. 2 (1991): 205-214.

Reviews recent developments in international finance and discusses their implications for Islamic finance.

0268 ZAMAN, S. M. HASANUZ. "Workman's Bonus: *Shari'ah* Arguments For and Against." *HI* 16, no. 2 (1993): 1993.

From an Islamic perspective, this essay examines the merits of the bonus system for workers.

0269 ZUBAIDI, SAMI. "The Politics of the Islamic Investment Companies in Egypt." *BSMES* 17, no. 2 (1990): 152-161.

Describes the rise of Islamic investment companies in Egypt, their activities, and Egyptian reactions to them.

C.   Women

0270   Abadan-Unat, Nermin. "The Impact of Legal and Educational Reforms on Turkish Women." *Women in Middle Eastern History*, 177-194. Eds. Nikki R. Keddie, and Beth Baron. New Haven and London: Yale University Press, 1991.

Through an examination of educational and regional reforms instigated by Kemal Ataturk, this article assesses the impact on the role of Turkish women from various classes in society. It describes how these secular reforms have recently come under attack by Islamists, and the fears that this phenomenon could roll back gains attained by women.

0271   Abdo, Nahla. "Nationalism and Feminism: Palestinian Women and the *Intifada* - No Going Back?" *Gender and National Identity: Women and Politics in Muslim Societies*, 148-170. Ed. Valentine M. Moghadam. London and New York: Karachi: Zed Books LTD: Oxford University Press, 1994.

By placing the Palestinian woman's struggle in historical perspective, this chapter seeks to discover what effects the *Intifada* has had on gender relations within Palestinian society.

0272   ABDULRAHIM, DIMA. "Islamic Law, Gender and the Policies of Exile, the Palestinians in West Berlin: A Case Study." *Islamic Family Law*, eds. Chibli Mallat, and Jane Conners. London: Graham & Trotman, 1990.

Based on field work in West Berlin, this article explores the transformation of a Palestinian family's interpretation of family law and understanding of male-female relationships.

0273   ABU ODEH, LAMA. "Post-Colonial Feminism and the Veil: Thinking the Difference." *FR* 43, no. 4 (1993): 26-37.

From the perspective of an Arab feminist, this article examines the topic of the veil in the Arab world.

0274   ABUKHALIL, AS'AD. "Toward the Study of Women and Politics and the Arab World: The Debate and the Reality." *FI* 13, no. 1 (1993): 3-22.

Examines the role of women in politics in the Arab world. Attributes the difficulties facing feminists to the society's lack of definition of women's role.

0275   ABU-LUGHOD, LILA. "The Romance of Resistance: Tracing Transformation of Power through Bedouin Women." *AE* 17, no. 1 (February 1990): 41-55.

Based on fieldwork conducted among bedouin women of Awlad Ali near the Libyan border in Egypt, this article examines different forms of resistance by these women. It examines the various power structures as the tribe becomes incorporated into the state of Egypt.

0276 ACCAD, EVELYNE. "Sexuality and Sexual Politics: Conflicts and Contradictions for Contemporary Women in the Middle East." *Third World Women and the Politics of Feminism*, 237-250. Eds. Chandra Talpade Mohanty, Ann Russo, and Lourdes Torres. Bloomington and Indianapolis: Indiana University Press, 1991.

Contends that to change gender relations in the Middle East, a sexual revolution should be "incorporated into political revolution."

0277 _____. "Sexuality, War, and Literature in Lebanon." *FI* 11, no. 2 (1991): 27-42.

Six novels concerning the Lebanese civil war are examined in order to demonstrate the relationship between sexuality, war, violence, power, love, and feminism as they relate to body, partner, family, political revolution, religion, and pacifism.

0278 AFKHAMI, MAHNAZ. "Women in Post-Revolutionary Iran: A Feminist Perspective." *In the Eye of the Storm: Women in Post-Revolutionary Iran*, 5-18. Eds. Mahnaz Afkhami, and Erika Friedl. Syracuse, NY: Syracuse University Press, 1994.

This chapter, written by the General Secretary of the former Woman's Organization of Iran, examines the impact of the changes in the status of women on the development of post-revolutionary Iran.

0279 AFKHAMI, MAHNAZ and ERIKA FRIEDL, eds. *In the Eye of the Storm: Women in Post Revolutionary Iran*, Syracuse, NY: Syracuse University Press, 1994.

This edited work stems from the proceedings of a conference entitled "Women in Post-Revolutionary Iran" convened by the Foundation for Iranian Studies and the Middle East Center of the University of Pennsylvania. The nine chapters provide information on diverse aspects of women's lives in the Iranian Islamic Republic. Articles included in this book explore topics such as women's education; the status of women and female children; women's issues in the Iranian Parliament; female labor participation; temporary marriage; the portrayal of women in classical and contemporary Persian literature; and women in the film industry in Iran. The work also offers two appendixes; one is a translation of excerpts from "The Legal Status of Woman in the Family in Iran" by Sima Pakzad and the second a selection of criminal laws concerning Iranian women.

0280 AFSHAR, HALEH. "Development Studies and Women in the Middle East: The Dilemmas of Research and Development." *Women in the Middle East: Perceptions, Realities and Struggles for Liberation*, 3-17. Ed. Haleh Afshar. New York: St. Martin's Press, 1993.

This introductory chapter asserts that Western methodologies, influenced by Western values, used in the study of Middle Eastern women have impeded true scholarly work in this field.

0281 _____. "Women and Work: Ideology Not Adjustment at Work in Iran." *Women and Adjustment Policies in the Third World*, 205-231. Ed. Haleh Afshar, and Carolyne Dennis. New York: St. Martin's Press, 1992.
Examines the implications of the limitations that economic and ideological factors place on women's work in Iran.

0282 _____, ed. *Women in the Middle East: Perceptions, Realities and Struggles for Liberation*, New York: St. Martin's Press, 1993.
This edited volume provides twelve chapters written by Middle Eastern women that address misperceptions about Middle Eastern women and seeks to show the reality of the status of the women of the Middle East. Divided into two sections, the first offers six chapters that discuss various aspects of Islam in women's lives. This includes chapters on marriage and divorce, employment, religious rituals, and a critique of Western perceptions of the "Oriental" female. The second section provides six articles that focus on women's struggle for liberation. Nawal El Saadawi traces the various women's resistance movements. Other chapters examine the resistance movements in Iran and Palestine as well as women's struggle in the context of Islamic fundamentalism.

0283 AFSHARI, M. REZA. "Egalitarian Islam and Misogynist Islamic Tradition: A Critique of the Feminist Reinterpretation of Islamic History and Heritage." *C*, no. 4 (1994): 13-33.
Offers a critique of the modern-day feminist interpretation of Islamic discourse and history.

0284 AGHAJANIAN, AKHBAR. "The Status of Women and Female Children in Iran: An Update from the 1986 Census." *The Oral History Collection of the Foundation for Iranian Studies*, 44-60. Eds. Gholam Reza Afkhami, and Seyyed Vali Reza Nasr. Washington, D.C.: Foundation for Iranian Studies, 1991.
The article compares Iranian government census data from 1976 and 1986 of the status of women as compared to men. The social indicators include: the literacy rate, school enrollment, employment, health and access to nutritional products, and the death rate of children.

0285 AHMED, LEILA. "Arab Culture and Writing Women's Bodies." *FI* (March 1989): 41-55.
This article explores how Islamic societies view women's bodies in various traditions both oral and written. The author points out that the way the West

handles topics of Islam and sexuality are quite different from those from Islamic societies.

0286 _____. "Early Islam and the Position of Women: The Problem of Interpretation." *Women in Middle Eastern History*, 58-73. Eds. Nikki R. Keddie, and Beth Baron. New Haven and London: Yale University Press, 1991.

Asserts that the formation of Islamic law during the Umayyad and Abbasid periods neglected the ethical egalitarian spirit of Islam. This, the author states, has led to the adaptation of the age's social mores which degraded women.

0287 AHMED, MUNIR D. "Muslim Women in an Alien Society: A Case Study of Germany." *JIMMA* 13, no. 1 (1992): 71-79.

Explores the responses of Muslim women living in Germany to the challenges they face as a minority in a Christian society.

0288 ALAM, SHAISTA AZIZ. "Purdah and the Qur'an." *III* 13, no. 4 (December 1990): 77-90.

Offers a comparison of the custom of *purdah* with Qur'anic injunctions to illustrate why a fresh examination of this topic is needed.

0289 ALSUWAIGH, SIHAM A. "Women in Transition: The Case of Saudi Arabia." *JCFS* 20, no. 1 (1989): 67-78.

Within the context of the impact of the socio-economic changes in Saudi Arabia, this article examines the status of Saudi Arabian women.

0290 ALTORKI, SOROYA. "Women, Development and Employment in Saudi Arabia: The Case of 'Unayzah." *Women and Development in the Middle East and North Africa*, 96-110. Eds. Joseph G. Jabbra, and Nancy W. Jabbra. Leiden: E.J. Brill, 1992.

Addresses the issue of female employment in Saudi Arabia and shows how they have long been employed in the agricultural, handicraft, and commercial sectors.

0291 AMYUNI, MONA TAKIEDDINE. "And Life Went On...in War-Torn Lebanon." *ASQ* 15, no. 2 (March 1993): 1-13.

A personal testimony written by a Lebanese woman of the impact of the war in Lebanon on the lives of those surrounding the author including women during the war. Also examines the images of women in Lebanon's war literature.

0292 _____. "Women in Contemporary Arabic and Francophone Fiction." *FI* 12, no. 2 (1993): 3-19.

Contending that literature mirrors as well as shapes reality during a period of flux, this article "recreates the female drama in the Arab world as incarnate by a few heroines during key periods of our contemporary history."

0293   ANEES, MUNAWAS A. "Circumcision: The Clitoral Inferno." *IC* 63, no. 3 (July 1989): 77-92.

Argues that various practices of genital mutilation have existed in many religions and cultures, not only in Islam, and have stemmed from different traditions. Explains that clitoridectomy is a pagan, pre-Islamic ritual that is not in line with Islamic teachings.

0294   ANTOUN, RICHARD T. "Litigant Strategies in an Islamic Court in Jordan." *Law and Islam in the Middle East*, 35-60. Ed. Daisy Hilse Dwyer. New York: Bergin & Garvey, 1990.

Providing six case studies, this article analyzes the connection between Islamic law and customary law regarding personal status cases brought to court by Jordanian peasants.

0295   ARAT, YESIM. "Islamic Fundamentalism and Women in Turkey." *MW* 80, no. 1 (January 1990): 17-24.

Examines the role of the ruling party, the Ava Partisi, in loosening the controls on religion in Turkey and investigates the influence of the journal *Kadin ve Aile* (Women and Family) in Turkish society, while weighing the progressive tendencies of the magazine.

0296   _____. *The Patriarchal Paradox: Women Politicians in Turkey*. New York: Fairleigh Dickinson University Press, 1989.

Examines the challenges faced by Turkish women in the transition from the private to the public sphere. Drawing upon field research, the author interviews male and female members of the Turkish parliament as well as female members of the municipality council. The first two chapters offer a historical overview of the Contemporary Turkish political situation. The subsequent chapters introduce those who were interviewed and assesses the challenges they face.

0297   AREBI, SADDEKA. "Gender Anthropology in the Middle East: The Politics of Muslim Women's Misrepresentation." *AJISS* 8, no. 1 (1991): 99-108.

Recommending a theory of gender that is tailored to Muslim women's experience, this article critiques gender anthropology in Muslim society.

0298   ASWAD, BARBARA C. "Attitudes of Immigrant Women and Men in the Dearborn Area Toward Women's Employment and Welfare." *Muslim*

Communities in North America, 501-519. Eds. Yvonne Yazbeck Haddad, and Jane Idleman Smith. New York: State University of New York Press, 1994.

This chapter assesses the impact of the perceptions and attitudes of immigrant Arab men and women in Dearborn, Michigan on the lives of Arab women especially focusing on female employment.

0299 _____. "Yemeni and Lebanese Muslim Immigrant Women in Southeast Dearborn, Michigan." *Muslim Families in North America*, 256-281. Eds. Earle H. Waugh, Sharon McIrvin Abu-Laban, and Regula Burckhardt Qureshi. Edmonton, Alberta: The University of Alberta Press, 1991.

This chapter, based on intensive interviews in 1984 with forty married immigrant women from South Lebanon and North Yemen living in Southeast Dearborn, Michigan, examines the change in the role of women through migration.

0300 AUGUSTIN, EBBA, ed. *Palestinian Women: Identity and Experience*, London and Atlantic Highlands, New Jersey: Zed Books, 1993.

This edited volume provides insight into the daily lives of Palestinian women during the Intifada. Divided into two sections, the first offers eight chapters that deal with "Women in Palestinian Society and Politics." These chapters examine social and political issues that have undergone dramatic change with the advent of the Intifada. Part two examines "Women in the Intifada." Here political activities, such as civil disobedience, and their effect on every day life are examined.

0301 BADRAN, MARGOT. "Competing Agenda: Feminists, Islam and the State in 19th and 20th Century Egypt." *Women, Islam and the State*, 201-236. Ed. Deniz Kandiyoti. Philadelphia: Temple University Press, 1991.

This article examines the competing discourses between the Islamists, feminists, and the state in nineteenth and twentieth century Egypt. The essay also traces how the various discourses have changed over time.

0302 _____. "Expressing Feminism and Nationalism in Autobiography: The Memoirs of an Egyptian Educator." *De/Colonizing the Subject: The Politics of Gender in Women's Autobiography*, 270-284. Eds. Julia Watson, and Sidonie Smith. Minneapolis: University of Minnesota Press, 1992.

Through the autobiography of Nubawiyya Musa, a leading Egyptian feminist in the early twentieth century, the author explores the conditions of Egyptian women at this time.

0303 _____. "From Consciousness to Activism: Feminist Politics in Early Twentieth Century Egypt." *Problems of the Middle East in Historical Perspective*. Ed. John Spagnolo. London: Ithaca Press, 1992.

Discusses the issues pertaining to women's rights and the activists that supported them in early twentieth century Egypt.

0304 _____. "Gender Activism: Feminists and Islamists in Egypt." *Identity Politics and Women: Cultural Reassertions and Feminisms in International Perspective*, 202-227. Ed. Valentine M. Moghadam. Boulder, CO: Westview Press, 1994.
Based on numerous interviews with feminists and Islamist women in Egypt, this chapter examines gender activism in Egypt.

0305 _____. "Independent Women, More Than a Century of Feminism in Egypt." *Arab Women: Old Boundaries, New Frontiers*, 129-174. Ed. Judith Tucker. Bloomington: University of Indiana, 1993.
This chapter traces feminism in Egypt from the last decades of the nineteenth century to the present day. The author contends that contrary to popular belief, Egyptian feminism began with upper class Egyptian women not men.

0306 BAFFOUN, ALYA. "Feminism and Muslim Fundamentalism: The Tunisian and Algerian Cases." *Identity Politics and Women: Cultural Reassertions and Feminisms in International Perspective*, 167-182. Ed. Valentine M. Moghadam. Boulder, CO: Westview Press, 1994.
This chapter compares and contrasts the status of women and the role that Islam plays in defining that status in Tunisia and Algeria.

0307 BARON, BETH. "The Making and Breaking of Marital Bonds in Modern Egypt." *Women in Middle Eastern History*, 275-291. Eds. Nikki R. Keddie, and Beth Baron. New Haven and London: Yale University Press, 1991.
This chapter examines the development of companion marriage in Egypt by tracing the patterns of middle and upper class urban Egyptians in the nineteenth and twentieth century.

0308 BAUER, JANET. "Conversations Among Iranian Political Exiles on Women's Rights: Implications for the Community-Self Debate in Feminism." *C*, no. 4 (1994): 1-12.
Looks at discussions of women's rights by Iranian political exiles and assesses the impact it has had on the Iranian women's movement.

0309 _____. "Ma'ssoum's Tale: The Personal and Political Transformation of a Young Iranian 'Feminist' and Her Ethnographer." *FS* 19, no. 3 (September 1993): 519-548.
Describes the developing feminist consciousness of a young female Iranian political activist.

0310 BENNOUNE, KARIMA. "Algerian Woman Confront Fundamentalism." *MR* (September 1994): 26-39.

This article discusses the violence committed against women in Algeria by Islamic fundamentalists. The author explains how Algerian women have joined together to confront violence by forming independent organizations and by participating in demonstrations.

0311 BOUATTA, CHERIFA. "Feminine Militancy: *Moudjahidates* During and After the Algerian War." *Gender and National Identity: Women and Politics in Muslim Societies*, 18-39. Ed. Valentine M. Moghadam. London and New Jersey: Karachi: Zed Books LTD: Oxford University Press, 1994.

Through interviews with two *moudjahidates* (female fighters), the author utilizes her skills as a social psychologist to portray Algerian women's perceptions about their role in the Algerian Revolution.

0312 BOUATTA, CHERIFA and DORIA CHERIFATI-MERABTINE. "The Social Representative of Women in Algeria's Islamist Movement." *Identity Politics and Women: Cultural Reassertions and Feminisms in International Perspective*, 183-201. Ed. Valentine M. Moghadam. Boulder, CO: Westview Press, 1994.

Explores what the Algerian Islamic Movement's perspective is toward women's status in society.

0313 BROUWER, L. "Binding Religion: Moroccan and Turkish Runaway Girls." *Islam in Dutch Society: Current Developments and Future Prospects*, 75-89. Eds. W. A. R. Shadid, and P.S. van Koningsveld. The Netherlands: Kok Pharos Publishing House, 1992.

Based on field research conducted on Muslim runaway girls, this chapter examines the divisions within the family that lead to girls running away and the role that Islam plays in this conflict.

0314 CAINKAR, LOUISE. "The Gulf War, Sanctions and the Lives of Iraqi Women." *ASQ* 15, no. 2 (March 1993): 15-51.

This study contends that Iraqi women replaced the high-tech industry infrastructure destroyed during the Gulf war. They do this by taking on physical labor associated with pre-industrial times. The article also examines the toll the war and post-war sanctions has placed on women.

0315 _____. "Palestinian Women in American Society: The Interaction of Social Class, Culture, and Politics." *The Development of Arab-American Identity*, 85-106. Ed. Ernest McCarus. Ann Arbor: The University of Michigan Press, 1994.

Drawing upon interviews with Palestinian women in the Chicago area, this study assesses their status in American society.

0316 _____. "Palestinian-American Muslim-Women: Living on the Margins of Two Worlds." *Muslim Families in North America*, 282-308. Eds. Earle H. Waugh, Sharon McIrvin Abu-Laban, and Regula Burckhardt Qureshi. Edmonton, Alberta: The University of Alberta Press, 1991.

This chapter, based on participant observation and life histories recounted to the author between 1982-1985, describes the lives of Palestinian Muslim women born or raised in Chicago.

0317 CALLAWAY, BARBARA and LUCY CREEVY. *The Heritage of Islam: Women, Religion, and Politics in West Africa*. Boulder and London: Lynne Rienner Publishers, 1994.

Examines the impact of Islam on the lives of West African women primarily from Nigeria and Senegal. This work explores the issue of how Muslim women in West Africa fare in comparison to Christian and animist women of the same region. The authors assess the role that Muslims play in the economy, the politics and the domestic realm as well as their level and access to training and education. This comparative study is placed within the particular historical, religious, political and socio-economic context of life in West Africa.

0318 CARMODY, LARDNER DENISE. "Islamic Women." *Women and World Religions*, 185-208. New Jersey: Prentice Hall, Inc., 1989.

This chapter examines Islamic traditions pertaining to Muslim women.

0319 CHERIET, BOUTHEINA. "Islamism and Feminism: Algeria's 'Rites of Passage' to Democracy." *State and Society in Algeria*, 171-215. Eds. John P. Entelis, and Philip C. Naylor. Boulder, CO: Westview Press, 1992.

An analysis of the political debate between the Islamic fundamentalists and feminists in Algeria placed within the larger debate of the democratic process.

0320 CHERIFATI-MERABTINE, DORIA. "Algeria at a Crossroads: National Liberation, Islamization and Women." *Gender and National Identity: Women and Politics in Muslim Societies*, 40-61. Ed. Valentine M. Moghadam. London and New Jersey: Karachi: Zed Books LTD: Oxford University Press, 1994.

This chapter explores the status of Algerian women during the French colonial period and the liberation struggle to discover how women were characterized and represented and what connections existed between this representation and the political sphere. In addition, the work examines the relationship between the woman's nationalist movement that developed following independence and the Islamic current.

0321 CHHACHHI, AMRITA. "Forced Identities: The State, Communalism, Fundamentalism and Women in India." *Women, Islam and the State*, 144-175. Ed. Deniz Kandiyoti. Philadelphia: Temple University Press, 1991.

The formation process of community identity and the effect on Muslim women in India is the focus of this study. The author contends that this process cannot be understood on its own merit but must be placed within the wider context of communalism, fundamentalism, and the interplay between the post-colonial state, capitalism, and patriarchy.

0322 CLANCY-SMITH, JULIA. "The House of Zainab: Female Authority and Saintly Succession in Colonial Algeria." *Women in Middle Eastern History*, 254-274. Eds. Nikki R. Keddie, and Beth Baron. New Haven and London: Yale University Press, 1991.

This chapter analyzes the part that Lalla Zainab played in directing the Rahmaniyya *zawiya* (Sufi lodge) in Algeria from 1897-1904. The author examines the story of Zainab to further understand the role of woman in North African *tariqas* (Sufi orders).

0323 CREEVY, LUCY. "The Impact of Islam on Women in Senegal." *JDA* 25, no. 3 (April 1991): 347-368.

To determine whether religious practices define women's position in Muslim societies. This article assesses the impact of Islam on women in Senegal.

0324 DAVIS, SUSAN SCHAEFER. "Impediments to Empowerment: Moroccan Women and the Agencies." *Women and Development in the Middle East and North Africa*, 111-121. Eds. Joseph G. Jabbra, and Nancy W. Jabbra. Leiden: E.J. Brill, 1992.

Contends that those who work on development projects have only served to limit women's participation in Moroccan society.

0325 DICKS, A. R. "New Lamps for Old: The Evolving Legal Position of Islam in China, With Special Reference to Family Law." *Islamic Family Law*, 347-385. Eds. Chibli Mallat, and Jane Conners. London: Graham & Trotman, 1990.

This essay explores the evolution of the accommodation between the Chinese and Islamic legal systems concerning family law matters.

0326 DJERBAL, DALILA and LOUISA AIT HAMOU. "Women and Democracy in Algeria." *ROAPE* 54 (July 1995): 106-111.

Recounts the growth of the Algerian womens' movement within the larger context of the Algerian experiment with democratization and the rise of Islamic political groups.

0327   DOI, ABDUR RAHMAN I. *Women in Shari'ah (Islamic Law)*. London: Ta-Ha Publishers Ltd, 1989.

This work seeks to explain the role of women in a Muslim society and their rights in the *shari'ah* (Islamic law). Looks at the following topics: marriage and sexual relations; polygyny; divorce; adultery; abortion; family planning; and economic issues. Also contains a chapter describing what he believes to be the failure of Western-influenced feminism in Egypt, Turkey, and Iran.

0328   DOUMATO, ELEANOR A. "Gender, Monarchy, and National Identity in Saudi Arabia." *BJMES* 19, no. 1 (1992): 31-47.

Explores the way in which patriarchal norms work in concert with national identity myths in Saudi Arabia.

0329   _____. "Women and the Stability of Saudi Arabia." *MERIP* 171 (July 1991): 34-37.

This article describes how the Kingdom's official definition of women in their society helps to legitimate the Monarchy and how women act as a barometer of Saudi stability.

0330   DUPREE, NANCY HATCH. "Afghanistan: Women, Society and Development." *Women and Development in the Middle East and North Africa*, 43-55. Eds. Joseph G. Jabbra, and Nancy W. Jabbra. Leiden: E.J. Brill, 1992.

Depicts the lives of Afghani women during the civil war and relates some of their experiences as refugees.

0331   DWYER, DAISY HILSE, Ed. *Law and Islam in the Middle East*, New York: Bergin & Garvey Publishers, 1990.

An edited volume of articles which examine Middle Eastern laws as adhered to by Muslims in different Middle Eastern states. It explores such diverse issues as: the Egyptian criminal justice system and its impact on women; the relative use of Islamic law versus customary law in conflict resolution and dispute behavior within the context of the Jordanian marital sphere; documentary practices in Yemen; criminal Islamic law in Libya; the legal reform efforts of secular and clerical lawyers and the procedures of conflict-resolution in Iran and the relationship between class and law in Lebanon.

0332   EARLY, EVELYN A. "Popular Baladi Islam: Processions and Vows." *Baladi Women of Cairo: Playing with an Egg and a Stone*, 85-130. Boulder & London: Lynne Rienner Publishers, 1993.

Describes popular Islam, defined as everyday religious practices that mix scriptural and local traditions, as practiced by Egyptian women in the *baladi* (traditional) quarters of Cairo.

0333 EDWARDS, KIM. "The Body as Evil." *UR* 50 (May 1992): 70-71.
Author relates her experience as a woman living in an Islamic country, Malaysia.

0334 ENGINEER, ASGHAR ALI. "Islam, Status of Women, and Social Change." *IMA* 21, no. 3 (1990): 180-199.
Advocates a re-reading and re-interpretation of the *shari'ah* (Islamic law) so that issues concerning women are better suited to contemporary times.

0335 _____. *The Rights of Women in Islam.* New York: St. Martin's Press, 1992.
Written by an Islamic theologian, this work calls for a reassessment of women's rights in Islam. Contends that all positions concerning women found in the *shari'ah* (Islamic law) must not be accepted blindly, especially if they contradict Qur'anic injunctions. Provides a historical overview of the position of women in the *jahiliya* (pre-Islamic period). The work then explores issues such as sexual and other aspects of equality; marital rights; and divorce from an Islamic reformist perspective. The final chapter presses the case for reform of Muslim personal law.

0336 ESFANDIARI, HALEH. "The Majles and Women's Issues in the Islamic Republic of Iran." *In the Eye of the Storm: Women in Post-Revolutionary Iran*, 61-79. Eds. Mahnaz Afkhami, and Erika Friedl. Syracuse, NY: Syracuse University Press, 1994.
This chapter provides an analysis of the debates on women's issues that took place in the Iranian Parliament during the writing of the new constitution and the first and second Parliament. The author also looks at the difficulties that the few women representatives faced when voicing the concerns of their female constituents.

0337 FALK, NANCY AUER. *Women and Religion in India: An Annotated Bibliography of Sources in English.* Kalamazoo, MI: New Issues Press, 1994.
Includes citations on Muslim women in India, Pakistan, and Bangladesh.

0338 FARHI, FARIDEH. "Sexuality and the Politics of Revolution in Iran." *Women and Revolution in Africa, Asia, and the New World*, 252-271. Ed. Mary Ann Tètreault. Columbia, SC: University of South Carolina Press, 1994.
Focusing on the revolution in Iran, this chapter looks at ways that women's bodies have been and continue to be the contested sphere through which the meaning of the revolution is defined and reinterpreted.

0339 FAUST, KIMBERLY, JOHN GULICK, SAAD GADALLA, and HIND KHATAB. "Women in the Egyptian Islamic Movement." *MW* 82, no. 1-2 (1992): 55-65.

Drawing upon empirical information, this essay provides an assessment of the female members of the Egyptian Islamic movement.

0340 FLUEHR-LOBBAN, CAROLYN. "Towards a Theory of Arab-Muslim Women as Activist in Secular and religious Movements." *ASQ* 15, no. 2 (March 1993): 87-106.

Through an analysis of the development of the status of women in Islamic and Arab culture, this article provides a theoretical model of the status of the modern Arab Muslim woman. Also focuses on the theme of Arab Muslims as activists.

0341 FREEDMAN, JENNIFER. "Women in Iraq." *AAA* 29 (June 1989): 42-46.

This article examines the elevated role that Iraqi women assumed during the Iran-Iraq war.

0342 FRIEDL, ERIKA. "The Dynamics of Women's Spheres of Action in Rural Iran." *Women in Middle Eastern History*, 195-214. Eds. Nikki R. Keddie, and Beth Baron. New Haven and London: Yale University Press, 1991.

Based on twenty years of field work in a tribal rural area of southwestern Iran, this chapter analyzes the relations between gender and economic activities.

0343 _____. "Sources of Female Power in Iran." *In the Eye of the Storm: Women in Post-Revolutionary Iran*, 151-179. Eds. Mahnaz Afkhami, and Erika Friedl. Syracuse, NY: Syracuse University Press, 1994.

This chapter examines the contradictory concept of the "oppressed - yet - powerful woman" and looks at how women maintain some form of control in a patriarchal society.

0344 EL GAWHARY, KARIM. "An Interview With Heba Ra'uf Ezzat: 'It Is Time to Launch a New Women's Liberation--an Islamic One.'" *MERIP* 191 (November 1994): 26-27.

Offers a discussion with Heba Ra'uf Ezzat, a young female Islamist intellectual who edits the women's page in *Al-Sha'b*, a weekly opposition newspaper published by a coalition of the Muslim Brotherhood and Labor party in Egypt. She articulates her views on women, politics and political sociology within an Islamic framework.

0345 GEADAH, YOLANDE. "Palestinian Women in View of Gender and Development." *Women and Development in the Middle East and North*

Africa, 43-55. Eds. Joseph G. Jabbra, and Nancy W. Jabbra. Leiden: E.J. Brill, 1992.

Illustrates how Palestinian women drew upon their experiences during the *intifada* and enhanced their role in Palestinian society.

0346 GERAMI, SHAHIN. "Privatization of Woman's Role in the Islamic Republic of Iran." *Religion and Political Power*, 99-118. Eds. Gustavo Benavides, and M. W. Daly. Albany: State University of New York Press, 1989.

The agenda of creating an Islamic society by the leaders of the Islamic Republic had as one of its central components the Islamization of the role of women. This chapter describes this process as the restoration of the traditional role of mother and wife and therefore keeping women out of the public sphere.

0347 _____. "The Role, Place, and Power of Middle-Class Women in the Islamic Republic." *Identity Politics and Women: Cultural Reassertions and Feminisms in International Perspective*, 329-348. Ed. Valentine M. Moghadam. Boulder, CO: Westview Press, 1994.

Provides insight into middle-class Iranian women's attitudes toward their role in the Islamic Republic of Iran.

0348 GHAIDA, DINA ABU. "Secular Feminism vs. Islamist Feminism in Palestine." *ASJ* 1, no. 2 (September 1993): 18-20.

Examines the relationship of the two impulses in Palestinian feminism--the secular or Islamist trend--with the family and Palestinian nationalism.

0349 GOODWIN, JAN. *Price of Honor: Muslim Women Lift the Veil of Silence on the Islamic World*. Boston / New York / Toronto / London: Little, Brown and Company, 1994.

Seeking to better understand what it is like to grow up as a woman in an Islamic society, the author travels to Afghanistan, Iran, Pakistan, the United Arab Emirates, Kuwait, Iraq, Saudi Arabia, Jordan, the West Bank and Gaza, and Egypt. The work looks at the effect of the rise of Islamic revivalism on the status of women in these societies.

0350 GRUENBAUM, ELLEN. "The Islamist State and Sudanese Women." *MERIP* 179 (November 1992): 29-32.

Based on fieldwork in Sudan, this essay examines the impact of the policies of the National Islamic Front on Sudanese women.

0351 GRZYMALA-MOSZEZYNKSA, HALINA. "Islam and Feminism in Poland." *JIMMA* 11, no. 1 (January 1990): 73-76.

Following a brief background of Islam in Poland, this article focuses on the status of Muslim women in contemporary Poland.

0352 HAERI, SHAHLA. "Divorce in Contemporary Iran: A Male Prerogative in Self-Will." *Islamic Family Law*, 55-70. Eds. Chibli Mallat, and Jane Conners. London: Graham & Trotman, 1990.

Using Iran as a case study, this article offers a critique of the institution of divorce in Islamic law and how the Islamic government has sought to change these procedures. Examines how the divorce laws affect female-male relationships.

0353 _____. "Obedience Versus Autonomy: Women and Fundamentalism in Iran and Pakistan." *Fundamentalisms and Society: Reclaiming the Sciences, the Family, and Education*, 181-213. Eds. Martin E. Marty, and R. Scott Appleby. Chicago and London: The University of Chicago Press, 1991.

Centered within the context of the dialectical relationship of secular reformers of the 1950s and 1960s and their religious counterparts of the 1970s and 1980s in Pakistan and Iran, this article examines the interaction between Islamic activists, who the author asserts, advocate formalized gender relations and urban middle-class Iranian and Pakistani women who are voicing their own interpretations of personal status laws.

0354 _____. "Temporary Marriage: An Islamic Discourse on Female Sexuality In Iran." *In the Eye of the Storm: Women in Post-Revolutionary Iran*, 98-114. Eds. Mahnaz Afkhami, and Erika Friedl. Syracuse, NY: Syracuse University Press, 1994.

This chapter compares and contrasts the ideological interpretations about institutions of temporary marriage and veiling of the Pahlavi and Islamic regimes.

0355 HAJ, SAMIRA. "Palestinian Women and Patriarchal Relations." *S* 12, no. 4 (June 1992): 761-778.

Drawing upon field research conducted with Palestinian women, this article looks at how patriarchal structures are "both reproduced and contested in the occupied territories."

0356 HALE, SONDRA. *Gender, Islam, and Politics in Sudan*, G.E. von Grunebaum Center for Near Eastern Studies, University of California, Los Angeles, Los Angeles, CA, 1992.

Presents an analysis of the Sudanese National Islamic Front's rise to power while focusing on the gender dynamics that facilitated this rise.

0357 _____. "Gender, Religious Identity, and Political Mobilization in Sudan." *Identity Politics and Women: Cultural Reassertions and Feminisms in International Perspective*, 145-166. Ed. Valentine M. Moghadam. Boulder, CO: Westview Press, 1994.

Explores how gender is politicized in Sudan by various means including the state's relationship with Islam and "the particular expression of gender in Islam."

0358 _____. "The Rise of Islam and Women of the National Islamic Front in the Sudan." *ROAPE* 52 (July 1992): 27-41.
Explores the activities of the National Islamic Front which was active in the democratic era of 1985-1989 and the forces of gender that helped bring this party to power. Contends that this group set in motion impulses that "trained women for the 'revolution' and is now betraying them."

0359 _____. "Transforming Culture or Fostering Second-Hand Consciousness? Women's Front Organizations and Revolutionary Parties--The Sudan Case." *Arab Women: Old Boundaries, New Frontiers*, 149-174. Ed. Judith Tucker. Bloomington: University of Indiana, 1993.
The role of Muslim Sudanese women in the Sudanese Communist party in the 1950's and 60's is the focus of this article. In addition, the paper also discusses the changing conditions of Northern Muslim Sudanese women and the effects of the legitimization of popular 'traditional culture'--including Islam-- on women.

0360 HAMMAMI, REMA. "Women, the Hijab and the Intifada." *MERIP* 164\65 (May 1990): 24-28.
This report describes the campaign to force women to wear the *hijab* (veil) in Gaza by some Hamas members. Also discusses the reaction (or lack thereof) of the Unified National Leadership of the Uprising to this problem.

0361 HANAWAY, WILLIAM L. "Half-Voices: Persian Women's Lives and Letters." *Women's Autobiographies in Iran*, 55-63. Ed. Afsaneh Najmabadi. Cambridge, MA: Harvard University Press, 1990.
Explains why autobiography writing is different in the West and why the Western style might not "suit Persian cultural literary categories."

0362 HATEM, MERVAT F. *The Demise of Egyptian State Feminism and the Politics of Transition (1980-1991)*, G.E. von Grunebaum Center for Near Eastern Studies, University of California, Los Angeles, CA, 1991.
Analyzes the implications of the demise of state feminism in the Middle East on its female population.

0363 _____. "Toward the Development of Post-Islamist and Post-Nationalist Feminist Discourses in the Middle East." *Arab Woman: Old Boundaries, New*

Frontiers, 29-48. Ed. Judith E. Tucker. Bloomington and Indianapolis: Indiana University Press, 1993.

Examines how some features of what the author defines as a conservative Arab social order have contributed to the emergence of new discourses on women.

0364 _____. "Egyptian Discourses on Gender and Political Liberalization: Do Secularist and Islamist Views Really Differ?" *MEJ* 48, no. 4 (1994): 661-676.

This article examines the secular liberal and political Islamist discourse on women in the public sphere in Egypt to determine where the two diverge or agree with one another.

0365 HEGLAND, MARY ELAINE. "Political Roles of Aliabad Women: The Public-Private Dichotomy Transcended." *Women in Middle Eastern History*, 215-230. Eds. Nikki R. Keddie, and Beth Baron. New Haven and London: Yale University Press, 1991.

Based on field work conducted in the village of Aliabad, Iran in 1978-1979, this chapter examines the lives of two primary groups of women--peasants and traders. The author asserts that the public-private ideology has been used to restrain and utilize women and their political activities.

0366 HÉLIE-LUCAS, MARIE-AIMÉE. "The Preferential Symbol for Islamic Identity: Women in Muslim Personal Laws." *Identity Politics and Women: Cultural Reassertions and Feminisms in International Perspective*, 391-407. Ed. Valentine M. Moghadam. Boulder, CO: Westview Press, 1994.

Contends that while Islamic movements are as diverse as the nations in which they originated, certain features resonate through all of them: "the quest for identity and the woman question." Discusses the impact of Muslim Personal laws have on over 450 million Muslim women.

0367 _____. "Women's Struggles and Strategies in the Rise of Fundamentalism in the Muslim World: From Entryism to Internationalism." *Women in the Middle East: Perceptions, Realities and Struggles for Liberation*, 206-241. Ed. Haleh Afshar. New York: St. Martin's Press, 1993.

Outlines the issues stemming from networking to help in the struggle of women in the Middle East and notes the success that networking has had in empowering these women.

0368 HERMANSEN, MARCIA K. "Two-Way Acculturation: Muslim Women in America Between Individual Choice (Liminality) and Community Affiliation (Communitas)." *The Muslims of America*, 188-201. Ed. Yvonne Yazbeck Haddad. New York and Oxford: Oxford University Press, 1991.

Examines the different ways that Muslim women in America express their Islamic belief and identity.

0369 HIGGINS, PATRICIA J. and PIROUZ SHOAR-GHAFFARI. "Women's Education in the Islamic Republic of Iran." *In the Eye of the Storm: Women in Post-Revolutionary Iran*, 19-43. Eds. Mahnaz Afkhami, and Erika Friedl. Syracuse, NY: Syracuse University Press, 1994.

This essay, utilizing Iranian government census data, assesses the government's goal with respect to education, the implementation of these aims and their effect upon post-revolutionary Iranian women. The article also compares educational policies with those of the pre-revolutionary era.

0370 HILLMAN, MICHAEL CRAIG. "An Autobiographical Voice: Forugh Farrokhzad." *Women's Autobiographies in Iran*, 33-54. Ed. Afsaneh Najmabadi. Cambridge, MA: Harvard University Press, 1990.

Addresses the issue of why Iranian women are less likely to write autobiographies than Iranian men. Also discusses the first poetry ever published by an Iranian woman "on her own."

0371 HOODFAR, HOMA. "Devises and Desires: Population Policy and Gender Roles in the Islamic Republic." *MERIP* 190 (September 1994): 11-17.

Argues that the population policy in Iran is not decided by Islamic ideology but by political and economic realities.

0372 HOWARD-MERRIAM, KATHLEEN. "Guaranteed Seats for Political Representation of Women: The Egyptian Example." *W&P* 10, no. 1 (1990): 17-42.

Based on interviews with 45 Egyptian female political activists and 15 years of fieldwork in Egypt, this article examines Egypt's experiment with guaranteed representation for women in the country's parliament.

0373 HUXLEY, ANDREW. "Khaek, Moro, Rohinga - The Family Law of Three South Asian Muslim Minorities." *Islamic Family Law*, 225-252. Eds. Chibli Mallat, and Jane Conners. London: Graham & Trotman, 1990.

This article discusses the minority status that was thrust upon the Khaek Muslims in Thailand, the Rohinga Muslims of Burma, and the Moro Muslims in the Philippines as well as the different cases of state recognition of Islamic family law that ensued.

0374 IMAM, AYESHA. "Politics, Islam, and Women in Kano, Northern Nigeria." *Identity Politics and Women: Cultural Reassertions and Feminisms in International Perspective*, 123-144. Ed. Valentine M. Moghadam. Boulder, CO: Westview Press, 1994.

Through a case study of Kano women in Nigeria, this article focuses on the topic of seclusion as a means of male control and women's political participation and power.

0375 INDA, JULES. "Behind the Veil Debate." *UR* 50 (March 1992): 23-26. Briefly explores the debates surrounding the wearing of the veil.

0376 JABBRA, JOSEPH G. and NANCY W. JABBRA, eds. *Women and Development in the Middle East and North Africa*, Leiden: E.J. Brill, 1992.
This edited volume of essays explores the status of women and development in the Middle East and North Africa. Examines issues of political, economic, and social empowerment of women. Presents studies on women in Iran, Egypt, Iraq, Morocco, Egypt, Saudi Arabia, Palestine, and Afghanistan.

0377 JALAL, AYESHI. "The Convenience of Subservience in Women and the State of Pakistan." *Women, Islam and the State*, 77-114. Ed. Deniz Kandiyoti. Philadelphia: Temple University Press, 1991.
Placing the state as the focus of analysis, this essay provides a historical overview of the interplay in the relationship between the Pakistani state and women. The chapter discusses how Islam has been used to legitimize the state and thereby affect the status of women.

0378 JAWAD H. A. "Woman and the Question of Polygamy in Islam." *IQ* 35, no. 4 (1991): 181-190.
Criticizes contemporary Western studies on Muslim women. It focuses on the issue of polygamy to debunk Western misconceptions by outlining conditions under which it must occur.

0379 JOSEPH, SUAD. "Brother/Sister Relationships: Connectivity, Love and Power in the Reproduction of Arab Patriarchy." *AE* 21, no. 1 (February 1994): 50-73.
This article explores brother-sister relationships in Borj Hammoud, Lebanon. The author asserts, contrary to widely-held beliefs that Arab brother-sister relationships are merely an extension of the father-daughter relationship, that this relationship is often based on mutual love in addition to power and violence.

0380 _____. "Connectivity and Patriarchy Among Urban Working Class Arab Families in Lebanon." *E* 21, no. 4 (December 1993): 452-484.
Based on field work in Lebanon, this essay analyzes the interrelationship between "connectivity and Arab patriarchy" of two refugee camp families in Lebanon. The work also assesses different approaches to Arab societies such as "individualist and corporatist."

0381 _____. "Elite Strategies for State Building: Women, Family, Religion and State in Iraq and Lebanon." *Women, Islam and the State*, 176-200. Ed. Deniz Kandiyoti. London: Macmillan, 1991.

Seeking to contribute to a fuller understanding of the relationship between religion, women, family, and the state in the Middle East, this article compares and contrasts two case studies which focus on the state-building plans of the Iraqi and Lebanese elites and policies affecting women and the family.

0382 _____. "Gender and Relationality Among Arab Families in Lebanon." *FS* 19, no. 3 (September 1993): 465-486.

Investigates the theory that women are more relationship-oriented than men. Discovers through an examination of Arab families in an urban working class neighborhood near Beirut that both women and men are involved with "patriarchal connectivity" defined as "relationships in which a person's boundaries are relatively fluid so that a person feels a part of significant others."

0383 KABEER, NAILA. "The Quest for National Identity: Women, Islam and the State in Bangladesh." *Women, Islam and the State*, 115-143. Ed. Deniz Kandiyoti. Philadelphia: Temple University Press, 1991.

An exploration of the interplay between culture and religion in the formation of Bengali national identity and in shaping political policies is the focus of this article. In addition, the author compares and contrasts the Islamization process in Bangladesh to the process in Iran and Pakistan and illustrates that the most striking differential is in the sphere of women's rights.

0384 KADIOGLU, AYSE. "Women's Subordination in Turkey: Is Islam Really the Villain?" *MEJ* 48, no. 4 (1994): 645-660.

This article asserts that the debate about veiling in Turkey by political Islamists, colonial feminists, and Kemalist intelligentsia has undermined the chance for an independent Turkish feminist discourse to develop from below.

0385 KAMALKHANI, ZAHRA. "Women's Everyday Religious Discourse in Iran." *Women in the Middle East: Perceptions, Realities and Struggles for Liberation*, 85-94. Ed. Haleh Afshar. New York: St. Martin's Press, 1993.

Provides a case study of religious rituals in Iran and demonstrates how Iranian women have used these rituals and ceremonies to enhance their position in society.

0386 KANDIYOTI, DENIZ. "End of the Empire: Islam, Nationalism, and Women in Turkey." *Women, Islam and the State*, 22-48. Ed. Deniz Kandiyoti. Philadelphia: Temple University Press, 1991.

This chapter contends that the emancipation of women in Turkey may only be understood through an exploration of the political transformation process of an empire based on the *millet* (religious and national communities) system to a secular nation-state.

0387 _____. "Islam and Patriarchy: A Comparative Perspective." *Women in Middle Eastern History*, 23-42. Eds. Nikki R. Keddie, and Beth Baron. New Haven and London: Yale University Press, 1991.

Asserting that gender relations have been influenced by the link between patriarchy and Islam, this article offers a comparative analysis of patriarchal systems in sub-Saharan Africa, the Middle East, and South and Southeast Asia.

0388 _____, ed. *Women, Islam and the State*. Philadelphia: Temple University Press, 1991.

This edited work explores the relationship between the status of women, Islam, and the State in the Middle East and South Asia. The book highlights the theory that state policies have had an important impact on the role of women and therefore must be examined to reach an adequate analysis of the status of women in the Middle East and South Asia. Authors utilize this concept in their studies of Turkey, Iran, Egypt, Lebanon, Iraq, Pakistan, Bangladesh, and India. The differing state formation process helps the reader to understand why the position of women varies from one country to the next.

0389 _____. "Women, Islam and the State." *MERIP* 173 (November 1991): 9-13.

This article explores the relationship between Islam, the state, and the politics of gender. The author distinguishes three primary characteristics that affect this relationship: the ties between Islam and cultural nationalism; international pressures that influence state policies; and the means of state control over local kin-based, religious, and sectarian communities.

0390 _____. "Women, Islam, and the State: A Comparative Approach." *Comparing Muslim Societies: Knowledge and the State in a World Civilization*, 237-260. Ed. Juan R. I. Cole. Ann Arbor: The University of Michigan Press, 1992.

This chapter examines whether Islam or the state is the primary variable in accounting for the vast differences in the conditions of women in Muslim societies. The author examines the role of Islam in nationalism and state building, the expansion of state apparatus into the realm of women and the family, and the international dimension of the role of the wealthy states and the ties of foreign aid. It illustrates how all these variables have had an impact on the lives of Muslim women.

0391 KARMI, GHADA. "The Saddam Hussein Phenomenon and Male-Female Relations in the Arab World." *Women in the Middle East: Perceptions,*

Realities and Struggles for Liberation, 146-157. Ed. Haleh Afshar. New York: St. Martin's Press, 1993.

Examines the Arab patriarchal family system and notes the problems it poses for women's liberation and on the Arab states themselves.

0392 KAWAR, AMAL. "National Mobilization, War Conditions, and Gender Consciousness." *ASQ* 15, no. 2 (March 1993): 53-67.

Examines the impact of war conditions and nationalism on the PLO's female leadership in Lebanon between 1971-1982.

0393 KNAUSS, PETER R. "Algerian Women Since Independence." *State and Society in Algeria*, 151-169. Eds. John P. Entelis, and Philip C. Naylor. Boulder, CO: Westview Press, 1992.

Asserting that French colonial policies reasserted and revived patriarchal norms, this chapter offers an analysis of the status of Algerian women since the Algerian Revolution.

0394 KOUSHA, MAHNAZ. "Women, History and the Politics of Gender in Iran." *C* 1 (September 1992): 25-37.

An examination of the political, social, and economic changes in the lives of Iranian women since 1925. In addition, the author assesses Iranian women's accomplishments since the Revolution.

0395 KUSHA, HAMID R. "Minority Status of Women in Islam: A Debate Between Traditional and Modern Islam." *JIMMA* 11, no. 1 (1990): 58-72.

Analyzes three different Islamic ideologies concerning the status of women--fundamentalist, reformist, and revolutionary.

0396 KUTTAB, DAOUD. "Women in Islam: An Interview with Hanan Riyan Bakri." *PIJ* 2 (1994): 94-98.

Through an interview with Hanan Riyan Bakri, considered an expert in Islamic law as well as a practicing Muslim, this work looks at the rights of Muslim women under Islamic law.

0397 KUTTAB, EILEEN S. "Palestinian Women in the *Intifada*: Fighting on Two Fronts." *ASQ* 15, no. 2 (March 1993): 69-85.

Examines Palestinian women's historical role in the Palestinian national struggle as well as during the *intifada*.

0398 LACAR, LUIS Q. "The Emerging Role of Muslim Women in a Rapidly Changing Society: The Philippine Case." *JIMMA* 13, no. 1 (January 1992): 80-98.

Discusses the prominent role that Filipino Muslim play in the Philippine Muslim community.

0399   LATEEF, SHAHIDA. *Muslim Women in India: Political and Private Realities*. London: Zed Press, Ltd., 1990.

Based on a survey conducted in nine major Indian cities, this study attempts to delineate the role and status of Muslim women in India in both the public and private spheres. It zeroes in on issues of education, literacy, social legislation, and purdah. The work places the material in its historical as well as economic and political context with an assessment of the participation of Muslim women in women's movements in addition to social and political action.

0400   LAZREG, MARNIA. "Gender and Politics in Algeria: Unraveling the Religious Paradigm." *S* 15, no. 4 (June 1990): 755-780.

Explores the role that religion plays in Algerian politics to better determine its impact upon women in Algerian society.

0401   MABRO, JUDY. *Veiled Half-Truths: Western Travelers' Perceptions of Middle Eastern Women*. London: I.B. Tauris & Co., Ltd., 1991.

This anthology is a selection of Western travelers' perceptions of Middle Eastern women during the 19th and early 20th centuries. Divided into twelve chapters, the work examines various topics concerning the role and status of Middle Eastern women and provides excerpts of Western writers to illustrate the misperceptions and stereotypes that existed then and have continued to this day.

0402   MACLEOD, ARLENE ELOWE. *Accommodating Protest: Working Women, the New Veiling and Change in Cairo*. New York: Columbia University Press, 1991.

This study examines the new veiling of lower middle class women in Cairo who leave their homes to enter the work place. The writer employs a case study of eighty five women to explore their beliefs and behavior. The work gives voice to many of the Egyptian women studied and their socio-cultural universe through discussions and interviews over a period of years. It evaluates the conflicting ideologies of lower middle class women who seek to blend economic pressures of modern life with traditional values. Within this context the writer examines the symbolism of the new veiling that many women have adopted in order to enter the work place while accommodating traditional power structures.

0403 MAHMOOD, TAHIR. "Islamic Family Law: Latest Developments in India."
Islamic Family Law, 295-320. Eds. Chibli Mallat, and Jane Conners. London:
Graham & Trotman, 1990.
This article examines the repercussions of the enactment of the Muslim
Women (Protection of Rights of Divorce) Act in India in 1986.

0404 MALLAT, CHIBLI. "Shi'ism and Sunnism in Iraq: Revisiting the Codes."
Islamic Family Law, 71-92. Eds. Chibli Mallat, and Jane Conners. London:
Graham & Trotman, 1990.
Examines the problems the 1959 Iraqi Code of Personal Status Law faced
around the time of its inception within the context of the Sunni-Shi'i divisions.

0405 MALLAT, CHIBLI, and JANE CONNERS, eds. *Islamic Family Law*, London:
Graham & Trotman, 1990.
An edited volume of essays dealing with various aspects of Islamic Family
Law. The articles have been adapted from a conference convened by the Centre
of Islamic and Middle East Law, the Centre of Near and Middle Eastern
Studies and the Law Department of the School of Oriental and African Studies,
University of London. Mallat begins with an introduction to Islamic family law
which explores the dynamics of a unified personal law system versus
community personal laws system in Muslim societies and societies where
Muslims are a minority. The following work is divided into three geographical
areas. The first part, which deals with the Middle East, offers chapters on the
Islamic inheritance system, a comparative look at the treatment of non-Muslim
minorities under Islamic law in the Middle East, divorce in Iran, and Islamic
law under Israeli occupation in the West Bank. The second section moves to
Europe and examines Muslim minorities within the context of Islamic family
law in Britain, Germany and France. The final portion, which analyzes Islamic
family law in South Asia, Southeast Asia and China, includes chapters on
diverse issues such as Islamic law in colonial India, family law of the southeast
Asian minorities of Thailand, Burma and the Philippines, the reforms of
Islamic family law in India and the impact of a uniform civil code on Indian
Muslims, Islamic family law in Pakistan and the legal position of Muslims in
China.

0406 MALTI-DOUGLAS, FEDWA. *Woman's Body, Woman's Word: Gender and
Discourse in Arabo-Islamic Writing*. Princeton: Princeton University Press,
1991.
Analyzes medieval and modern texts in which woman's body and word are
linked. This work, divided into nine chapters, offers arguments that outline the
themes that define and delimit the representation of women in Arabo-Islamic
writing. The first five chapters discuss specific examples of medieval writings
of Arab literary prose including 1000 and One Nights, Ibn Tufayl's Male

Utopia, the writings of Ibn al-Wardi and al-Suhrawardi as well as philosophical commentaries and anecdotal collections. This section demonstrates that during this time period woman's voice was often heard, however, the writer behind her voice was usually male. Chapters six through nine examine contemporary writers such as Nawal al-Sa'adawi, Taha Hussein, 'Abla al-Ruwayni and Fadwa Tuqan and illustrates how these authors are writing within the Arabo-Islamic tradition in order to subvert it.

0407   MANASRA, NAJAH. "Palestinian Women: Between Tradition and Revolution." *Palestinian Women: Identity and Experience*, 7-21. Ed. Ebba Augusten. London and New Jersey: Zed Books, 1993.

This chapter explores the different life stages of Palestinian women and describes the roles that they are expected to play. The essay also looks at some family laws--divorce, marriage, and inheritance--and their impact on Palestinian women.

0408   MARCUS, JULIE. *A World of Difference: Islam and Gender Hierarchy in Turkey*. London and Atlantic Highlands, NJ: Zed Books, 1992.

This study of Islam and gender in Aegean Turkey examines the effects of the incorporation of the Ottoman economy into the developing world economy had on gender hierarchy. In a critique of modern ethnography, the author analyzes the politics of the 19th century European travelers' accounts and portraits of the Middle East and concludes that central to the Western construct of the orient are women and sexuality. This comparative analysis of the construction of female space in both Turkey and the West argues that gender systems play a fundamental role in the organization of societies and culture. Marcus depicts the gender hierarchy as divided between the men who have their sacred structural center in the mosque and anti-structural center in the pilgrimage to Mecca. Women, on the other hand, have corresponding centers at *mevlid* recitals in the home and in pilgrimages to local shrines.

0409   MATORY, J. LORAND. "Rival Empires: Islam and the Religions of Spirit Possession Among the 'OYO'-Yoruba." *AE* 21, no. 3 (August 1994): 495-515.

This case study looks at the relationship between Islam and spirit possession as practiced by the 'OYO'-Yoruba women of West Africa.

0410   MCCLOUD, BEVERLY THOMAS. "African-American Muslim Women." *The Muslims of America*, 177-187. Ed. Yvonne Yazbeck Haddad. New York and Oxford: Oxford University Press, 1991.

Based upon oral history research of a community in Philadelphia, this chapter examines the problems faced by African American women who have converted to Islam.

0411 MEHDI, R. "The Offense of Rape in the Islamic Law of Pakistan." *IJSL* 18, no. 1 (1990): 19-29.

Examines the legal issues surrounding rape in Pakistan's Islamic law.

0412 MEHDID, MALIKA. "A Western Invention of Arab Womanhood: The 'Oriental' Female." *Women in the Middle East: Perceptions, Realities and Struggles for Liberation*, 18-58. Ed. Haleh Afshar. New York: St. Martin's Press, 1993.

Traces Western literary images of Middle Eastern women and discusses the harmful impact these stereotypical perceptions have had on these women.

0413 MENSKI, WERNER F. "The Reform of Islamic Family Law and a Uniform Civil Code for India." *Islamic Family Law*, 253-294. Eds. Chibli Mallat, and Jane Conners. London: Graham & Trotman, 1990.

This article explores the degree to which Islamic family laws were changed in India and assesses the desirability of a uniform civil code.

0414 MERNISSI, FATIMA. *Dreams of Trespass: Tales of a Harem*. Reading, Massachusetts: Addison-Wesley Publishing Company, 1994.

Set in Morocco, this fictional novel is the story of a young girl raised in a harem. The author vividly depicts the life and personalities of the characters and presents a clear image of the role of women in a harem society.

0415 _____. *The Veil and the Male Elite: A Feminist Interpretation of Women's Rights in Islam*. Reading, MA: Addison-Wesley, 1991.

Examines the question of whether Islam is opposed to women's rights. To do this the author provides the reader with a dramatic re-reading of early Islamic texts that pertain to the role of women such as the Hadith and Tabari's commentary on the Qur'an. Mernissi, through scriptural analysis and an examination of social space, slavery, warfare, inheritance, violence, sexual practices and the hijab in early Islam demonstrates how the early texts have been manipulated by the male elite to receive and retain political legitimacy. Throughout this analysis the author insists that the male elites have in fact manipulated memory and history and not the texts themselves.

0416 MILANI, FARZANEH. "Veiled Voices: Women's Autobiographies in Iran." *Women's Autobiographies in Iran*, 1-16. Ed. Afsaneh Najmabadi. Cambridge, MA: Harvard University Press, 1990.

Discusses the difficulties faced by Iranian female writers who express themselves in autobiographies.

0417 _____. *Veils and Words: The Emerging Voices of Iranian Women Writers*. Syracuse, NY: Syracuse University Press, 1992.

Focuses on Iranian female writers who have explored new ideas concerning veiling and unveiling. Her survey includes three genres of lyric poetry, short stories, and novels from the 19th century to the present. The main thesis of this work is that women's literary articulations are determined by cultural and historical circumstances. The first section of this work is a socio-historical overview in Iranian cultural and literary history. The second portion is an analysis of the poetry of four Iranian women. The concluding portion of this work focuses solely on the poetry of Simin Behbahani which the author asserts is representative of neotraditional feminism. This poetry is also read against the backdrop of the Iranian Revolution as an example of the tensions between tradition and modernity.

0418 MIR-HOSSEINI, ZIBA. "Women, Marriage and the Law in Post-Revolutionary Iran." *Women in the Middle East: Perceptions, Realities and Struggles for Liberation*, 59-84. Ed. Haleh Afshar. New York: St. Martin's Press, 1993.

Examines the institution of marriage in Iran and asserts that Iranian women have developed methods to counter the negative aspects of the *shari'ah* concerning marriage and divorce.

0419 MOGHADAM, FATEMEH E. "Commoditization of Sexuality and Female Labor Participation in Islam: Implications for Iran 1960-90." *In the Eye of the Storm: Women in Post-Revolutionary Iran*, 80-97. Eds. Mahnaz Afkhami, and Erika Friedl. Syracuse, NY: Syracuse University Press, 1994.

Using the paradigm of commoditization, the author analyzes laws and practices relating to the concept of female sexuality in Iran.

0420 MOGHADAM, VALENTINE M. "Fundamentalism and the Woman Question in Afghanistan." *Fundamentalism in Comparative Perspective*, 126-151. Ed. Lawrence Kaplan. Amherst: The University of Massachusetts Press, 1992.

This article argues that the Soviet intervention in Afghanistan and the world attention it has generated, concealed the primary nature of the conflict: one between modernization and tradition, which is between patriarchy and women's emancipation.

0421 _____, ed. *Gender and National Identity: Women and Politics in Muslim Societies*, London and Atlantic Highlands, New Jersey: Karachi: Zed Books LTD: Oxford University Press, 1994.

This edited collection of articles examines the role that woman play in national identity formation in Muslim societies. Composed of seven chapters, the first outlines the themes of the book and discusses the role that the debate over the rights of women has played in political movements and the relationship between feminism and dominant ideologies including socialism, nationalism, and Islamic fundamentalism. The second chapter highlights the role of the Algerian *Moujahidates* (freedom fighters) during and after Algeria's liberation struggle. The third chapter also deals with Algeria and explores the relationship between the national liberation struggle, Islamization, and women. The fourth chapter discusses the woman's movement in Bangladesh within the framework of the Bangladesh national struggle and the rising Islamic fundamentalist movement. The fifth chapter examines the 'woman question' in Afghanistan and illustrates the difficulties that this issue raises for the different leaders in Afghanistan due to the weakness of the state and embedded patriarchal values. The sixth chapter demonstrates how historical, political, economic, social, cultural, and religious factors have all combined to shape the Iranian feminist movement. The final chapter assesses the impact of the *intifada* on the Palestinian woman's movement, specifically how these changes, brought about because of the struggle, will shape gender relations and Palestinian society at large.

0422   _____, ed. *Identity Politics and Women: Cultural Reassertions and Feminists in International Perspective*, Boulder, CO: Westview Press, 1994.
    This edited volume looks at the issue of "identity politics," which is defined as "discourses and movements organized around questions of religious, ethnic, and national identity." The majority of the essays in this work focus on movements that are seeking to take over power and are religious in nature and defined as Muslim "fundamentalist." The Islamic "fundamentalist" movements selected for this study have an agenda for women. The chapters examine the interaction between women, identity, and culture from all over the world. The volume also explores the women who are active participants in these movements and those who are totally opposed to them. It details the causes behind the rise of these movements and its ideology and goals. The work also seeks to address the question of why many of the members of these groups are preoccupied with gender issues, specifically women's place in society.

0423   _____. *Modernizing Women: Gender and Social Change in the Middle East*. Boulder & London: Lynne Rienner Publishers, 1993.
    This work explores the process of social change in the Middle East, North Africa, and Afghanistan and examines the impact of this change on the roles and status of women. Chapters deal with issues such as economic development and women's employment; the impact of revolution and reform measures on women's roles in society; the patriarchal structure of the Middle Eastern family and the changes occurring due to economic development and demographic transition; the causal factors behind the rise of Islamic fundamentalism, the impact on women and women's diverse responses; an analysis of female fertility, education, employment and literacy rates in post-Revolutionary Iran;

and, an overview of women's struggle in Afghanistan within the context of a tribal, patriarchal society with a weak central state.

0424 _____. "Reform, Revolution, and Reaction: The Trajectory of the 'Woman Question' in Afghanistan." *Gender and National Identity: Women and Politics in Muslim Societies.* Ed. Valentine M. Moghadam. London and Atlantic Highlands, New Jersey: Karachi: Zed Books LTD: Oxford University Press, 1994.

Through a historical analysis of the 'woman question' in Afghanistan, this chapter examines the troubles that the issues of woman's emancipation and rights have had in Afghani society particularly during the war.

0425 _____. "The Reproduction of Gender Inequality in Muslim Societies: A Case Study of Iran in the 1980s." *WD* 19, no. 10 (October 1991): 1335-1349.

The author uses social, economic, and demographic data to document the disadvantages of women in the Iranian Islamic Republic.

0426 _____. "Revolution, Islamist Reaction, and Women in Afghanistan." *Women and Revolution in Africa, Asia, and the New World,* 211-235. Ed. Mary Ann Tètreault. Columbia, SC: University of South Carolina Press, 1994.

Contends that the international and geopolitical nature of the Soviet invasion and occupation of Afghanistan cloaked the underlying roots of the conflict: strife between the "modernizers and traditionalists, and between women's emancipation and patriarchy." Focuses on the contention over the issue of women's rights as well as the significance of gender issues for both sides of the conflict.

0427 MOGHISSI, HAIDEH. "Women in the Resistance Movement in Iran." *Women in the Middle East: Perceptions, Realities and Struggles for Liberation,* 158-171. Ed. Haleh Afshar. New York: St. Martin's Press, 1993.

Traces the experiences of the political left in Iran prior to the Revolution and examines the difficulties faced by Iranian women in terms of active participation in the national struggle.

0428 MOHSEN, SAFIA K. "Women and Criminal Justice in Egypt." *Law and Islam in the Middle East,* 15-34. Ed. Daisy Hilse Dwyer. New York: Bergin & Garvey, 1990.

Examines how Egyptian women are treated, either as victims or offenders, in the various stages of the Egyptian criminal justice system. Explores six different criminal cases.

0429 MOLYNEUX, MAXINE. "The Law, the State and the Socialist Policies with Regard to Women: The Case of the People's Democratic Republic of Yemen

1967-1990." *Women, Islam and the State*, 237-271. Ed. Deniz Kandiyoti. Philadelphia: Temple University Press, 1991.

Through an analysis of family law reform in the PDRY, this chapter explores the relationship between Islam, socialism, and women.

0430 AL MUGHNI, HAYA. *Women in Kuwait: The Politics of Gender*. London: Saqi Books, 1993.

A study of women's organizations in Kuwait set in the context of the issues of class, tribe, and politics. Discusses the impact of oil wealth; the institutionalization of the state on the role of women, as well as the challenge of the growth of the Islamic revivalist movement and its impact on the future prospects for women.

0431 MULE, PAT and DIANE BARTHEL. "The Return to the Veil: Individual Autonomy Vs. Social Esteem." *SF* 7, no. 2 (1992): 323-332.

Explores the recent phenomenon of donning the veil by Egyptian women as a means to obtain a degree of autonomy and self esteem.

0432 MUMTAZ, KHAWAR. "Identity Politics and Women: 'Fundamentalism' and Women in Pakistan." *Identity Politics and Women: Cultural Reassertions and Feminisms in International Perspective*, 228-242. Ed. Valentine M. Moghadam. Boulder, CO: Westview Press, 1994.

This chapter explores the "religious right" in Pakistan and its manifestation in the political sphere. The work then examines the "fundamentalist women," their origins, ideology, and goals and aims.

0433 NAFICY, AZAR. "Images of Women in Classical Persian Literature and the Contemporary Iranian Novel." *In the Eye of the Storm: Women in Post-Revolutionary Iran*, 115-130. Eds. Mahnaz Afkhami, and Erika Friedl. Syracuse, NY: Syracuse University Press, 1994.

This chapter analyzes images of women in classical Persian literature and compares them with those presented in contemporary Iranian novels in order to evaluate the changes in the literary portrayal of women.

0434 NAFICY, HAMID. "Veiled Vision/Powerful Presences: Women in Post-Revolutionary Iranian Cinema." *In the Eye of the Storm: Women in Post-Revolutionary Iran*, 131-150. Eds. Mahnaz Afkhami, and Erika Friedl. Syracuse, NY: Syracuse University Press, 1994.

The author traces the historical background of Iranian women's participation in Iranian film-making, the emergence of women film directors and examines how the film industry deals with the government's demand for sexual modesty.

0435 NAJMABADI, AFSANEH. "A Different Voice: Taj os-Saltaneh." *Women's Autobiographies in Iran*, 17-32. Ed. Afsaneh Najmabadi. Cambridge, MA: Harvard University Press, 1990.

Surveys the memoirs of Taj as-Sultaneh, a Qajar princess, to discern how the ideas of Iranian women writers were created as well as how these ideas differed from their male counterparts.

0436 _____. "Hazards of Modernity and Morality: Women, State, and Ideology in Contemporary Iran." *Women, Islam and the State*, 48-76. Ed. Deniz Kandiyoti. Philadelphia: Temple University Press, 1991.

This chapter explores the 'woman question' as appropriated by the Pahlavi regime; the interplay between transformation of the state and the new meanings given to the 'woman question'; and the shift into Islamic politics with differing views concerning the status of women in an Islamic society.

0437 _____. "Veiled Discourse--Unveiled Bodies." *FS* (September 1993): 487-518.

Through an examination of women's social functions, "genre literature, and bodily disciplines," this article views the "woman question" in the debates concerning modernization and Islamic discourse in late 19th and early 20th century Iran.

0438 _____, ed. *Women's Autobiographies in Iran*, Cambridge, MA: Harvard University Press, 1990.

This collection of essays are the result of a conference focusing on biographies and autobiographies in 19th and 20th century Iranian history. Offers four essays that portray female autobiographical voices in Iran.

0439 NELSON, CYNTHIA. "Biography and Women's History: On Interpreting Doria Shafik." *Women in Middle Eastern History*, 310-333. Eds. Nikki R. Keddie, and Beth Baron. New Haven and London: Yale University Press, 1991.

Through an examination of the life of Egyptian feminist Doria Shafik, this chapter addresses issues of changing boundaries between the biographer and the women studied.

0440 OLCOTT, MARTHA BRILL. "Women and Society in Central Asia." *Soviet Central Asia*, 235-254. Ed. William Fierman. Boulder, CO: Westview Press, 1991.

Contends that seventy years of communist rule has failed to fully integrate women into the changing life of Central Asia. Also discusses the role that Islam plays in their day to day lives.

0441 ONG, AIHWA. "State versus Islam: Malay Families, Women's Bodies, and the Body Politic in Malaysia." *AE* 17, no. 2 (May 1990): 258-276.

The social effects of state policies and Islamic revivalism on ideals of Malay womanhood, identity and kinship is the central thesis of this study.

0442 PAPPS, IVY. "Attitudes to Female Employment in Four Middle Eastern Countries." *Women in the Middle East: Perceptions, Realities and Struggles for Liberation*, 96-116. Ed. Haleh Afshar. New York: St. Martin's Press, 1993.

Offers the results of a survey conducted on women and another on employers in the countries of Egypt, Jordan, Morocco, and Turkey as part of a World Bank study of female employment. Uses these results to make some observations concerning the connection between female employment and Islam.

0443 PEARL, DAVID. "Executive and Legislative Amendments to Islamic Family Law in India and Pakistan." *Islamic Law and Jurisprudence*, 199-220. Ed. Nicholas Heer. Seattle and London: University of Washington Press, 1990.

This essay explores the significant impact of Muslim Family Laws Ordinance 1961 on the political and social life of Pakistan since its enactment. In addition, the article examines the impact of this legislation on Muslim family law in India.

0444 _____. "Three Decades of Executive, Legislative and Judicial Amendments to Islamic Family Law in Pakistan." *Islamic Family Law*, 321-338. Eds. Chibli Mallat, and Jane Conners. London: Graham & Trotman, 1990.

Examines the reasons behind the various amendments to Islamic family law in Pakistan over the past thirty years.

0445 PETERSON, J. E. "The Political Status of Women in the Arab Gulf States." *MEJ* 43, no. 1 (1989): 34-50.

Addresses the topic of women's political and public participation in the Gulf states.

0446 PETHERBRIDGE, SALLY. "This is Not the Dawn: Women and Islamisation in Pakistan." *Politics of the Future: The Role of Social Movements*, 355-377. Eds. Christine Jennett, and Randa G. Stewart. Melbourne, Australia: Macmillan, 1989.

Through an examination of the Women's Action Forum, Pakistan's first feminist organization, this article looks at the impact of Islamization on women's status.

0447 POPE, JULIET J. "The Emergence of a Joint Israeli-Palestinian Women's Peace Movement During the *Intifada*." *Women in the Middle East:*

Perceptions, Realities and Struggles for Liberation, 172-184. Ed. Haleh Afshar. New York: St. Martin's Press, 1993.

Examines the joint peace activities undertaken by Palestinian and Israeli women during the first two years of the *intifada*.

0448   RAMAZANI, NESTA. "Women in Iran: The Revolutionary Ebb and Flow." *MEJ* 47, no. 3 (June 1993): 409-428.

Examines the early excesses and repression of the Iranian revolution and later reformist governments. Through an investigation of personal status laws and the roles of women in the political institutions, the author argues that since the revolution the Iranian government has quietly introduced progressive reforms concerning the status of women. However, the writer states that much remains to be done.

0449   RASSAM, AMAL. "Popular Ideology and Women in Iraq: Legislation and Cultural Constraints." *Women and Development in the Middle East and North Africa*, 82-95. Eds. Joseph G. Jabbra, and Nancy W. Jabbra. Leiden: E.J. Brill, 1992.

Depicts the programs adopted by the Ba'thi state to provide greater rights for Iraqi women.

0450   RAZAVI, SHAHRASHOUB. "Women, Work and Power in the Rafsanjani Basin of Iran." *Women in the Middle East: Perceptions, Realities and Struggles for Liberation*, 117-136. Ed. Haleh Afshar. New York: St. Martin's Press, 1993.

Based on field research carried out in two Iranian villages between September 1988 and August 1989, this chapter examines the "gender division of labor" and the relationship between economic conditions and gender.

0451   REEVES, MINOU. *Female Warriors of Allah: Women and the Islamic Revolution*. New York: E.P. Dutton, 1989.

This book helps the reader understand the role of Iranian women in the Islamic revolution in Iran. Moreover, the author delves into the topic of the female Iranian soldiers and martyrs. Explores reasons behind female support for the revolution and motivation to become soldiers for the cause. In addition, the work examines the rise and depth of Islamic revivalism in the Muslim world and then focuses on the Islamic revolution in Iran.

0452   RUSSELL, MONA L. "The Female Brain Drain, the State, and Development in Egypt." *Women and Development in the Middle East and North Africa*, 122-142. Eds. Joseph G. Jabbra, and Nancy W. Jabbra. Leiden: E.J. Brill, 1992.

Depicts the picture of what happens when a state cannot employ its educated female population.

0453 SAADAWI, NAWAL EL. "Women's Resistance in the Arab World and in Egypt." *Women in the Middle East: Perceptions, Realities and Struggles for Liberation*, 139-145. Ed. Haleh Afshar. New York: St. Martin's Press, 1993.
Explores the various women's resistance movements in the Arab world.

0454 SABBAGH, SUHA. "The Rights of Women in the Future State of Palestine: An Interview with Yasser Arafat Conducted in Tunis on 3 July 1989." *ASQ* 15, no. 2 (March 1993): 107-115.
Through an interview with Yassir Arafat, this article looks at the Chairman of the PLO's views on gender issues and the role of women in a Palestinian state.

0455 SABBAGH, SUHA and GHADA TALHAMI, eds. *Images and Reality: Palestinian Women Under Occupation and in the Diaspora*, Washington, DC: The Institute for Arab Women's Studies, Inc., 1990.
This edited volume contains five articles which were presented at a conference on Palestinian women sponsored by the Palestinian Human Rights Campaign in 1986. Seeks to inform the general public on Arab feminism in general and Palestinian feminism in particular.

0456 SALEM, NEHAD. "Women's Rights in the Arab Nation." *JAA* 9, no. 1 (1990): 36-41.
Analyzes the data concerning the reality of women's rights in the Arab world.

0457 SANAD, JAMAL and MARK TESSLER. "Women and Religion in a Modern Islamic Society: The Case of Kuwait." *Religious Resurgence and Politics in the Modern World*, 195-218. Ed. Emile Sahliyeh. Albany, NY: State University of New York Press, 1990.
Using Kuwait as a case study and based on a survey conducted on five hundred and fifty Kuwaiti women in 1984, this chapter analyzes the connections between Islamic orientations and views concerning the role of women in society.

0458 SANASARIAN, ELIZ. "The Politics of Gender and Development in the Islamic Republic of Iran." *Women and Development in the Middle East and North Africa*, 56-68. Eds. Joseph G. Jabbra, and Nancy W. Jabbra. Leiden: E.J. Brill, 1992.
Depicts how many men lost much of their political power in post-revolutionary Iran yet attained more power over women. Also shows how more women are questioning their role in society.

0459 SEIKALY, MAY. "Women and Social Change in Bahrain." *IJMES* 26, no. 3 (August 1994): 415-426.
Discusses the status of Bahraini women to determine whether this status has changed with the changes in society.

0460 SHAHEED, FARIDA. "Controlled or Autonomous: Identity and the Experience of the Network, Women Living under Muslim Laws." *S* 19, no. 4 (June 1994): 997-1019.
Through an examination of women, Islam, and the law, this article traces the development and strategies of the international organization, Women Living under Muslim Laws.

0461 SHAHIDIAN, HAMMED. "The Iranian Left and the "Woman Question"' in the Revolution of 1978-79." *IJMES* 26, no. 2 (May 1994): 223-247.
Addresses the changing relationship between the Iranian left and the questions of women's rights in Iran.

0462 _____. "National and International Aspects of Feminist Movements: The Example of the Iranian Revolution of 1978-79." *C*, no. 2 (1993): 33-53.
Using the example of the Iranian women's movement, this article assesses the concept of sisterhood on an international sphere. Examines how race, class, and gender influence the solidarity of the global women's movement.

0463 SHARONI, SIMONA. "Gender and Middle East Politics." *FFWA* 17, no. 2 (1993): 59-74.
Drawn from examples of the struggles of women in the Middle East, this essay seeks to define concepts of peace and security.

0464 SHIRAZI-MAHAJAN, FAEGHEH. "The Politics of Clothing in the Middle East: The Case of *Hijab* in Post-Revolution Iran." *C*, no. 2 (1993): 54-63.
Using the example of the hijab (veil) in post-revolutionary Iran, this essay assesses the relationship between politics and clothing.

0465 SOBHAN, SALMA. "National Identity: Fundamentalism and the Women's Movement in Bangladesh." *Gender and National Identity: Women and Politics in Muslim Societies*, 63-80. Ed. Valentine M. Moghadam. London and Atlantic Highlands, New Jersey: Karachi: Zed Books LTD: Oxford University Press, 1994.
Through a historical survey of Bangladesh, this chapter examines the impact of Islamic fundamentalism on Bengali women.

0466 SOSEBEE, STEPHEN J. "The Palestinian Woman's Movement and the Intifada: A Historical and Current Analysis." *AAA* 32 (March 1990): 81-91.

Based on interviews with Palestinian men and women in the Occupied
Territories in 1990 and on recent studies on Palestinian women, this essay
explores the Palestinian women's movement before and during the *intifada* to
assess the changes made by the national struggle.

0467 SPELLBERG, DENISE A. "Political Action and Public Example: 'A'isha and
the Battle of the Camel." *Women in Middle Eastern History*, 45-57. Eds. Nikki
R. Keddie, and Beth Baron. New Haven and London: Yale University Press,
1991.
Recounts how the political participation of 'A'isha, the favorite wife of the
Prophet Muhammad, in the Battle of the Camel led 9th-century historians to
argue for constraints to be placed on women's role in politics.

0468 SPRATT, JENNIFER E. "Women and Literacy in Morocco." *AAAPSS* 520
(March 1992): 121-132.
This article investigates the gender gap in literacy and education in Morocco.
The author utilizes statistics to evaluate recent programs in Morocco, and the
role that education, labor, and women's health play in determining literacy
rates. The conclusion offers some recommendations for improvement.

0469 STOWASSER, BARBARA F. "Women's Issues in Modern Islamic Thought."
Arab Woman: Old Boundaries, New Frontiers, 3-28. Ed. Judith E. Tucker.
Bloomington and Indianapolis: Indiana University Press, 1993.
Presents the interpretations of modern Islamic thinkers and writers on
women's issues. The author divides the literature into three categories:
modernists, conservatives, and fundamentalists or integrationists.

0470 _____. *Women in the Qur'an, Traditions, and Interpretations*. New York and
Oxford: Oxford University Press, 1994.
Through an examination of Islamic texts, this work analyzes the Qur'an's
female characters whom the author states are "a living part of the contemporary
Islamic religious worldview." By a comparison of the medieval and
contemporary interpretations of the women of the Qur'an, the book
demonstrates that the Muslim outlook and the way they define themselves have
been shaped by history. Divided into two parts, the first offers chapters on
Eve; the women of Noah, Lot, and Abraham; Zulaykha; women in Moses' life;
the Queen of Sheba Bilqis, and Mary. The second part looks at the Prophet's
wives as they appear in the Qur'an and the Hadith. The final chapter looks at
contemporary Islamic interpretations.

0471 STRUM, PHILLIPPA. "The Threat of Fundamentalism." *The Women are
Marching: The Second Sex and the Palestinian Revolution*, 215-228.
Brooklyn, NY: Lawrence Hill Books, 1992.

This chapter examines the effect that the relationship between fundamentalism and feminism has had on the lives of Palestinian women.

0472 SULEIMAN, MICHAEL W. "Political Orientation of Young Tunisians: The Impact of Gender." *ASQ* 15, no. 1 (December 1993): 61-80.

Based on the results of a 1988 survey of female and male Tunisian youths between 9-17 years, this article assesses the influence of gender on political and cultural practices and values in Tunisia.

0473 SULLIVAN, EARL T. "Democratization and Changing Gender Roles in Egypt." *AAA* 36 (March 1991): 16-18.

This essay is taken from a discussion in a panel on "Democratization in the Middle East." The work discusses the role that women play in the democratization process in Egypt and the conditions or obstacles they face in securing their participation.

0474 TAVAKOLI-TARGHI, MOHAMMAD. "Women of the West Imagined: The *Farangi* Other and the Emergence of the Woman Question in Iran." *Identity Politics and Women: Cultural Reassertions and Feminisms in International Perspective*, 98-120. Ed. Valentine M. Moghadam. Boulder, CO: Westview Press, 1994.

A historical study that illustrates the relationship between discourse in the European woman as the "other" and the emergence of the "woman question" in Iran.

0475 TÈTREAULT, MARY ANN. "Civil Society in Kuwait: Protected Spaces and Women's Rights." *MEJ* 47, no. 2 (1993): 275-291.

Discusses women's role in Kuwaiti society and examines the change in their status since the Iraqi invasion.

0476 _____. "Whose Honor? Whose Liberation? Women and the Reconstruction of Politics in Kuwait." *Women and Revolution in Africa, Asia, and the New World*, 297-315. Ed. Mary Ann Tètreault. Columbia, SC: University of South Carolina Press, 1994.

Contends that the best way to institutionalize democratic norms in Kuwait is to extend political rights to women in Kuwait.

0477 THOMAS, EDWARD H. "Ali Shari'ati on the Role of the Muslim Woman." *MW* 81, no. 1 (1991): 1-8.

Provides a translation of Ali Shari'ati's thoughts on women. The author asserts that he was "not for sexual freedom."

0478 THORNHILL, TERESA. "The Interrogation of Women 'Security' Detainees by the Israeli General Security Service." *Women in the Middle East: Perceptions, Realities and Struggles for Liberation*, 185-205. Ed. Haleh Afshar. New York: St. Martin's Press, 1993.

Based on field research conducted in 1990, this article provides a comparison of the interrogation methods used on Palestinian and Israeli women detainees.

0479 TLEMÇANI, RACHID. "The Rise of Algerian Women: Cultural Dualism and Multi-Party Politics." *Women and Development in the Middle East and North Africa*, 69-81. Eds. Joseph G. Jabbra, and Nancy W. Jabbra. Leiden: E.J. Brill, 1992.

Although Algerian women's participation in the Algerian Revolution was honored, this chapter shows why they did not receive greater rights following the war.

0480 TOHIDI, NAYEREH. "Gender and Islamic Fundamentalism: Feminist Politics in Iran." *Third World Women and the Politics of Feminism*, 251-267. Eds. Chandra Talpade Mohanty, Ann Russo, and Lourdes Torres. Bloomington and Indianapolis: Indiana University Press, 1991.

This chapter assesses the historical, socio-economic, cultural, religious, and political factors in Iran that have impacted the development of the Iranian feminist movement.

0481 _____. "Modernity, Islamization, and Women in Iran." *Gender and National Identity: Women and Politics in Muslim Societies*, 110-147. Ed. Valentine M. Moghadam. London and Atlantic Highlands, New Jersey: Karachi: Zed Books LTD: Oxford University Press, 1994.

Examines the impact that modernization and Islamization policies have had on the status of women in Iran.

0482 TOPRAK, BINNAZ. "Women and Fundamentalism in Turkey." *Identity Politics and Women: Cultural Reassertions and Feminisms in International Perspective*, 293-306. Ed. Valentine M. Moghadam. Boulder, CO: Westview Press, 1994.

This chapter contends that the Islamic movement in Turkey is defined by its concern for the role of women in society.

0483 TUCKER, JUDITH and RAMLA KHALIDI. *Women's Rights in the Arab World*, Middle East Report and Information Project, Washington, DC, 1908.

Through the eyes of Arab women, this paper examines gender and power issues.

0484 TURABI, HASAN. *Women in Islam and Muslim Society*. London: Milestones (London) Publishers, 1991.

Divided into four chapters, this work by Hasan Turabi, the leader of the National Islamic Front in Sudan, offers an Islamist perspective on the role of women in Muslim societies.

0485 WADUD-MUHSIN, AMINA. *Qur'an and Woman*. Kuala Lumpur: Penerbit Fajar Bakti SND.BHD., 1992.

A Muslim feminist analysis of the concept of woman in the Qur'an. Contends that the meaning of the Qur'an must be perpetually re-interpreted and proceeds to prove that the text does not discriminate against women, rather, it is the interpreters who have misinterpreted its meaning.

0486 WALDMAN, MARILYN ROBINSON. "Reflections on Islamic Tradition, Women, and Family." *Muslim Families in North America*, 309-325. Eds. Earle H. Waugh, Sharon McIrvin Abu-Laban, and Regula Burckhardt Qureshi. Edmonton, Alberta: The University of Alberta Press, 1991.

This chapter, offering a historian's perspective, examines Muslim families and the differing roles of Muslim women in North American societies.

0487 WALTHER, WIEBKE. *Women in Islam*. Princeton and New York: Marcus Wiener Publishing, 1993.

This work, which focuses on women of the Middle East including Turkey and Iran, explores the issue of women and Islam from a historical viewpoint. It offers a historical review of Islamic history and follows with an analysis of Muslim women in Islamic law, the Qur'an, and in tradition. The work moves on to discuss Muslim women's lives within the family and society, in Islamic history, culture and literature. Women's search for identity from a historical standpoint is the topic of the final chapter. This work includes illustrations of Muslim women in Mughal, Iranian and Ottoman art as well as a bibliography of women in the Middle East.

0488 WEISS, A. M. "Benazir Bhutto and Future of Women in Pakistan." *AS* 30 (1990): 433-445.

Examines the policies of Benazir Bhutto as they impact on the future of Pakistani women.

0489 WELCHMAN, LYNN. "Family Law under Occupation: Islamic Law and the Shari'a Courts in the West Bank." *Islamic Family Law*, 93-115. Eds. Chibli Mallat, and Jane Conners. London: Graham & Trotman, 1990.

Provides an analysis of the personal status law in the West Bank under Israeli military occupation since 1967. The author examines how the *shari'a* courts have adjusted to occupation and the manner in which the occupation has influenced the operation of the courts and the application of personal status law.

0490 WING, ADRIEN KATHERINE. "Palestinian Women: Their Future Legal Rights." *ASQ* 16, no. 1 (December 1994): 55-73.
This article examines the potential legal reforms that will improve the legal status of Palestinian women in a future Palestinian state.

0491 YEGANEH, NAHID. "Women, Nationalism and Islam in Contemporary Political Discourse in Iran." *FR* 44 (1993): 3-18.
Briefly explores the historical ties between Islam and Iranian nationalism and its impact upon Iranian women.

0492 ZAKARIA, RAFIQ. *Women and Politics in Islam: The Trial of Benazir Bhutto.* New York, NY: Horizons Press, 1989.
This fictional novel evolves around a trial involving Pakistan's first female prime minister, Benazir Bhutto. During the course of the trial, legendary scholars and political leaders from Islamic history decide if it is proper for a woman to be prime minister of a country. This book offers a unique perspective on the concept of the role of women in Muslim societies over the course of history.

0493 ZUHUR, SHERIFA. *Revealing, Reveiling: Islamist Gender Ideology in Contemporary Egypt.* Albany: State University of New York Press, 1992.
Adopting a Jungian framework, this work examines how contemporary Egyptian women perceive themselves, their identity and their social and political environment. Zuhur provides a historical background on the role of women in Islam and the contemporary Egyptian Islamic movement and examines much of the literature on this topic. The author has interviewed fifty Egyptian women, representing a wide range of ages and classes, about their self-image and their views on Islam and society. It offers a glimpse into the multiplicity and diversity of views and ideas of contemporary Egyptian women and their perceptions of themselves.

D. Democracy

0494 ABUKHALIL, AS'AD. "A Viable Partnership: Islam, Democracy and the Arab World." *Altered States: A Reader in the New World Order*, 239-247. Eds. Phyllis Bennis, and Michel Moushabeck. New York: Olive Branch Press, 1993.
Addresses the issue of democracy in the Arab world and the compatibility of Islam and democracy in the 'new world order.'

0495   ADDI, LAHOUARI. "Algeria's Democracy Between the Islamists and the Elite." *MERIP* 175 (March 1992): 36-38.
    This essay asserts that for the democratic process to move forward in Algeria, Islam must be depoliticized.

0496   _____. "Islamicist Utopia and Democracy." *AAAPSS* 524 (November 1992): 120-130.
    Through the Algerian experience, this article examines the democratic period in an Islamic society. The author asserts that Islam, as a public religion, is incompatible with democracy because of the Islamist utopia which aims to maintain society's communal structures while rejecting the independence of the political sphere. The writer also states that Islamist utopias have stood in the way of both democracy and modernization in Algeria.

0497   AL AKIM, HASSAN. "Islam and Democracy: Mutually Reinforcing or Incompatible?" *Power-Sharing Islam?*, 77-89. Ed. Azzam Tamimi. London: Liberty for Muslim World Publications, 1993.
    Contending that Islam and democracy are "mutually reinforcing," this chapter explores the characteristics of an Islamic state including the principles of democracy, consultation, and leadership and examines how they should mix with election procedures in a democratic Islamic state.

0498   AMAWI, ABLA. "Democracy in Jordan." *MERIP* 172 (January 1992): 26-29.
    Through a discussion of the political liberalization measures in Jordan, this article explores the impact of the gains of the Islamist parties in the elections of 1989 on the democratic process.

0499   BAHZUT, GAWDAT. "Democracy in the Middle East: The American Connection." *SCT* 17, no. 1 (1994): 87-96.
    Discusses the prospects for democracy in the Middle East and offers policy options on how the U.S. should deal with Islamic political movements.

0500   BAKER, RAYMOND. "Islam, Democracy, and the Arab Future: Contested Islam in the Gulf Crisis." *The Gulf War and the New World Order*, 473-501. Eds. Tareq Y. and Jacqueline S. Ismael Ismael. Gainesville: University of Florida Press, 1994.
    Asserts that by examining the Gulf war and the role that Islam played in uniting and mobilizing the people, Islam can "not be fairly generalized as either predictably irrational or undemocratic."

0501   BIANCHI, ROBERT. "Islam and Democracy in Egypt." *CH* 88, no. 535 (February 1989): 93-97, 104.

The author contends that the Mubarak regime is willing to reach an accommodation with its religious opposition because the regime has realized that aspects of Islam and democracy are compatible.

0502   BRUMBERG, DANIEL. "Islamic Fundamentalism, Democracy, and the Gulf War." *Islamic Fundamentalisms and the Gulf Crisis*, 186-208. Ed. James Piscatori. The United States of America: The American Academy of Arts and Science, 1991.
Assesses the possibility for democratic reforms to continue in the aftermath of the Gulf war.

0503   DUNN, MICHAEL COLLINS. "Islamist Parties in Democratizing States: A Look at Jordan and Yemen." *MEP* 2, no. 2 (1993): 16-27.
Compares and contrasts the experiences of the Islamist parties in the democratization process in Jordan and Yemen. Seeks to illustrate that political Islam and democracy are not inherently incompatible and that each Islamic movement must be examined within the political context of its own country.

0504   _____. "Revivalist Islam and Democracy: Thinking about the Algerian Quandary." *MEP* 1, no. 2 (1992): 16-22.
Through a brief examination of the Algerian case, the article seeks to answer questions of whether political revivalist Islam is able to coexist with democracy and democratic principles.

0505   ENTELIS, JOHN P. "Islam, Democracy, and the State: The Reemergence of Authoritarian Politics in Algeria." *Islamism and Secularism in North Africa*, 219-251. Ed. John Ruedy. New York: St. Martin's Press, 1994.
Seeks to understand why the "populist response" to the canceling of the first democratic elections in Algeria and the reimposition of the authoritarian regime was not the same as in the attempted coup in Russia in 1991.

0506   ENTELIS, JOHN P. and LISA J. ARONE. "Algeria in Turmoil: Islam, Democracy and the State." *MEP* 1, no. 2 (1992): 23-35.
Offers an analysis of Algeria's brief experiment with democracy and gives reasons for its failure.

0507   ESPOSITO, JOHN L. "Islam and the Challenge of Democracy." *Under Siege*, 129-145. Ed. Richard Bulliet. New York: Columbia University, 1994.
Through an examination of the compatibility of Islam and democracy, this chapter assesses some of the recent attempts toward political liberalization in the Muslim world.

0508 _____. "Islamic Movements, Democratization, and U.S. Foreign Policy." *Riding the Tiger: The Middle East Challenge After the Cold War*, 187-210. Eds. Phebe and William Lewis Marr. Boulder, CO: Westview Press, 1993.

This chapter examines the organizational structures of the contemporary Islamic movements through an assessment of their ideology, political agendas, and attitudes toward democracy as well as their influence on the foreign policy decisions of the United States.

0509 ESPOSITO, JOHN L. and JAMES P. PISCATORI. "Democratization and Islam." *MEJ* 45, no. 3 (June 1991): 427-40.

Explores the question of Islam's compatibility with democracy. Begins with an overview of the parliamentary experience in a number of Muslim countries. The article then outlines various interpretations of democracy by Muslim thinkers such as: Sayyid Qutb, Ali Belhadj, Abu al-A'la al-Mawdudi, and Rashid Ghannouchi. The authors conclude that democracy has become a part of Muslim political thought and discourse.

0510 FARLEY, JONATHAN G. "Algeria: Democracy On Hold." *CR* 26, no. 2 (March 1993): 130-135.

This article examines the divisions within Algeria's body politic and assesses the likelihood for democratic reforms to continue.

0511 HERMIDA, ALFRED. "Democracy Derailed." *AR* (March 1992): 13-17.

Examines the victory of the FIS in the 1990 municipal elections in Algeria, the army intervention in the election process, the banning of the FIS, and the state of emergency that followed.

0512 AL-HIBRI, AZIZAH Y. *Islamic Constitutionalism and the Concept of Democracy.* New York: American Muslim Foundation, 1992.

Explores the concepts of democracy and constitutionalism in Islamic law, concluding that neither principle is antithetical to Islam.

0513 HUDSON, MICHAEL C. "Arab Regimes and Democratization: Responses to the Challenge of Political Islam." *InS* 29, no. 4 (October 1994): 3-27.

Provides an analysis of the possibilities that exist for democratization in the Arab world by examining the Islamic trend and the various reactions to calls for democracy by the Arab regimes as well as the regimes' interaction with the Islamic trend.

0514 KRAMER, GÜDRUN. "Islamist Notions of Democracy." *MERIP* 183 (July 1993): 2-14.

Challenging the assumption that there is one political Islamic doctrine, this article utilizes Arabic sources written by Islamic intellectuals and analyzes the debate on the compatibility of Islam and democracy.

0515 KRAMER, MARTIN. "Islam vs. Democracy." *Com* 95, no. 1 (January 1993): 35-42.

This article begins with a denouncement of scholars who have written objective critiques of Islamic resurgence. Provides a perspective of the dangers that Islamic movements pose for peace and stability in the Middle East region as well as an argument of why Islam and liberal democracy are incompatible.

0516 LEWIS, BERNARD. "Islam and Liberal Democracy." *AM* (February 1993): 89-98.

Examines the relationship between Islam and liberal democracy. Seeks to illustrate that from a political perspective Islam and liberal democracy are incompatible.

0517 LOWRIE, ARTHUR L., ed. *Islam, Democracy, the State and the West: A Round Table with Dr. Hasan Turabi.* Tampa, FL: The World and Islam Studies Enterprise, 1993.

This work, the proceedings of a round table discussion held with Hasan Turabi in 1992, provides Dr. Turabi's thoughts on topics such as the Western misperception of Islamic revivalism and the shape of an Islamic state.

0518 MERNISSI, FATIMA. *Islam and Democracy: Fear of the Modern World.* Reading, MA: Addison-Wesley, 1992.

An artfully forged argument for the necessity of Middle Eastern governments to introduce democratic practices and allow the people of the region to participate in politics. This work examines the reasons for the refusal of Middle East governments and religious elites to implement democracy and analyzes how they align themselves with Western elites in order to prevent true political reform. The writer catalogues the fears which are an impediment to self fulfillment of Muslim societies: the foreign West, the Imam, democracy, freedom of thought, individualism, the past and the present. Islam and democracy is set against the stage of the Gulf War which the author asserts was devastating because it laid bare the divisions within Islamic societies. The second theme which runs through this book is the notion that without equality throughout Islamic societies the nations will never be able to realize their true capabilities.

0519 MONSHIPOURI, MAHMOOD and CHRISTOPHER G. KUKLA. "Islam, Democracy and Human Rights: The Continuing Debate in the West." *MEP* 3, no. 2 (1992): 22-39.

An examination of the compatibility and divergence between Islam and democracy. Using assessments of human rights conditions in Algeria, Iran, Pakistan and the Sudan as a basis for analysis, the author examines the current situation in these countries where the debate on Islam and democracy is engaged.

0520 MORTIMER, ROBERT A. "Algeria: The Clash between Islam, Democracy, and the Military." *CH* 92, no. 570 (January 1993): 37-41.

Examines the rise of Islamism in Algeria; the Islamic Salvation Front (FIS); the municipal and provisional elections and their annulment; and President Boudiaf's assassination. The author contends that the military and the Islamists have squeezed out the secular democrats.

0521 _____. "Islam and Multiparty Politics in Algeria." *MEJ* 45, no. 4 (1991): 575-593.

Analyzing the balance of power in Algeria between the army, state and society, this article describes the process of Algeria's transformation from a one-party system to a multi-party democracy. It details the results of the June 1990 elections, the strong showing of the Islamic Salvation Front (FIS), the complications generated by the Gulf war on the electoral process, and the imposition of martial law by the army in the wake of a FIS victory after the first round of elections.

0522 MOUSSALLI, AHMAD S. "Hasan al-Turabi's Islamist Discourse on Democracy and *Shura*." *MES* 30, no. 1 (January 1994): 52-63.

From a hearing held before the U.S. Congress on Islamic fundamentalism in Africa, this essay examines Hasan al-Turabi's views on democracy.

0523 NASR, SEYYED VALI REZA. "Democracy and the Crisis of Governabilty in Pakistan." *AS* 32, no. 6 (June 1992): 81-90.

An analysis that seeks to identify the factors behind the weakness of the democratization process in Pakistan since 1988.

0524 OLAYIWOLA, ABDUR RAHMAN O. "Democracy in Islam." *IC* 65, no. 2-3 (1991): 63-83.

Though a detailed Qur'anic analysis, this article argues that Islam is entirely democratic and that there are similarities and deep differences between Islamic and Western concepts of the term.

0525 PARIS, JONATHAN A. S. "When to Worry in the Middle East." *Orbis* 37, no. 4 (September 1993): 553-565.

This essay argues that due to the 'Islamic fundamentalist threat,' it is not always in America's best interest to promote democracy in the Middle East.

0526 SADOWOSKI, YAHYA. "The New Orientation and the Democracy Debate."
      MERIP 183 (July 1993): 14-27.
      Provides a critique of the new Orientalist approach to understanding Islamic
      societies, Islamic movements, and the democratic experience within these
      societies.

0527 SAVORY, ROGER M. "Islam and Democracy: The Case of the Islamic
      Republic of Iran." *The Islamic World: From Classical to Modern Times*,
      821-843. Eds. C. E. Bosworth, Charles Issawi, Roger Savory, and
      A.L.Udovitch. Princeton, NJ: The Darwin Press, Inc., 1989.
      Through a case study of the Islamic Republic of Iran, this chapter addresses
      the topic of the compatibility of Islam and democracy.

0528 SHAHIN, EMAD ELDIN. "Algeria: The Limits to Democracy." *MEI* 8
      (January 1992): 10-19.
      Examines the events that led to the rise of the Islamic Salvation Front (FIS),
      the social background of the FIS, the movement's aims and objectives,
      ideology, and political organization

0529 SISK, TIMOTHY D. *Islam and Democracy*. Washington D.C.: United States
      Institute of Peace Press, 1992.
      A brief examination of the relationship between religion and politics in
      general, the international wave of democratization in the late twentieth century
      as well as an overview of different political interpretations of the compatibility
      of Islam and democracy. The work analyzes the role of Islamic movements in
      Iran, Algeria, Jordan, the Gulf, and the Palestinian National Movement. Islam
      and Democracy concludes with three possible future scenarios of the
      relationship of Islam and politics: the abandonment of fundamentalism,
      continued compromise and confrontation and a new synthesis of Islamic
      practices and democratic concepts.

0530 EL SOLH, RAGHID. "Islamist Attitudes Towards Democracy: A Review of
      the Ideas of al-Ghazali, al-Turabi, and 'Amara." *BJMES* 20, no. 1 (1993):
      57-63.
      Surveys the opinions that three Muslim intellectuals have on the issue of
      democracy between the period of 1985-1990. Asserts that Islamists are divided
      into three categories: those who reject democracy, those believe that Islam is
      compatible with democracy, and those who accept certain principles of
      democracy. Contends that these three intellectuals represent either the second
      or third groups.

0531 TURABI, HASAN. "Islam, Democracy, the State and the West." *MEP* 1, no.
      3 (1992): 49-60.

This article is a summary of a lecture and round table discussion with Hasan Turabi, prepared by Louis J. Cantori and Arthur Lowrie. Dr. Turabi presents his views on the contemporary Islamic movement; Islam and democracy; Islam and foreign policy; Islam and women; Islam and the Palestine question; and Islam and Arab nationalism.

0532   VOLL, JOHN OBERT and JOHN L. ESPOSITO. "Islam's Democratic Essence." *MEQ* 1, no. 3 (September 1994): 3-11.
Examines Islamic heritage in order to illustrate that many elements of Islam are compatible with democracy.

0533   WRIGHT, ROBIN. "Islam, Democracy and the West." *FA* 71, no. 3 (June 1992): 131-45.
Explores the Islamist transformation from illegal underground groups to one that participates in democratic experiments in Algeria and Central Asia. The author prescribes that the U.S. encourage the democratic process in order to avoid the radicalization of the Islamic movements.

0534   _____. "Islam's New Political Face." *CH* 90, no. 552 (January 1991): 25-28, 35-36.
An examination of the importance of Islam in Middle Eastern political spheres is the focus of this article. The author states that the developments in the Maghrib and 'Arab Heartland' indicate that Islam and democracy may not be incompatible.

0535   ZARTMAN, I. WILLIAM. "Democracy and Islam: The Cultural Dialectic." *AAAPSS* 524 (November 1992): 181-91.
Views the current history of Islam as a cultural dialectic between modern and authentic synthesis. The synthesis arises only to be challenged by a new authentic synthesis which today is political Islam. Asserting that democracy arises as a critique of prevalent conditions and a quest for government. The article states that democracy and Islam are not inherently incompatible and offers prescriptions for finding a synthesis between the two.

0536   ZUBAIDA, SAMI. "Islam, the State and Democracy: Contrasting Conceptions of Society in Egypt." *MERIP* 179 (November 1992): 2-10.
Offers an examination of the relationship between the Islamic associations and the state in Egypt.

II.   AFRICA

0537 CHRISTELOW, ALLAN. "The Muslim Judge and Municipal Politics in Colonial Algeria and Senegal." *Comparing Muslim Societies: Knowledge and the State in a World Civilization*, 133-162. Ed. Juan R. I. Cole. Ann Arbor: The University of Michigan Press, 1992.

Addresses the issue of the degree to which religious groups may maintain their legal practices and still receive political equality within an integrated national polity. Compares and contrasts the differing experiences in Algeria and Senegal by looking at the role of history, Muslim courts, the politics of colonial municipalities, the role of the law, and military conscription.

0538 HUNWICK, JOHN O., ed. *Religion and National Integration in Africa: Islam, Christianity, and Politics in the Sudan and Nigeria*, Evanston, Illinois: Northwestern University Press, 1992.

This edited volume is a collection of articles which were presented at a conference in May 1988 under the auspices of the Program of African Studies, Northwestern University. The focus of this work is Sudan and Nigeria and explores the problems raised by Muslim-Christian loyalties as well as class and ethnic tensions. The introduction provides a brief update on the situation in Sudan and Nigeria since the conference. The first paper discusses the role that Islam plays in national integration in Sudan. The second article relates to the identity crisis in Sudan and offers some suggestions on how the divide between the fighting factions can be bridged. The second portion of this work is concerned with Nigeria and offers perspectives on the role of Islam in political life and the instability caused by Muslim-Christian tensions. The final paper poses philosophical problems in the relationship between religion and the state.

0539 NAUDE, J. A. "South Africa: The Role of a Muslim Minority in a Situation of Change." *JIMMA* 13, no. 1 (January 1992): 17-32.

This article outlines the debates within the Muslim minority community concerning their participation in political life in South Africa.

0540 NKRUMAH, GORKEH GAMAL. "Islam in Southern Africa." *ROAPE* 52 (November 1991): 94-97.

Asserts that the rising anti-apartheid movement in South Africa led to increased social awareness which in turn helped foster a more militant Islamic activism.

0541 PARRATT, SAROJ J. "Muslims in Botswana." *AFS* 48, no. 1 (1989): 71-81.

Explores the role of Islam in the Southern African state of Botswana. Traces the origin of Botswana Muslims, attempts to Africanize Islam, and prospects for Islam to spread in Botswana.

0542   SANNEH, LAMIN. "Religion, Politics, and National Integration: A Comparative African Perspective." *Religion and National Integration in Africa: Islam, Christianity, and Politics in the Sudan and Nigeria*, 151-166. Ed. John O. Hunwick. Evanston, Illinois: Northwestern University Press, 1992.

Discusses the interaction between religion and politics in the issue of national integration and authority in Nigeria and Sudan.

0543   TURABI, HASSAN AL. "The Implications for U.S. Policy of Islamic Fundamentalism in Africa." *MEAJ* 1, no. 1 (June 1992): 4-10.

Presents the opening statement of Dr. Hassan al-Turabi before the U.S. House Foreign Affairs Africa Subcommittee Hearing concerning Islamic fundamentalism in Africa.

0544   VAWDA, SHAHID. "The Emerging of Islam in an African Township." *AJISS* 7, no. 4 (1994): 532-547.

Drawing upon ethnographic research conducted in townships located near Durban, South Africa, this article examines the South African Muslim population.

0545   VOLL, JOHN OBERT. "Religion and Politics in Islamic Africa." *The Religious Challenge to the State*, 209-238. Eds. Matthew C. Moen, and Lowell S. Gustafson. Philadelphia: Temple University Press, 1992.

Through an analysis of four different African countries--Egypt, Sudan, Nigeria, and South Africa--where Muslim majority and minority statuses differ. The author assesses the impact of Islamic ideology as a political force and the implications for the nation-state in Africa.

A.   East Africa

0546   ABDULLAH, ABDURAHMAN. "Political Islam in Somalia." *MEAJ* 1, no. 3 (March 1993): 44-55.

Analyzes the Somali Islamist movement within the context of other Islamic movements, and through the occasional communiques of the Somali movements. It examines how the movement's traditional background has led to increased support for its cause.

0547   AZEVEDO, MARIO and GWENDOLYN S. PRATER. "The Minority Status of Islam in East Africa: A Historico-Sociological Perspective." *JIMMA* 12, no. 2 (July 1991): 482-497.

Focusing on Kenya, Mozambique, and Tanzania, this article examines the impact of Islam (a minority religion) on the populations of East Africa.

0548 LAMBEK, MICHAEL. "Certain Knowledge, Contestable Authority: Power and Practice on the Islamic Periphery." *AE* 17, no. 1 (1990): 23-40.

This study examines the relationship between religious texts and 'textual authority' in local Islamic practice in Mayotte, Comoro Islands, East Africa.

0549 _____. "The Practice of Islamic Experts in a Village on Mayotte." *JRA* 20, no. 1 (1990): 20-40. Analyzes the discipline of Islamic knowledge and the experts who practice it on the island of Mayotte off the coast of East Africa.

0550 MANDIVENGA, EPHRAIM. "Islam in Tanzania: A General Survey." *JIMMA* 11, no. 2 (July 1990): 311-320.

Traces the spread of Islam from the late eighteenth hundreds until contemporary times in Tanzania where Muslim are a significant portion of the country's population.

B.   North Africa

0551 ABRAMSON, GARY. "Rise of the Crescent." *AR* 37, no. 2 (March 1992): 18-21.

This article assesses Islamic fundamentalist power in the countries of North Africa following the army take over in Algeria.

0552 ANDERSON, LISA. "Obligations and Accountability: Islamic Politics in North Africa." *DA* 120, no. 3 (June 1991): 93-112.

This essay examines how the various political Islamic movements in North Africa have been shaped by specific social, religious, economic, and political events in modern-day North Africa.

0553 _____. "Tunisia and Libya: Responses to the Islamic Impulse." *The Iranian Revolution: Its Global Impact*, 157-176. Ed. John L. Esposito. Miami: Florida International University Press, 1990.

Examines how the influence of the Iranian revolution on Tunisia and Libya accelerated Islamic political activist trends already in existence.

0554 BURGAT, FRANCOIS and WILLIAM DOWELL. *The Islamic Movement in North Africa*. Austin: University of Texas Press, 1993.

Explores the complex and contested nature of Islamic political ideologies and the goals and practices that are advocated by those who articulate this ideology in North Africa. The authors examine the wide variety of this new Islamic political discourse. An overview of the terminology given to the Islamic political phenomena and the transition from nationalism to Islamism is followed by an examination of the role of Islam in Libya, Morocco, Tunisia and

Algeria. This work gives voice to many of the leaders of North Africa's Islamic movements such as Morocco's Abdessalam Yassine and Tunisia's Rachid Ghannouchi.

0555 CHATER, KHALIFA. "A Rereading of Islamic Texts in the Maghrib in the Nineteenth and Early Twentieth Centuries: Secular Themes or Religious Reformism." *Islamism and Secularism in North Africa*, 37-51. Ed. John Ruedy. New York: St. Martin's Press, 1994.
Examines the *fatwa*s (legal rulings) issued during the nineteenth and early twentieth century to shed light on the different characteristics of the Islamic reform movement in North Africa.

0556 DEEB, MARY-JANE. "Islam and the State in Algeria and Morocco: A Dialectical Model." *Islamism and Secularism in North Africa*, 275-287. Ed. John Ruedy. New York: St. Martin's Press, 1994.
Using Morocco and Algeria as case studies, this article provides a theory that explains why Islamic movements are powerful in some Muslim countries and not in others.

0557 _____. "North African Migrants in France: Caught Between a Rock and a Hard Place." *MQ* 4, no. 4 (September 1993): 96-104.
Looks at the relationship between North African migrants and their former colonial ruler, France. Examines why North Africans migrate to France and why France seeks to cut this tie.

0558 FARLEY, JONATHON G. "The Maghreb's Islamic Challenge." *WT* 47 (August 1991): 148-151.
Offers a brief comparison of the Islamic experience in Morocco, Tunisia, and Algeria.

0559 HERMASSI, ELBAKI. "The Political and the Religious in the Modern History of the Maghrib." *Islamism and Secularism in North Africa*, 87-99. Ed. John Ruedy. New York: St. Martin's Press, 1994.
Provides a historical overview of the relationship between Islam and politics in North Africa during the twentieth century.

0560 LAYACHI, AZZEDINE and ABDEL-KADER HAIRECHE. "National Development and Political Protest: Islamists in the Maghreb Countries." *ASQ* 14, no. 2-3 (March 1992): 69-92.
This article examines the factors which have contributed to the rise of Islamic movements in the North African countries of Algeria, Morocco, and Tunisia. The authors find a strong correlation between severe economic problems, westernization and secularization policies and the rise of Islamic movements as popular protest against the Maghribi regimes.

0561 MOORE, CLEMENT HENRY. "Political Parties." *Polity and Society in Contemporary North Africa*, 42-70. Eds. I. William Zartman, and William Mark Habeeb. Boulder, CO: Westview Press, 1993.

Through a discussion of the political parties in North Africa, this article also touches on the role that the Islamic movement plays in each of the countries' political sphere.

0562 RUEDY, JOHN, ed. *Islamism and Secularism in North Africa*, New York: St. Martin's Press, 1994.

This edited volume examines the points of convergence and divergence between religious and secular movements in the North African countries of Algeria, Libya, Morocco, and Tunisia. Scholars from the United States, Europe, and North Africa explore this issue from many different vantage points including economics, sociology, anthropology, and political science. Divided into three parts, the first provides six chapters that deal with the Islamic-secular "encounters in historical perspective." The second part provides five articles and looks at the "Islamist challenge" in the differing North African states. The final part has five chapters that examine the State's "responses to the Islamic revival."

0563 TOZY, MOHAMMED. "Islam and the State." *Polity and Society in Contemporary North Africa*, 102-122. Eds. I. William Zartman, and William Mark Habeeb. Boulder, CO: Westview Press, 1993.

This article compares the role of Islam in North Africa and asserts that following independence movements of Morocco, Algeria, and Tunisia have gone through many of the same historical experiences concerning the relationship between Islam and the state. This includes secularization programs following independence; the incorporation of Islam in political legitimacy; the rise of strong Islamic movements; state control over the instruments of expression; and "diffusion of the Muslim religion." Also contains a brief section on Islam in Libya.

0564 VENEMA, BERNHARD. "Islamic Resurrection in North Africa: Backgrounds and Variations." *Power and Prayer: Religious and Political Processes in Past and Present*, 251-256. Eds. Mart Baz, and Adrianus Koster. Amsterdam: VU University Press, 1993.

Providing background on the evolution of Islamic movements in North Africa, this chapter explains why the Islamic movement in Algeria is stronger than those in Tunisia and Morocco.

1. *Algeria*

0565 ABRAMSON, GARY. "Rise of the Crescent." *AR* 37, no. 2 (March 1992): 18-21.

This article assesses Islamic fundamentalist power in the countries of North Africa following the army take over in Algeria.

0566 AKACEM, MOHAMMED. "Algeria: In Search of an Economic and Political Future." *MEP* 2, no. 2 (1993): 50-60.

Analyzes the transition from a one-party political system to a multi-party system, the factors leading to the rise of the Islamic movement FIS, the implications of the electoral success of FIS on Algeria's neighbors and the West, as well as the Algerian economic situation.

0567 BEKKAR, RABIA. "Taking up Space in Tlemcen: The Islamist Occupation of Urban Algeria." *MERIP* 179 (November 1992): 11-15.

Rabia Bekkar, an urban sociologist who has spent twelve years conducting fieldwork in Tlemcen, Algeria, provides a local perspective on the program of the Islamic Salvation Front (FIS).

0568 BEN EISSA, RACHID. "The Algerian Experiment." *Power-Sharing Islam?*, 141-143. Ed. Azzam Tamimi. London: Liberty for Muslim World Publications, 1993.

This brief chapter blames the West for the failure of the democratic experience in Algeria.

0569 BRUMBERG, DANIEL. "Islam, Elections, and Reform in Algeria." *JOD* 2, no. 1 (December 1991): 58-71.

Provides background on the Algerian experience that led up to the 1991 National Assembly elections.

0570 DUNN, MICHAEL COLLINS. "Algeria's Agony: The Drama So Far, The Prospects for Peace." *MEP* 3, no. 3 (1994): 145-156.

Offers a review of the Algerian crisis and looks at the prospects for the future.

0571 DURAN, KHALID. "The Second Battle of Algiers." *Orbis* 33 (June 1989): 403-421.

This article discusses the October 1988 riots in Algeria and offers an analysis of the causal factors behind the riots.

0572 ELTAYEB, SALAH EL DIN ELZEEN. "Ulama and Islamic Renaissance in Algeria." *AJISS* 6, no. 2 (1989): 257-288.

Examines the role that the Islamic renaissance played in the Algerian liberation war.

0573 ENTELIS, JOHN P. "The Crisis of Authoritarianism in North Africa: The Case of Algeria." *POC* 41 (May 1992): 71-81.
This article examines the problems in Algeria adapting to political liberalization, the rise of the Islamic Salvation Front (FIS), and the military takeover following the first round of elections.

0574 _____. "US -- Maghreb Relations in a Democratic Age: The Priority of Algeria." *MEI* 8 (January 1992): 31-35.
This essay makes the case for the U.S. government to promote the legitimation of moderate Islamic groups. The author asserts that if the FIS in Algeria was to take over it would not necessarily be detrimental for the United States.

0575 HADDAM, ANWAR N. "The Political Experiment of the Algerian Islamic Movement and the New World Order." *Power-Sharing Islam?*, 127-140. Ed. Azzam Tamimi. London: Liberty for Muslim World Publications, 1993.
Traces the experience of the Algerian Islamic Movement (FIS) in Algerian politics and provides a framework of FIS's political agenda.

0576 HERMIDA, ALFRED. "Death in Algiers." *AR* 37, no. 2 (March 1992): 49-53.
Examines the assassination of Algeria's President Mohamed Boudiaf, the crackdown by the military on the FIS, and the retaliation of the FIS against state targets and officials.

0577 _____. "Democracy Derailed." *AR* (March 1992): 13-17.
Examines the victory of the FIS in the 1990 municipal elections in Algeria, the army intervention in the election process, the banning of the FIS, and the state of emergency that followed.

0578 HOLSINGER, DONALD C. "Islam and State Expansion in Algeria: Nineteenth-Century Saharan Frontiers." *Islamism and Secularism in North Africa*, 3-21. Ed. John Ruedy. New York: St. Martin's Press, 1994.
Looks at the way Islam defined various events in Algeria during the 19th century.

0579 IRATNI, BELCACEM and MOHAND SALAH TAHI. "The Aftermath of Algeria's First Free Local Elections." *GO* 26, no. 4 (1991): 466-479.
This article provides the results of the local elections of 12 June 1990 in Algeria. The essay discusses the victory of the FIS, how each party fared in certain districts, the disruption of the Gulf war on the elections, the

gerrymandering that took place before the legislative elections, and the state of siege that followed.

0580 KNAUSS, PETER R. "Algerian Women Since Independence." *State and Society in Algeria*, 151-169. Eds. John P. Entelis, and Philip C. Naylor. Boulder, CO: Westview Press, 1992.

Asserting that French colonial policies reasserted and revived patriarchal norms, this chapter offers an analysis of the status of Algerian women since the Algerian Revolution.

0581 LABAT, SÈVERINE. "Islamisms and Islamists: The Emergence of New Types of Politico-Religious Militants." *Islamism and Secularism in North Africa*, 103-121. Ed. John Ruedy. New York: St. Martin's Press, 1994.

Through an examination of the Algerian experience, the author asks the question of whether the current radical stage of the Islamic movement is its dying phase or the movement is one that will be forever hostile to the separation of religion and state.

0582 LAYACHI, AZZEDINE. "Algerian Crisis, Western Choices." *MEQ* 1, no. 3 (September 1994): 55-62.

Provides background on Algeria's current crisis, Algerian President Zeroual's efforts to find a solution to the conflict, and three possible scenarios for the future.

0583 LEWIS, WILLIAM H. "Algeria: The Failed Revolution." *MQ* 3, no. 4 (September 1992): 66-74.

Discusses the rise of the Algerian Islamic movement, the FIS, and the country's subsequent failed attempt at democratization.

0584 MAGHRAOUI, ABDELSLAM. "Problems of Transition to Democracy: Algeria's Short-Lived Experiment with Electoral Politics." *MEI* 8 (July 1992): 20-26.

Highlights the political events in Algeria during the 1991 elections. Offers an analysis of reasons given for the success of the Islamic Salvation Front (FIS) in the Algerian context.

0585 NOAKES, GREG. "Islamism vs. the State in Algeria." *MEAJ* 1, no. 3 (March 1993): 14-28.

Explores how the Islamic movement in Algeria has evolved since independence. Also discusses the difficulties that the movement faces and how these challenges will be met.

0586 ROBERTS, HUGH. "Algeria Between Eradicators and Conciliators." *MERIP* 198 (July 1994): 24-27.

Offers an analysis of the deep divisions among the ruling elites and the Islamist parties. Examines the difficulties Algerian President Lamine Zeroual has faced within the government and army in attempts at reconciliation. Also demonstrates how the Islamic party has radicalized since the banning of elections and assesses the strengths and weaknesses of the various factions.

0587 _____. "The Algerian State and the Challenge of Democracy." *GO* 27 (1992): 433-454.

Asserts that a re-evaluation of the events in Algeria that led up to the recent elections is necessary in order to understand Algerian politics and the popularity of the Islamic Salvation Front.

0588 _____. "Doctrinaire Economics and Political Opportunism in the Strategy of Algerian Islamism." *Islamism and Secularism in North Africa*, 123-147. Ed. John Ruedy. New York: St. Martin's Press, 1994.

Examines the economic problems in Algeria that helped induce the current crisis and asks why the FIS, as a populist Islamic movement, did not present an economic agenda.

0589 _____. "From Radical Mission to Equivocal Ambition: The Expansion and Manipulation of Algerian Islamism, 1979-1992." *Accounting for Fundamentalisms: The Dynamic Character of Movements*, 428-489. Eds. Martin E. Marty, and R. Scott Appleby. Chicago and London: The University of Chicago Press, 1994.

Analyzes the dynamic development of the Algerian Islamic movement represented by the Islamic Salvation Front (FIS) through an examination of the character and history of Algerian politics.

0590 _____. "A Trial of Strength: Algerian Islamism." *Islamic Fundamentalisms and the Gulf Crisis*, 131-154. Ed. James Piscatori. The United States of America: The American Academy of Arts and Science, 1991.

Discusses how the Gulf crisis disrupted the election procedure in Algeria, radicalized the Algerian people and united the nation against the Western-led coalition. Also illustrates how events in Algeria during this time caused the Algerian Prime Minister, Mouloud Hamrouche, to overreach himself and contribute to the current volatile situation. Provides a brief background of the principle Algerian Islamic parties at that time; the Islamic Salvation Front (FIS), Hamas, and the Movement of Islamic Resistance (MNI).

0591 RUEDY, JOHN. "Continuities and Discontinuities in the Algerian Confrontation with Europe." *Islamism and Secularism in North Africa*, 73-85. Ed. John Ruedy. New York: St. Martin's Press, 1994.

Argues that the emergence of the Islamic movement in Algeria is a manifestation of earlier "contradictions in the Algerian experience that have existed for centuries."

0592 SCHEMN, PAUL. "Hope for Algeria?: Renewed Possibility for Dialogue May Spell an End to the Country's Agony." *MEI* 10, no. 6 (September 1994): 44-48.

Examines recent developments in the bloody struggle between the Algerian government and armed Islamic groups. Offers a description of the Group Islamique Armée (GIA), an analysis of Western interests in Algeria as well as French and Algerian relations.

0593 TAHI, MOHAND SALAH. "The Arduous Democratisation Process in Algeria." *JMAS* 30, no. 3 (1992): 397-419.

Describes the tenuous election process in Algeria that led up to the military suppression. Includes profiles on the major parties, the FIS, FLN, and Kabyle party.

0594 TLEMÇANI, RACHID. "Chadli's Perestroika." *MERIP* 163 (March 1990): 14-17.

Discusses President Chadli Benjedid's economic and political reform measures. Also offers a brief examination of the rise of the Islamic movement, FIS.

0595 VANDEWALLE, DIRK. "At The Brink: Chaos In Algeria." *WPJ* 9, no. 4 (1991): 705-717.

Examines the Algerian political and economic quagmire which has resulted since the cancellation of the legislative elections in 1992. Focuses on the structural process of economic, political and ideological disintegration, which the author asserts, began when the country became independant.

0596 ZEBIRI, KATE. "Islamic Revival in Algeria: An Overview." *MW* 83, no. 3-4 (July 1993): 203-226.

This article provides an overview of recent events in Algeria and examines Islamic political parties; official versus popular Islam; the leaders and programs of the Islamic Salvation Front (FIS); and the role of Emir Abdel Kadir Islamic University in the Algerian Islamic resurgence.

0597 ZOUBIR, YAHIA H. "The Painful Transition from Authoritarianism in Algeria." *ASQ* 15, no. 3 (June 1993): 83-110.

Through an examination of the political system in Algeria, this article looks at the difficulties facing the process of democratization in Algeria.

2. *Libya*

0598 DEEB, MARIUS K. "Militant Islam and Its Critics: The Case of Libya." *Islamism and Secularism in North Africa*, 187-197. Ed. John Ruedy. New York: St. Martin's Press, 1994.

This article explains why an Islamic movement, similar to the groups that have emerged in Algeria, Tunisia, Egypt, and Syria, has not evolved in Libya.

0599 MAYER, ANN ELIZABETH. "Reinstating Islamic Criminal Law in Libya." *Law and Islam in the Middle East*, 99-114. Ed. Daisy Hilse Dwyer. New York: Bergin & Garvey, 1990.

Examines the extent to which Islamic criminal law has been implemented in the Libyan legal system. Asserts that the implementation of Islamic law is particular to Libyan historical and political circumstances.

0600 SAMMUT, DENNIS. "Libya and the Islamic Challenge." *WT* 50, no. 4 (1994): 198-200.

The essay examines why Libya has not faced the same kinds of problems with an Islamic opposition as have its North African neighbors.

3. *Morocco*

0601 COMBS-SCHILLING, M. E. *Sacred Performance: Islam, Sexuality, and Sacrifice*. New York: Columbia University Press, 1989.

Based upon field research conducted in Morocco, this work contends that religious rituals are the underpinning of the Moroccan monarchy. Containing five sections and 17 chapters, the first part illustrates the power of rituals. Part two examines what the author terms as "the consolidation of political and sexual culture in Islam." The third part examines the arrival of Islam in Morocco and the birth of the monarchy. Part four focuses on the role of culture and ritual practices in the survival of the Moroccan monarchy. The final section centers on contemporary Morocco and brings the analysis to the present time.

0602 COOPER, MARTHA. "The Islamic Movement of Morocco." *ASJ* 1, no. 1 (March 1993): 4-5.

Discusses the elements which led to the rise of an Islamic movement in Morocco and given the current situation, the movement's future.

0603 EICKELMAN, DALE F. "The Art of Memory: Islamic Education and Social Reproduction." *Comparing Muslim Societies: Knowledge and the State in a*

World Civilization, 97-132. Ed. Juan R. I. Cole. Ann Arbor: The University of Michigan Press, 1992.

Using a Durkheimian framework, this chapter describes and analyzes the cognitive style of Islamic learning as existed in Marrakesh, Morocco in the 1920s and 1930s. The article considers how forms of transmission of knowledge in society shaped social and cultural change. The author achieves this by examining Qur'anic schools for elementary education and a profile of the Yusufiyya school for higher education.

0604 _____. "Re-Imagining Religion and Politics: Moroccan Elections in the 1990s." *Islam and Secularism in North Africa*, 253-273. Ed. John Ruedy. New York: St. Martin's Press, 1994.

This article explores the electoral process and procedures that began in Morocco in 1992 with municipal and parliamentary elections.

0605 EL MANSOUR, MOHAMED. "Salafis and Modernists in the Moroccan Nationalist Movement." *Islamism and Secularism in North Africa*, 54-71. Ed. John Ruedy. New York: St. Martin's Press, 1994.

Provides analysis of the role that the Salafi movement played in Morocco's bid for independence.

0606 MUNSON, HENRY, JR. "Morocco's Fundamentalists." *GO* 26, no. 3 (June 1991): 331-344.

Based on interviews with members of Morocco's Islamic movement as well as their publications, this article describes the trends of the Islamic movement and reason's behind their "political inefficacy."

0607 _____. "The Political Role of Islam in Independent Morocco (1970-1990)." *North Africa: Nation, State, and Region*, 187-202. Ed. George Joffé. London: Routledge, 1993.

Three types of Moroccan Islamic Movements--traditional, as represented by Al-Fqih al-Zamzami; moderate, as represented by 'Abd al-Salam Yassin; and radical, as represented by Abd al-Karim Muti--is the focus of this analysis. The author concludes that none of these groups can compete with the religious legitimacy assumed by King Hasan.

0608 _____. *Religion and Power in Morocco*. New Haven and London: Yale University Press, 1993.

Based on Arabic texts from the 17th through the twentieth century and on ethnographic field world over several years in Morocco, the author argues that the political role of Islam cannot be understood without reference to its religious foundation. This work seeks to trace the evolution of the role of political Islam in Morocco, focusing on a series of conflicts between rulers and those who seek to overthrow an unjust leader. Chapter one provides two interpretations of the 17th century scholar-cum-saint al-Hasan al-Yusi--one by the anthropologist Clifford Geertz and the other by the author. Chapter two explores the political and religious roles of sultans and scholars in pre-colonial Morocco. The third chapter investigates the myth of the righteous man of God as represented by Sidi Muhammad bin 'Abd al-Kabir al-Kattani who was put to death in 1909 by Sultan Mulay 'Abd al-Hafidh. The next chapter discusses popular religion, orthodoxy, and Salafi scripturalism. Chapter five argues that previous interpretations by Geertz and Elaine Combs-Schilling over-emphasize the religious significance of the monarchy in late twentieth century Moroccan Islam and fail to take into account the importance of force and fear. The sixth chapter provides an analysis of the Islamic movements that have challenged the rule of Hasan II. The conclusion summarizes the differences between the author's historical and anthropological analysis and that of Geertz in his book *Islam Observed*.

0609 SHAHIN, EMAD EL DIN. "Secularism and Nationalism: The Political Discourse of 'Abd al-Salam Yassin." *Islamism and Secularism in North Africa*, 167-186. Ed. John Ruedy. New York: St. Martin's Press, 1994.

Through a discussion of the Islamic movement in Morocco, the author relays the ideology of Islamist 'Abd al-Salam Yassin which the author has termed as modernist.

4. *Tunisia*

0610 HALLIDAY, FRED. "Tunisia's Uncertain Future." *MERIP* 163 (March 1990): 25-27.

This essay examines the relationship between the Tunisian secular state and the rising Islamist challenge.

0611 HERMASSI, ELBAKI. "The Islamicist Movement and November 7." *Tunisia: The Political Economy of Reform*, 193-204. Ed. I. William Zartman. Boulder and London: Lynne Rienner Publishers, 1991.

This chapter examines the MTI, the Islamic party in Tunisia, and the pivotal date of November 7, 1987 when the Tunisian President Bourguiba was overthrown and the party rejected its revolutionary character and sought to work within the legal mainstream of the political system.

0612 MAGNUSON, DOUGLAS K. "Islamic Reform in Contemporary Tunisia: Unity and Diversity." *Tunisia: The Political Economy of Reform*, 169-192. Ed. I. William Zartman. Boulder and London: Lynne Rienner Publishers, 1991.

Based on three years of anthropological study, this chapter focuses on three Tunisian Islamic groups--the Group of the Call and Communication, the movement of the Islamic Way, and the Progressive Islamists--seeking to reform the Islamic system. The author examines the diversity and commonalities of the groups that came out of the same broad Islamic reform movement. In addition, the work provides a framework to compare and characterize these groups within the larger Islamic reform movement.

0613   PERKINS, KENNETH J. "'The Masses Look Ardently to Istanbul': Tunisia, Islam, and the Ottoman Empire, 1837-1931." *Islamism and Secularism in North Africa*, 23-36. Ed. John Ruedy. New York: St. Martin's Press, 1994.
   Examines the relations between the rulers in Tunisia and the Ottoman Sultans during the nineteenth and early twentieth centuries.

0614   SULEIMAN, MICHAEL W. "Political Orientation of Young Tunisians: The Impact of Gender." *ASQ* 15, no. 1 (December 1993): 61-80.
   Based on the results of a 1988 survey of female and male Tunisian youths between 9-17 years, this article assesses the influence of gender on political and cultural practices and values in Tunisia.

0615   ZARTMAN, I. WILLIAM. "The Conduct of Political Reform: The Path Toward Democracy." *Tunisia: The Political Economy of Reform*, 9-28. Ed. I. William Zartman. Boulder and London: Lynne Rienner Publishers, 1991.
   Provides a "structural analysis" of the various forces that both compete and cooperate with each other in Tunisia's attempt to transform the political system towards democracy.

0616   ZGHAL, ABDELKADER. "The New Strategy of the Movement of the Islamic Way: Manipulation or Expression of Political Culture." *Tunisia: The Political Economy of Reform*, 205-220. Ed. I. William Zartman. Boulder and London: Lynne Rienner Publishers, 1991.
   Defends the theory that the Islamist phenomenon in Tunisia is an offshoot of the nationalist movement and a reaction to its institutionalization.

C.   West Africa

0617   AJETUNMOBI, MUSA ALI. "The Place of Islamic Law in the Constitution of the Federal Republic of Nigeria." *HI* 14, no. 1 (March 1991): 67-82.
   Examines the degree to which the recommendations of the author outlining certain difficulties associated with the application of Islamic law in the 1979 constitution were carried out and added to the 1989 constitution in Nigeria.

0618 BAH, MOHAMMAD ALPHA. "The Status of Muslims in Sierra Leone and Liberia." *JIMMA* 12, no. 2 (July 1991): 464-481.

Through an examination of the role of Islam in two West African countries, this article seeks to discover why Muslims play a larger role in commercial areas than in the political sphere.

0619 BIRAI, M. UMAR. "Islamic Tajdid and the Political Process in Nigeria." *Fundamentalisms and the State: Remaking Polities, Economies, and Militance*, 184-203. E. Martin Marty, and R. Scott Appleby, eds. Chicago and London: The University of Chicago Press, 1991.

Based on interviews with a number of leading Nigerian sheikhs, this article offers an analysis of the political, religious, and cultural aspects of the Nigerian Islamic movement.

0620 DANMOLE, H. D. "Islam and Party Politics in Lagos: A Study of the United Muslim Party 1953-1966." *JIMMA* 11, no. 2 (1990): 334-346.

Focuses on how the United Muslim Party influenced political affairs in Lagos, Nigeria in the 1950s and 1960s.

0621 AL FARIRI YUSUFF, SALAMAN. "The Commercialization of Knowledge in Nigeria and its Impact on the Muslims." *IC* 65, no. 1 (January 1991): 63-73.

Criticizes the U.S. model of education used in Nigeria and its effects on traditional Nigerian values.

0622 GAMBARI, IBRAHIM A. "Islamic Revivalism in Nigeria: Homegrown or Externally Induced?" *The Iranian Revolution: Its Global Impact*, 302-316. Ed. John L. Esposito. Miami: Florida International University Press, 1990.

Seeks to discover whether the rise of Islamic revivalism in Nigeria was based on internal circumstances or was directly attributed to the Iranian revolution.

0623 _____. "The Role of Religion in National Life: Reflections on Recent Experience in Nigeria." *Religion and National Integration in Africa: Islam, Christianity, and Politics in the Sudan and Nigeria*, 85-99. Ed. John O. Hunwick. Evanston, IL: Northwestern University Press, 1992.

Discusses the roles that the various Christian denominations as well as Islam play in Nigerian society.

0624 HUNWICK, JOHN. "An African Case Study of Political Islam: Nigeria." *AAAPS* 524 (November 1992): 143-155.

This article focuses on the close symbiosis between Islam and political power in Nigeria. The author asserts that an end to the violence in Nigeria is predicated upon the implementation of democracy, the support for the *shari'ah* among Yourba Muslims, and external influences.

0625 KANE, OUSMANE. "Izala: The Rise of Muslim Reformism in Northern Nigeria." *Accounting for Fundamentalisms: The Dynamic Character of Movements*, 490-512. Eds. Martin E. Marty, and R. Scott Appleby. Chicago and London: The University of Chicago Press, 1994.
    Situated within the political, economic, and social evolution of Nigeria, this article examines the origins, evolution, leadership policies and the eventual fragmentation of the Izala Islamic movement.

0626 OHADIK, DON. "Muslim-Christian Conflict and Political Instability in Nigeria." *Religion and National Integration in Africa: Islam, Christianity, and Politics in the Sudan and Nigeria*, 101-123. Ed. John O. Hunwick. Evanston, IL: Northwestern University Press, 1992.
    Explores the religious struggle between Muslims and Christians in Nigeria and assesses the impact on Nigerian politics.

0627 OLAYIWOLA, ABDUR RAHMAN O. "Nationalism and Nation Building in Islam." *IQ* 34, no. 2 (1990): 101-114.
    This paper looks at concepts of nationalism and nation-building from Islamic perspective with special reference for religious co-existence and tolerance in Nigeria.

0628 OLAYIWOLA, RAHMAN O. "The Impact of Islam on the Conduct of Nigerian Foreign Relations." *IQ* 33, no. 1 (1989): 17-33.
    An examination of the impact of Islam on Nigerian foreign relations, especially countries of the Islamic world is the central focus of this study.

0629 OYEWESO, SIYAN. "The State and Religion in a Plural Society: The Nigerian Experience." *IC* 63, no. 4 (October 1989): 65-80.
    With the purpose of developing the proper role of the state and religion, particularly the role of politicians, this article focuses on the historical roots of Christian-Muslim rivalry and the points of convergence and divergence in Nigeria's pluralistic society.

0630 SODIQ, YUSHAU. "Application of Islamic Law in Nigeria: A Case Study." *HI* 17, no. 2 (June 1994): 55-76.
    Based on judgements of several court cases in Northern Nigeria in 1989, this article investigates to what extent the judges adhered strictly to the letter of Islamic law.

0631 TURNER, H. W. "New Religious Movements in Islamic West Africa." *ICMR* 4, no. 1 (1993): 3-35.

Explores the new religions that have developed in West Africa through their interaction with Islam.

III. THE AMERICAS

0632 ABRAHAM, NABEEL. "Anti-Arab Racism and Violence in the United States." *The Development of Arab-American Identity*, 155-213. Ed. Ernest McCarus. Ann Arbor: The University of Michigan Press, 1994.

Explores the sources of violence targeted against Arab Americans.

0633 ABU-LABAN, SHARON MCIRVIN. "The Coexistence of Cohorts: Identity and Adaptation Among Arab-American Muslims." *ASQ* 11, no. 2&3 (March 1989): 45-63.

This article surveys Arab Muslim immigrants in America examining the three waves of immigration and categorizing the patterns they display. It assesses a variety of experiences that affect Arab-American Muslim solidarity.

0634 _____. "Family and Religion Among Muslim Immigrants and their Descendants." *Muslim Families in North America*, 6-31. Eds. Earle H. Waugh, Sharon McIrvin Abu-Laban, and Regula Burckhardt Qureshi. Edmonton, Alberta: The University of Alberta Press, 1991.

This chapter is based on census data on Muslim immigrants as well as interviews with many Muslims in the North American community over a period of thirty years. It examines some of the commonalities and diversities among Muslim immigrants in North America. The author argues that the relationship between religion and family has been different for each family and thereby has affected family forms of Muslims in North America.

0635 ADENEY, MARIAM, and KATHRYN DEMASTER. "Muslims in Seattle." *Muslim Communities in North America*, 195-208. Eds. Yvonne Yazbeck Haddad, and Jane Idleman Smith. New York: State University of New York Press, 1994.

This essay identifies and examines the development of the major Muslim centers in Seattle. The chapter also looks at the Vietnamese, Cambodian, Druze, and African American Muslims as well as the tensions between the Muslim and non-Muslim community.

0636 AHMED, GUTBI MAHDI. "Muslim Organizations in the United States." *The Muslims of America*, 11-24. Ed. Yvonne Yazbeck Haddad. New York and Oxford: Oxford University Press, 1991.

Provides a historical overview of the organizational makeup of Sunni Muslims in America, offering insight into the formative period of the community.

0637 AKBAR, MUHAMMAD. "Muslims in the United States: History, Religion, Politics and Ethnicity." *JIMMA* 12, no. 2 (1991): 433-449.

Seeks to raise further inquiry about Muslims in the U.S. through an examination of identity, religion, and Christian-Muslim relations in the U.S.

0638 AKBAR, NA'IM. "Family Stability Among African-American Muslims." *Muslim Families in North America*, 213-231. Eds. Earle H. Waugh, Sharon McIrvin Abu-Laban, and Regula Burckhart Qureshi. Edmonton, Alberta: The University of Alberta Press, 1991.

This chapter focuses on the African-American Muslim community with a North American identity and examines how they are forging new social processes to bring a Muslim dynamic into their homes.

0639 EL AMIN, MUSTAFA. *The Religion of Islam and the Nation of Islam: What Is the Difference?* Newark, NJ: El-Amin Productions, 1990.

Contains a comparative analysis of the fundamental teachings of the Nation of Islam and mainstream Islam. The thirteen chapters discuss topics such as history; the concept of God; the last messenger of Allah; the dress code; Satan; judgement day; fasting; and prayers.

0640 BARAZANGI, NIMAT HAFEZ. "Acculturation of North American Arab Muslims: Minority Relations on Worldview Relations." *JIMMA* 11, no. 2 (1990): 373-390.

Drawing upon interviews conducted with Arab Muslims in Toronto, Buffalo, New York City, and Washington D.C., this essay analyzes Arab American Muslim religiosity and perceptions of Islam.

0641 _____. "Islamic Education in the United States and Canada: Conception and Practice of the Islamic Belief System." *The Muslims of America*, 157-174. Ed. Yvonne Yazbeck Haddad. New York and Oxford: Oxford University Press, 1991.

Based upon interviews with forty immigrant Muslim families in five major North American cities, this chapter compares and contrasts four different Islamic and Western world views and provides an examination of Islamic education in North America.

0642 _____. "Parents and Youth: Perceiving and Practicing Islam in North America." *Muslim Families in North America*, 132-147. Eds. Earle H. Waugh,

Sharon McIrvin Abu-Laban, and Regula Burckhardt Qureshi. Edmonton, Alberta: The University of Alberta Press, 1991.

This chapter, focusing on a sample of Arab Muslim youth between the ages of fourteen to twenty-two and their parents in North America, examines how they perceive themselves as Muslims and as Arabs in Canadian and American societies.

0643 BARBOZA, STEVEN. *American Jihad: Islam after Malcolm X.* New York: Doubleday, 1994.

Beginning with the death of Malcolm X, this work explores Islam in America. Seeking to explain "the pulse of Islamic society in America," the author includes portraits as well as interviews with 55 American Muslims that show the "jihad" or struggle that each has had in forging an Islamic identity for themselves in the United States. It illustrates the sometimes striking difference between American-born converts and immigrants from Islamic societies. Also, the book provides chapters on the origins and rise of the Nation of Islam and interviews with Warith Deen Muhammad and Louis Farrakhan.

0644 BA-YUNUS, ILYAS. "Muslims in North America: Mate Selection as an Indicator of Change." *Muslim Families in North America*, 232-249. Eds. Earle H. Waugh, Sharon McIrvin Abu-Laban, and Regula Burckhardt Qureshi. Edmonton, Alberta: The University of Alberta Press, 1991.

This chapter compares and contrasts the mate selection process of North American Muslim immigrants with that of those from traditional Islamic societies.

0645 BILGÉ, BARBARA. "Voluntary Associations in the Old Turkish Community of Metropolitan Detroit." *Muslim Communities in North America*, 381-405. Eds. Yvonne Yazbeck Haddad, and Jane Idleman Smith. New York: State University of New York Press, 1994.

The article analyzes metropolitan Detroit's old Turkish community institutions and examines how they helped in the adaptation process to American society. The essay also looks at the group's ties with Turkey, their identity, and values.

0646 CARSON, CLAYBORNE. *Malcolm X: The FBI File.* New York: Carroll and Graf Publishers, Inc., 1991.

An edited version of the more than thirty-six hundred pages of the FBI file on Malcolm X. Includes an introductory chapter on Malcolm and the American state.

0647   CHELKOWSKI, PETER J. and FRANK J. KOROM. "Community Process and the Performance of Muharram Observances in Trinidad." *DR* 38, no. 2 (June 1994): 150-174.
Begins with a brief historical overview of the event which is the foundation of the Muharram ritual. This article examines the various interpretations of the Muharram observances practiced by both the rural and urban Muslim population of Indian descent on the Caribbean island of Trinidad.

0648   _____. "Rituals/Muharram in Trinidad: A Festive Mourning." *IM* 13, no. 2 (January 1993): 54-63.
This article describes the ritual Muharram, a procession commemorating the death of Hussein the grandson of the Prophet Muhammed by the Muslim Indian population of the island of Trinidad.

0649   CONE, JAMES H. *Martin and Malcolm and America: A Dream or a Nightmare*. Maryknoll, NY: Orbis Books, 1991.
An examination of the relationship of Martin Luther King Jr. and Malcolm X and their struggle against racism as well as their vision of justice in American society.

0650   CURTIS, R. M. MUKHTAR. "Urban Muslims: The Formation of the Dar ul-Islam Movement." *Muslim Communities in North America*, 51-73. Eds. Yvonne Yazbeck Haddad, and Jane Idleman Smith. New York: State University of New York Press, 1994.
This article articulates the appeal of the Nation of Islam among African Americans in the 1940's and 1950's and examines the origins and evolution of the Dar ul-Islam movement in the U.S. and the factors that contributed to its dissolution.

0651   DENNY, FREDERICK M. "The Legacy of Fazlur Rahman." *The Muslims of America*, 96-108. Ed. Yvonne Yazbeck Haddad. New York and Oxford: Oxford University Press, 1991.
Traces the life and writings of Fazlur Rahman, the deceased Pakistani scholar, focusing on three main aspects of his work--"the philosophical-theological, the moral-ethical, and the religious-communal."

0652   AL DISUQI, RASHA. "The Muslim Image in Contemporary American Fiction." *IS* 31, no. 2 (1992):
Examines exaggerated depictions of Muslims in American literature.

0653   ESPOSITO, JOHN L. "Ismail R. al-Faruqi: Muslim Scholar-Activist." *The Muslims of America*, 65-79. Ed. Yvonne Yazbeck Haddad. New York and Oxford: Oxford University Press, 1991.

Provides an overview of the intellectual journey of the Palestinian scholar Ismail al-Faruqi from Arabism to a broader view of Islam as an integrating element of religion and culture. Illustrates the importance of his familiarity with Christian theological discourse in his interfaith dialogue.

0654 FA'IK, ALA. "Issues of Identity: In Theater of Immigrant Community." *The Development of Arab-American Identity*, 107-118. Ed. Ernest McCarus. Ann Arbor: The University of Michigan Press, 1994.

Examines the development of Arab drama and shows how it has been representative of the Arab American experience.

0655 FARRAKHAN, LOUIS. *A Torchlight for America*. Chicago: FCN Publishing CO., 1993.

Contains the essential teachings of Louis Farrakhan. It depicts America as "on her deathbed'" and charts a means for the salvation of African Americans under real leadership, and through reforms of the educational system, of the economy and of morality. It presents a new vision for America.

0656 FERRIS, MARK. "To 'Achieve the Pleasure of Allah': Immigrant Muslim Communities in New York City 1893-1991." *Muslim Communities in North America*, 209-230. Eds. Yvonne Yazbeck Haddad, and Jane Idleman Smith. New York: State University of New York Press, 1994.

This chapter discusses the historical development and ethnic composition of the Muslim community of New York.

0657 FRIEDLANDER, JONATHAN. "The Yemenis of Delano: A Profile of a Rural Islamic Community." *Muslim Communities in North America*, 423-444. Eds. Yvonne Yazbeck Haddad, and Jane Idleman Smith. New York: State University of New York Press, 1994.

This narrative, based on ethnographic research, examines the historical development of the Yemeni Muslims who settled in the agricultural town of Delano, California.

0658 GALLEN, DAVID. *Malcolm X: As They Knew Him*. New York: Carroll and Graf Publishers, Inc., 1992.

Includes excerpts written by twenty five women and men whose lives have been touched by Malcolm X, including Maya Angelou, Mike Wallace, and Alex Haley. The second part contains excerpts from his speeches, while the third part provides a re-assessment of his life by six authors.

0659 GARDELL, MATTIAS. "The Sun of Islam Will Rise in the West: Minister Farrakhan and the Nation of Islam in the Latter Days." *Muslim Communities in North America*, 15-49. Eds. Yvonne Yazbeck Haddad, and Jane Idleman Smith. Albany: State University of New York Press, 1994.

This article offers an introductory overview of the Nation of Islam and its leader Minister Louis Farrakhan. Provides historical background of the movement and discusses some of the more controversial claims against the Nation of Islam and its leader.

0660   HADDAD, YVONNE YAZBECK. "American Foreign Policy in the Middle East and Its Impact On the Identity of Arab Muslims in the United States." *The Muslims of America*, 217-235. Ed. Yvonne Yazbeck Haddad. New York and Oxford: Oxford University Press, 1991.

Looks at how American foreign policy decisions in the Middle East has affected Muslims in America and helped shape how they perceive themselves.

0661   _____. "The Challenge of Muslim 'Minorityness': The American Experience." *The Integration of Islam and Hinduism in Western Europe*, eds. W. A. R. Shadid, and P.S. van Koningsveld. Kampen, The Netherlands: Kok, 1991.

Addresses issues facing Muslim minorities through the experience of Muslims in America.

0662   _____. "Maintaining the Faith of the Fathers: Dilemmas of Religious Identity in the Christian and Muslim Arab-American Communities." *The Development of Arab-American Identity*, 61-84. Ed. Ernest McCarus. Ann Arbor: The University of Michigan Press, 1994.

Presents a picture of the importance that religion plays in Arab-American communities. Catalogues the differing Arab communities in the U.S. and provides information on their historical background as well as the influence that each group wields.

0663   _____. Ed. *The Muslims of America*, New York and Oxford: Oxford University Press, 1991.

This edited volume of scholarly essays on the growing U.S. Muslim community attempts to heighten public awareness of Islam as well as provide ideas that may lead to a better understanding of this community. Organized into six sections, the first looks at the organizational structures and estimates of Muslims in the United States. Section two provides different "Perceptions of Muslims in the United States." The third section traces the ideology and discourse of three Islamic scholars in America. The fourth section examines "Islamic activity" be it religious, political, or both. The fifth section provides essays on the Muslim women's perspective of what it means to be a Muslim woman in America. The final section examines identity issues.

0664 HADDAD, YVONNE YAZBECK and JANE IDLEMAN SMITH. "The Druze in the United States." *MW* (January 1991): 111-132.

Begins with a discussion of the origins and doctrines of the Druze then continues with an examination of the community in North America, especially their role during the U.S. involvement in the Lebanese civil war. Also analyzes issues of identity in the community.

0665 _____. *Mission to America: Five Islamic Sectarian Movements in the United States*. Gainesville: University of Florida Press, 1993.

An examination of five North American Muslim communities: the Druze, the Ahmadiyya, the Moorish Science Temple of America, the Ansaru Allah community, and the United Submitters International. All of these sectarian groups claim to be the true believers of Islam. This work explores the identities of these communities and discusses how they integrate with practitioners of mainstream Islam and American society.

0666 _____, eds. *Muslim Communities in North America*, Albany: State University of New York Press, 1994.

Provides a detailed examination of the issues facing Muslim society and institutions in North America. The work, a collection of 22 essays, deals with topics including: the growing Islamic community among African Americans; prejudice and racism; difficulties faced trying to maintain a strong ethnic and religious identity while assimilating into mainstream America; and the changing role of Muslim women in North America. Separated into three sections, the first discusses Islamic communities which are organized around specific beliefs or a charismatic leader. The second section provides a sampling of the Islamic groups in various metropolitan areas of the United States. The third section describes how various communities have adapted to life in America.

0667 HAINES, BYRON L. "Perspectives of the American Churches on Islam and the Muslim Community in North America." *The Muslims of America*, 39-52. Ed. Yvonne Yazbeck Haddad. New York and Oxford: Oxford University Press, 1991.

Through official and unofficial statements of various Christian churches in America, this chapter looks at their perceptions of American Muslims and the religion of Islam.

0668 HAKIM, JAMEELA A. "History of the First Muslim Mosque of Pittsburgh, Pennsylvania." *Islam in North America: A Sourcebook*, 153-163. Eds. Micheal A. Köszegi, and J. Gordan Melton. New York and London: Garland Publishing, Inc., 1992.

Traces the establishment of the first Muslim Mosque in Pennsylvania.

0669 HAMDANI, DAOOD HASSAN. "Muslim and Christian Life in Canada." *Islam in North America: A Sourcebook*, 253-263. Eds. Michael A. Köszegi, and J. Gordon Melton. New York and London: Garland Publishing, Inc., 1992.

Examines how the Muslim community in Canada interacts with the largely Christian population.

0670 HASHEM, MAZEN. "Assimilation in American Life: An Islamic Perspective." *AJISS* 8, no. 1 (1991): 83-97.

Using Milton Gordon's paradigm of assimilation, this essay explores aspects of cultural, identificational, civic, marital, and structural assimilation of Muslims in America.

0671 HERMANSEN, MARCIA K. "The Muslims in San Diego." *Muslim Communities in North America*, 169-194. Eds. Yvonne Yazbeck Haddad, and Jane Idleman Smith. New York: State University of New York Press, 1994.

This chapter offers a look at the historical development of the Muslim community in San Diego and examines the diversity of their community centers and mosques.

0672 _____. "Two-Way Acculturation: Muslim Women in America Between Individual Choice (Liminality) and Community Affiliation (Communitas)." *The Muslims of America*, 188-201. Ed. Yvonne Yazbeck Haddad. New York and Oxford: Oxford University Press, 1991.

Examines the different ways that Muslim women in America express their Islamic belief and identity.

0673 HOGBEN, W. MURRAY. "Marriage and Divorce Among Muslims in Canada." *Muslim Families in North America*, 154-184. Eds. Earle H. Waugh, Sharon McIrvin Abu-Laban, and Regula Burckhardt Qureshi. Edmonton, Alberta: The University of Alberta Press, 1991.

The author, coming from the viewpoint of a 'participant observer,' examines issues of marriage such as family intermarriage, polygyny, and arranged marriages among Muslims in Canada.

0674 HUSAIN, ASAD and HAROLD VOGELAAR. "Activities of the Immigrant Muslim Communities in Chicago." *Muslim Communities in North America*, 231-257. Eds. Yvonne Yazbeck Haddad, and Jane Idleman Smith. New York: State University of New York Press, 1994.

Based on oral traditions, early Muslim newspapers, dissertations, newsletters, and published materials of various Chicago Muslim organizations, this chapter outlines the waves of the Muslim immigrants to Chicago. In addition, the article explores the Muslim community centers and their organizational activities.

0675 HUSEBY-DARVAS, EVA VERONIKA. "'Coming to America': Dilemmas of Ethnic Groups since the 1880s." *The Development of Arab-American Identity*, 9-22. Ed. Ernest McCarus. Ann Arbor: The University of Michigan Press, 1994.

Offers a framework of the waves of immigrants who came to America in the 1880s in order to enable future researchers to compare the Arab American experience.

0676 JOHNSON, STEVE A. "The Muslims of Indianapolis." *Muslim Communities in North America*, 259-277. Eds. Yvonne Yazbeck Haddad, and Jane Idleman Smith. New York: State University of New York Press, 1994.

This chapter offers a brief history of Islamic institutions in Indiana including African American Islamic institutions and the immigrant Muslim communities. The article also examines relations between the various Muslim groups.

0677 _____. "Political Activity of Muslims in America." *The Muslims of America*, 111-124. Ed. Yvonne Yazbeck Haddad. New York and Oxford: Oxford University Press, 1991.

Surveys political activity of Muslims in America and explains the hesitancy of Muslims to engage in political activity and shows some of the difficulties that Muslims have had when dealing with Christian Arabs in political organizations.

0678 KASHEM, MAZEN. "Assimilation in American Life: An Islamic Perspective." *AJISS* 8, no. 1 (March 1991): 83-97.

Examines various aspects of assimilation, arguing that certain processes must be adopted to maintain cultural and religious identity but that Muslims should invest efforts in total civic assimilation.

0679 KELLEY, RON. *Irangeles: Iranians in Los Angeles*, Berkeley: University of California Press, 1992.

This blend of text and photography seeks to improve the American understanding of the Iranian community of Los Angeles and of the origins of the Islamic Republic of Iran. Divided into seven chapters, the work provides interviews in each. Topics studied include: Iran prior to immigration to the United States; identity and diversity; social and gender issues; economics; politics; culture; and "The Photography of Irangeles."

0680 _____. "Muslims in Los Angeles." *Muslim Communities in North America*, 135-167. Eds. Yvonne Yazbeck Haddad, and Jane Idleman Smith. New York: State University of New York Press, 1994.

This essay explores the widely varying differences among the Muslims of Los Angeles. The author looks at the mosques of L.A.; the conflict within the community; political, religious, and cultural fragmentation; and the cultural and class gaps between African American Muslims and Muslim immigrants from traditional Islamic societies.

0681   KLY, Y. N. "The African-American Muslim Minority: 1776-1900." *JIMMA* 10, no. 1 (January 1989): 152-160.
Through an examination of the evolution of the African American community, this article looks at three primary factors which contributed to its development.

0682   KOLARS, CHRISTINE. "Masjid ul-Mutkabir: The Portrait of an African Orthodox Muslim Community." *Muslim Communities in North America*, 475-499. Eds. Yvonne Yazbeck Haddad, and Jane Idleman Smith. New York: State University of New York Press, 1994.
This chapter examines the African American Muslim community in Poughkeepsie, New York. The author looks at their mosque, the Masjid ul-Mutkabir, its activities and the role that Islam plays in their lives and in the process of their identity formation. The article also briefly touches on relations with other Islamic communities in the area.

0683   KÖSZEGI, MICHAEL A. "The Sufi Order in the West: Sufism's Encounter With the New Age." *Islam in North America: A Sourcebook*, 211-222. Eds. Michael A. Köszegi, and J. Gordon Melton. New York and London: Garland Publishing, Inc., 1992.
Explores one Sufi organization in America founded by Hazrat Inayat Khan.

0684   LAHAJ, MARY. "The Islamic Center of New England." *Muslim Communities in North America*, 293-315. Eds. Yvonne Yazbeck Haddad, and Jane Idleman Smith. New York: State University of New York Press, 1994.
This chapter discusses the historical development of the New England Islamic Center and its community from its inception as the Arab American Banner Society in 1937.

0685   LINCOLN, C. ERIC. *The Black Muslims in America*. Grand Rapids, MI: Trenton, NJ: William B. Eerdmans Publishing Company: Africa World Press, Inc., 1994.
This updated third edition is a sociological study of the black Muslim movement in America. Traces the history of the movement including the Nation of Islam following the death of its founder Elijah Muhammad in 1975. Includes the steps taken by his son Wallace Deen Muhammad to bring the movement towards mainstream Islam and the emergence of Louis Farrakhan as the new leader of the Nation of Islam.

0686 MACKENZIE, CLAYTON G. "Muslim Primary Schools in Trinidad and Tobago." *IQ* 33, no. 1 (1989): 5-16.

This article traces the historical development and assesses the future prospects of the Muslim educational system in Trinidad and Tobago.

0687 MCCARUS, ERNEST. *The Development of Arab-American Identity*. Ed. Ann Arbor: The University of Michigan Press, 1994.

Presents a collection of essays that explore the topic of Arab Americans. Chapters provide studies on the early immigration experience, racism, violence, Arabs in the political realm, Palestinian women, and identity.

0688 MCDONOUGH, SHEILA. "Muslims in Montreal." *Muslim Communities in North America*, 317-334. Eds. Yvonne Yazbeck Haddad, and Jane Idleman Smith. New York: State University of New York Press, 1994.

This chapter illustrates how the ethnic, linguistic, and sectarian diversity of the Montreal Muslim community has not stood in the way of their goal to transcend differences and forge a common Muslim identity.

0689 MOORE, KATHLEEN M. "New Claimants to Religious Tolerance and Protection: A Case Study of American and Canadian Muslims." *AJISS* 6, no. 1 (1989): 135-142.

Explores the Muslim experience in Canada and the U.S. and discusses their attempts to become a part of American and Canadian society.

0690 _____. "The Case for Muslim Constitutional Interpretive Activity in the United States." *AJISS* 7, no. 1 (1990): 65-76.

Beginning with a review of the ways in which Muslims in America adopt a litigation as a method to participate in American politics, the article examines the impact of this strategy.

0691 _____. "Muslim Commitment in North America: Assimilation or Transformation." *AJISS* 11, no. 2 (June 1994): 223-244.

Provides a profile of American Muslims, focusing on their recent litigation efforts and identity.

0692 _____. "Muslims in Prison: Claims to Constitutional Protection of Religious Liberty." *The Muslims of America*, 136-156. Ed. Yvonne Yazbeck Haddad. New York and Oxford: Oxford University Press, 1991.

Provides an analysis of the experience of Muslims in the American prison system and their ability to freely practice their religion.

0693 NAFF, ALIXA. "The Early Arab Immigrant Experience." *The Development of Arab-American Identity*, 23-36. Ed. Ernest McCarus. Ann Arbor: The University of Michigan Press, 1994.

Explores the experience of the early waves of Arab migration to the United States.

0694 NAFICY, HAMID. *The Making of Exile Cultures: Iranian Television in Los Angeles*. Minneapolis: University of Minnesota Press, 1993.

The product of a ten year study of Iranian TV programs in Los Angeles is enriched by interviews with the producers. It attempts an analysis of concepts of exile and identity, exploring the means by which the community is transformed through opposition and resistance to domination by the host culture as well as the social values it carried from the home country.

0695 NURUDDIN, YUSUF. "The Five Percenters: A Teenage Nation of Gods and Earth." *Muslim Communities in North America*, 109-132. Eds. Yvonne Yazbeck Haddad, and Jane Idleman Smith. New York: State University of New York Press, 1994.

This chapter examines the historical development, the organizational make-up, the ideology and worldview of the Five Percenters, a group that split from the Nation of Islam in 1964.

0696 NYANG, SULAYMAN S. "Convergence and Divergence in an Emergent Community: A Study of Challenges Facing U.S. Muslims." *The Muslims of America*, 236-249. Ed. Yvonne Yazbeck Haddad. New York and Oxford: Oxford University Press, 1991.

Studies the challenges facing American Muslims through an examinations of their differences and similarities.

0697 POSTON, LARRY A. "Da'wah in the West." *The Muslims of America*, 125-135. Ed. Yvonne Yazbeck Haddad. New York and Oxford: Oxford University Press, 1991.

Traces the historical movement of Muslim missionaries in America and divides them into those who wish to protect the ideals of the Islamic community and those who actively engage in missionary work.

0698 _____. "The Future of *Da'wah* in North America." *AJISS* 8, no. 3 (1991): 501-511.

Assesses the success of Muslim missionary work in America.

0699 RAGOONATH, BISHNU. "The Failure of the Abu Bakr Coup: The Plural Society, Cultural Traditions and Political Development in Trinidad." *JCCP* 31, no. 2 (July 1993): 33-53.

Investigating background events and the aftermath of the 1990 coup, the author shows how Trinidad's pluralism prevented the success of the coup as the people of Trinidad lined up according to their race and religion.

0700 RASHID, SAMORY. "Islamic Aspects of the Legacy of Malcolm X." *AJISS* 10, no. 1 (1993): 60-71.
Examines the phenomenon of Malcolm X and analyzes the significance of the Muslim leader and the Islamic aspects that remain following his death.

0701 ROSS-SHERIF, FARIYAL. "Elderly Muslim Immigrants: Needs and Challenges." *Muslim Communities in North America*, 407-421. Eds. Yvonne Yazbeck Haddad, and Jane Idleman Smith. New York: State University of New York Press, 1994.
Based on ethnographic research that included discussions with elderly Muslims from South Asia and South Asian Muslims immigrating from Africa, this article provides information on the lives and challenges of the elderly Muslim community in America.

0702 ROSS-SHERIF, FARIYAL and AZIM NANJI. "Islamic Identity, Family, and Community: The Case of the Nizari Ismaili Community." *Muslim Families in North America*, 101-117. Eds. Earle H. Waugh, Sharon McIrvin Abu-Laban, and Regula Burckhardt Qureshi. Edmonton, Alberta: The University of Alberta Press, 1991.
This chapter examines how the Nizari Isma'ili Muslim immigrants in North America draw upon their religious traditions to forge new social institutions in order to adapt them to their new lives.

0704 SABAGH, GEORGES and MEHDI BOZORGMEHR. "Secular Immigrants: Religiosity and Ethnicity Among Iranian Muslims in Los Angeles." *Muslim Communities in North America*, 445-473. Eds. Yvonne Yazbeck Haddad, and Jane Idleman Smith. New York: State University of New York Press, 1994.
Using the Iranian Muslims of Los Angeles as a test case, this chapter challenges the assumption that religion reinforces ethnicity among immigrants.

0705 SACHEDINA, ABDULAZIZ A. "A Minority within a Minority: The Case of the Shi'a in North America." *Muslim Communities in North America*, 3-14. Eds. Yvonne Yazbeck Haddad, and Jane Idleman Smith. New York: State University of New York Press, 1994.
This essay explores the immigrant Shi'i communities in North America offering a glimpse of the role that the traditional religious structure plays in a functioning Shi'i society.

0706 SARMA, JONATHAN D. "The American Jewish Experience and the Emergence of the Muslim Community in America." *AJISS* 9, no. 3 (1992): 370-382.

Explores the changes in the American Jewish community with the rise of the American Muslim community.

0707 SCHUBEL, VERNON. "The Muharram Majlis: The Role of a Ritual in the Preservation of Shi'a Identity." *Muslim Families in North America*, 118-131. Eds. Earle H. Waugh, Sharon McIrvin Abu-Laban, and Regula Burckhardt Qureshi. Edmonton, Alberta: The University of Alberta Press, 1991.

This chapter looks at the role of the *Muharram Majlis* (lamentation assembly) in the preservation of the Shi'a identity in North America.

0708 SEARLE, CHRIS. "The Muslimeen Insurrection in Trinidad." *RC* 33, no. 2 (October 1991): 29-43.

The author examines the events surrounding the attempted coup by Abu Bakr's "Jamaat al-Muslimeen" group in Trinidad and Tobago, as well as the coup's causes and its aftermath.

0709 SHAFIQ, MUHAMMAD. *Growth of Islamic Thought in North America: Focus on Isma'il Raji al-Faruqi*. Brentwood, MD: Amana Publications, 1994.

Presents the development and the importance of the work of the Islamic thinker Isma'il Al-Faruqi. Demonstrates why the murder of Al-Faruqi and his wife was devastating to the Muslim community. Al-Faruqi's work had explored the difficulties facing the Muslim world and offered answers to some of these problems.

0710 SHINGIETY, ABUBAKER AL. "The Muslim as the 'Other': Representation and Self-Image of the Muslims in America." *The Muslims of America*, 53-61. Ed. Yvonne Yazbeck Haddad. New York and Oxford: Oxford University Press, 1991.

Centering on the experience of the Nation of Islam, this chapter illustrates the relationship between the way the Muslims view themselves and how the West perceives Islam.

0711 SMITH, JANE I. "Seyyed Hossein Nasr: Defender of the Sacred and Islamic Traditionalism." *The Muslims of America*, 80-95. Ed. Yvonne Yazbeck Haddad. New York and Oxford: Oxford University Press, 1991.

Traces the works of Seyyed Hossein Nasr, the Iranian scholar of Islam, and illustrates how Nasr advocates Islamic traditionalism over fundamentalism, modernism, rationalism, and evolution.

0712 SONN, TAMARA. "Diversity in Rochester's Islamic Community." *Muslim Communities in North America*, 279-292. Eds. Yvonne Yazbeck Haddad, and Jane Idleman Smith. New York: State University of New York Press, 1994.

Based primarily on interviews with people from differing Islamic groups in the Rochester region, this article presents some observations about the diversity of that Muslim community.

0713 STOCKTON, RONALD. "Ethnic Archetypes and the Arab Image." *The Development of Arab-American Identity*, 119-154. Ed. Ernest McCarus. Ann Arbor: The University of Michigan Press, 1994.

Through a study of hundreds of cartoons that stereotype Arabs, this essay classifies the different types of pejorative stereotypes and the intentions of those who promote them.

0714 STONE, CAROL L. "Estimate of Muslims Living in America." *The Muslims of America*, 25-36. Ed. Yvonne Yazbeck Haddad. New York and Oxford: Oxford University Press, 1991.

Based upon 1980 Census Bureau emigration statistics, this chapter offers a projection of American Muslims today. Contends that approximately 4 million Muslims live in the U.S. today and major Muslim communities are found in Illinois, California, and New York.

0715 SULEIMAN, MICHAEL W. "Arab-Americans and the Political Process." *The Development of Arab-American Identity*, 37-60. Ed. Ernest McCarus. Ann Arbor: The University of Michigan Press, 1994.

Provides a historical survey of the experience of Arab Americans in the political sphere.

0716 TRIX, FRANCES. "Bektashi Tekke and the Sunni Mosque of Albanian Muslims in America." *Muslim Communities in North America*, 359-380. Eds. Yvonne Yazbeck Haddad, and Jane Idleman Smith. New York: State University of New York Press, 1994.

This chapter offers a brief description of the Detroit-based Albanian Mosque, the first in America, and the Albanian Bektashi Tekke, a Sufi center of the Bektashi Order also based in Detroit. The article begins with the history of the immigration of Albanian Muslims to America and discusses the development of their organization's growth. The essay also provides information on each institution's functions, leadership, membership, as well as their relationship with each other.

0717 VOLL, JOHN OBERT. "Islamic Issues for Muslims in the United States." *The Muslims of America*. Ed. Yvonne Yazbeck Haddad. New York: Oxford University Press, 1991.

Examines the way in which Muslims in America deal with challenges faced because of their Islamic identity.

0718 WALBRIDGE, LINDA S. "Confirmation of Shi'ism in America: An analysis of Sermons in the Dearborn Mosques." *MW* 83, no. 3-4 (July 1993): 248-262.

Offers a brief overview of the history of the Lebanese Shi'a in Dearborn Michigan and a survey of the content and styles of sermons delivered in Dearborn Shi'a mosques.

0719 _____. "The Shi'a Mosques and their Congregations in Dearborn." *Muslim Communities in North America*, 337-357. Eds. Yvonne Yazbeck Haddad, and Jane Idleman Smith. New York: State University of New York Press, 1994.

Examines the role the Shi'a mosques played in uniting and dividing the Shi'a community in Dearborn, Michigan.

0720 WALDMAN, MARILYN ROBINSON. "Reflections on Islamic Tradition, Women, and Family." *Muslim Families in North America*, 309-325. Eds. Earle H. Waugh, Sharon McIrvin Abu-Laban, and Regula Burckhardt Qureshi. Edmonton, Alberta: The University of Alberta Press, 1991.

This chapter offers a historian's perspective and examines Muslim families and the differing roles of Muslim women in North American societies.

0721 WAUGH, EARLE H. "North America and the Adaption of the Muslim Tradition: Religion Ethnicity, and the Family." *Muslim Families in North America*, 68-95. Eds. Earle H. Waugh, Sharon McIrvin Abu-Laban, and Regula Burckhardt Qureshi. Edmonton, Alberta: The University of Alberta Press, 1991.

Analyzes the relationship of religion and ethnicity as experienced by Muslim immigrants who are in the process of adaptation to a new North American community.

0722 WAUGH, EARLE H., SHARON MCIRVIN ABU-LABAN, and REGULA BURCKHARDT QURESHI, eds. *Muslim Families in North America*, Calgary: The University of Alberta Press, 1991.

This edited work examines the significance of Islam and its impact on the lives of Muslims in North America. Divided into four sections, the first offers three studies which delineate the boundaries within which North American Muslims live. The first article provides an analysis of the relationship between family and religion among Muslim immigrants. The second chapter looks at the scriptural framework for the Muslim family and the third chapter examines the interplay between religion and ethnicity among North American Muslims. The second part examines the importance of conveying tradition from one generation to another as a means of preserving their identity. It offers studies on the Nizari Ismaili Muslims; the role of the lamentation assembly among North American Shi'a Muslims of South Asian origin; and how Arab Muslim youth and their parents perceive themselves in North American society. The third section examines the institution of marriage and family among Muslims living in North American societies. Offers chapters on marriage and divorce among Canadian Muslims; marriage strategies among North American Muslims of Pakistani and Indian origin; family stability among African American Muslims; and a comparative study of the mate selection process of Muslims in North American societies and those from traditional Islamic societies. The fourth part offers three papers which examine the dynamic relationship between Muslim women's roles, the family and Islam in North America. The first offers a study on Muslim women of Dearborn, Michigan; the second focuses on Palestinian women living in Chicago; and the third offers a historian's perspective on the role of women, family, and Islam in North American societies.

0723 WEBB, GISELA. "Tradition and Innovation in Contemporary American Islamic Spirituality: The Bawa Muhaiyaddeen Fellowship." *Muslim Communities in North America*, 75-108. Eds. Yvonne Yazbeck Haddad, and Jane Idleman Smith. New York: State University of New York Press, 1994.

Explores the historical development of the mystical side of Islam, personified in the Bawa Muhaiyaddeen Fellowship, as it has evolved in its American context. Examines the spiritual dimension, ideology, demographic trends, and future prospects for the movement.

0724 ZOGBY, JOHN J. "Islam's Image in American Public Opinion." *MEAJ* 2, no. 1 (March 1994): 23-31.

Looks at the portrayal of Muslims in America by the U.S. media.

IV.   ASIA

0725 AGWANI, M. S. *Religion and Politics in West Asia*. New Delhi: Vikas Publishing House PVT LTD, 1992.

Explores the interaction between politics and religion in the Muslim communities of West Asia. The first chapter introduces the social and economic picture as well as the impact of the growth of secular education on these societies. The second chapter surveys recent research about the interplay between Islam and the state through the development of Muslim societies. The third chapter examines the development of Islamic revivalism. The fourth chapter examines the Islamic revival in the contemporary period and its implication for the societies of west Asia.

0726 CANFIELD, ROBERT L. "Theological 'Extremism' and Social Movements in Turko-Persia." *Turko-Persia in Historical Perspective*, 132-160. Ed. Robert L. Canfield. Cambridge: Cambridge University Press, 1991.

From a historical perspective, this chapter explores the social movements that had doctrinal beliefs which were outside the mainstream of orthodox Islam in the Turko-Persia region.

0727 FULLER, GRAHAM E. *Islamic Fundamentalism in the Northern Tier Countries*. Santa Monica, CA: Rand, 1991.

This survey, prepared for the U.S. Under secretary of Defense for Policy, is the combination of a series of reports assessing Islamic fundamentalism in Turkey, Iran, Afghanistan and Pakistan. The work examines the causal factors behind the rise of Islamic activism within the political and socio-economic context of each of these countries. The survey seeks to determine the nature of Islamic fundamentalist policy should they take over power in Turkey, Afghanistan or Pakistan. The impact of Iran on these neighbors is also discussed. The author concludes with an assessment of the implications for U.S. policy.

0728 GABORIEAU, MARC. "Muslim Minorities in Nepal." *The Crescent in the East*, 79-101. Ed. Raphael Israeli. London: Curzon Press Ltd., 1989.

This chapter explores the Muslim minority community in Nepal and examines their position in Nepali society as well as the form of Islam to which they adhere.

0729 ISRAELI RAPHAEL, ed. *The Crescent in the East: Islam in Asia Major*, London: Curzon Press Ltd., 1989.

This edited volume of essays surveys the diversity and unity of the broad spectrum of Muslims in Asia. The work begins with an overview of the book and then discusses the significance of Islam in Iranian national identity. This follows with an examination of the Muslim Afghani groups and depicts their struggle against the Soviet based regime in Kabul. The next chapter on South Asia offers a brief overview of Muslims living on the Indian sub-continent, the creation of Pakistan and Bangladesh. Pakistan is further explored from a socio-political angle. The issue of how Muslims fare as a minority is analyzed with case studies of Muslims in Nepal, Burma, Thailand, the Philippines, Malaysia, Indonesia, and China.

0730 MARSOT, ALAIN-GERARD. "Political Islam in Asia: A Case Study." *AAAPSS* 524 (November 1992): 156-69.

Asserts that Islamic resurgence exists in every Asian country that Muslims inhabit. Focusing on the Muslims in South Asia and Southeast Asia, this article reviews patterns of Islamic conversions, European colonization, and the size of their populations. Provides case studies of Islamic activism in Pakistan, Bangladesh, India, Indonesia, and Malaysia and finds that Islamic revivalism has its basis in the traumatic changes of modernization and that Islam actually leads the movements toward decolonization.

0731 MALIK, IFTIKHAR H. "Islam, the West and Ethnonationalism: A Comparative Analysis of Contemporary Central and South Asia." *AJISS* 9, no. 1 (March 1992): 51-68.
Analyzes the roles of Islam and ethnic nationalism in identity formation and politics of contemporary, post Cold War Central and South Asia.

0732 _____. "Issues in Contemporary South and Central Asian Politics: Islam, Ethnicity, and the State." *AS* 32, no. 10 (October 1992): 888-901.
Examines the role that Islam and ethnicity play in South and Central Asian politics.

0733 MUTALIB, HUSSIN. "Islamic Revivalism in ASEAN States: Political Implications." *AS* 30, no. 9 (September 1990): 877-891.
The author first analyzes Islamic resurgence as a global phenomenon and then examines the political implications of this revival on the association of Southeast Asian nations in general and Malaysia in particular.

0734 REZUN, MIRON. "Iran and Afghanistan: With Specific Reference to Their Asian Policies and Practices." *JAAS* 25, no. 1-2 (January 1990): 9-26.
The article examines the relations of Iran and Afghanistan with Muslim and non-Muslim neighbors in Southwest Asia.

0735 VON DER MEHDEN, FRED R. "Malaysian and Indonesian Islamic Movements and the Iranian Connection." *The Iranian Revolution: Its Global Impact*, 233-254. Ed. John L. Esposito. Miami: Florida International University Press, 1990.
Focusing on government relations, state attempts to contain the impact of the Islamic revolution on their respective societies, and the popular reaction to the revolution, this article assesses the impact of the revolution on Malaysia and Indonesia.

A.   Central Asia

0736 ABDUVAKHITOV, ABDUJABAR. "Islamic Revival in Uzbekistan." *Russia's Muslim Frontiers*, 70-100. Ed. Dale Eickelman. Bloomington, IN: Indiana University Press, 1993.

Traces the origins of Uzbekistani Islamic revivalism that begins in the 1970's. This revivalism, spurred on by the disillusionment with the Soviet state, paved the way for the creation and strength of the Islamic Renaissance Party of Uzbekistan.

0737 _____. "The Jadid Movement and Its Impact on Contemporary Central Asia." *Central Asia: Its Strategic Importance and Future Prospects*, 65-76. Ed. Hafeez Malik. New York: St. Martin's Press, 1994.

Traces the history of the Jadid (modernist) movement and discusses its current influence in Central Asia. The article argues that the movement, nearly destroyed during the Stalinist era, is increasingly gaining supporters in Central Asia.

0738 ALGAR, HAMID. "Shaykh Zaynullah Rasulev: The Last Great Naqshabandi Shaykh of the Volga-Urals Region." *Muslims in Central Asia: Expressions of Identity and Change*, 112-133. Ed. Jo-Ann Gross. London: Duke University Press, 1992.

Analyzes the importance of Shaykh Zaynullah Rasulev, twentieth century leader of the Khalidi Sheikhs in the Volga-Urals region, in establishing an Islamic identity and community. The essay also examines the influence of Shaykh Rasulev on the formation process of Muslim identity among the Kazakhs, Tartars, and Bashkirs.

0739 ALTOMA, REEF. "The Influence of Islam in Post-Soviet Kazakhstan." *Central Asia in Historical Perspective*, 164-181. Ed. B. Manz. Boulder, CO: Westview Press, 1994.

Through an analysis of the role of Islam in Kazakhstan's politics, the author asserts that although wide interest in Islamic politics exists, the country's leaders follow a more secular agenda.

0740 ATKIN, MURIEL. "Religious, National, and Other Identities in Central Asia." *Muslims in Central Asia: Expressions of Identity and Change*, 46-72. Ed. Jo-Ann Gross. London: Duke University Press, 1992.

Explores the link between religious, national, ethnic, tribal, and socio-economic ties in the process of identity formation of the peoples of central Asia.

0741 _____. *The Subtlest Battle: Islam and Soviet Tajikistan*. Philadelphia, PA: Foreign Policy Research Institute, 1989.

Offers a case study of Islam in the former Soviet Union republic of Tajikistan. Assesses whether Islam is an active political force through an examination of the role that Islam plays in everyday life. Also looks at the extent to which Islamic political activism in Iran and Afghanistan influences politics in Tajikistan. Further chapters analyze the domestic and external elements that influence or encourage Islamic identification as well as the Soviet system that has tried to control Islamic activism.

0742 _____. "The Survival of Islam in Soviet Tajikistan." *MEJ* 43, no. 4 (1989): 605-18.

Illustrates how Islam has retained a broad following in Central Asia despite the attacks of the Soviet state in an effort to bring about domestic adaptation. Through a case study of Tajikistan, the article analyzes both state-sanctioned Islam and grassroots movements. Provides an examination of local holy men and women, unofficial means of spreading information, local practices, and holy places. The author concludes that Muslims in Tajikistan found ways to adapt to the Soviet system instead of allowing outsiders to manipulate them.

0743 BENNIGSEN, ALEXANDRE. "Islam and Political Power in the USSR." *Religion and Political Power*, 69-82. Eds. Gustavo Benavides, and M. W. Daly. Albany: State University of New York Press, 1989.

Discusses the paradoxical and often complicated relationship that the Soviet state had with the two faces of Islam under its power. This ranges from cooperation with an obedient but weak official Islam while trying to destroy the more powerful popular sufi movements. This chapter covers the policies towards its Muslim subjects in Turkmenistan, Kazakhastan, Kirgizia, Uzbekistan, and Tajikistan.

0744 BENNIGSEN, ALEXANDRE, PAUL B. HENZE, GEORGE K. TANHAM, and S. ENDERS WIMBUSH. *Soviet Strategy and Islam*. London: The Macmilan Press LTD, 1989.

This book, which had its origin in a study by the associates of Foreign Area Research Inc. for the Office of Net Assessment of the US Department of Defense, explores the beginnings and development of the Soviet Union's belief that the Islamic world carried a unique set of geo-strategic problems requiring special measures. The work also examines Soviet attempts to create and implement these measures believing that this would help achieve their short- and long-term political objectives.

0745 CANFIELD, ROBERT L. "The Collision of Evolutionary Process and Islamic Ideology in Greater Central Asia." *Afghanistan and the Soviet Union*, eds. Milan Hauner, and Robert L. Canfield. Boulder, CO: Westview Press, 1989.

Examines two sources of change in Greater Central Asia that will affect its political landscape--Soviet expansionism and Islamic ideology.

0746 CRITCHLOW, JAMES. "Islam and Nationalism in Soviet Central Asia." *Religion and Nationalism in Soviet and East European Politics*, 196-219. Ed. Pedro Ramet. Durham and London: Duke University Press, 1989.

 Explores the role that Islam plays in the Soviet Union despite attempts by the government to stamp it out.

0747 _____. "Nationalism and Islamic Resurgence in Uzbekistan." *Central Asia: Its Strategic Importance and Future Prospects*, 233-248. Ed. Hafeez Malik. New York, NY: St. Martin's Press, 1994.

 Discusses the role of Islam in the independent state of Uzbekistan. The author analyzes the Islamic movement in Uzbekistan and its relations with other Muslim countries.

0748 DUNN, MICHAEL COLLINS. "Central Asian Islam: Fundamentalist Threat or Communist Bogeyman." *MEP* 2, no. 1 (1993): 35-43.

 Seeks to answer the question of whether Islamic fundamentalism is a real phenomenon in the states of the former Soviet Union or whether it is a *bête noire* created by former communist leaders to maintain their hold on power.

0749 EICKELMAN, DALE F., ed. *Russia's Muslim Frontiers: New Directions in Cross-Cultural Analysis*, Bloomington and Indianapolis: Indiana University Press, 1993.

 This edited volume is derived from workshops held in Moscow and Leningrad and conferences held in New Hampshire and Washington D.C. Reflects the work of U.S. and Soviet scholars who study the Muslim community in Central Asia, South Asia, and the Middle East and the product of their discussion of Islamic religion and politics. Divided into four sections, they provide insight into the relationship between Islam and politics in Central Asia, Afghanistan, Iran, and Pakistan. Also offers perspectives of U.S. and Soviet policy regarding the Middle East during the Cold War.

0750 EICKELMAN, DALE F. and KAMRAN PASHER. "Muslim Societies and Politics: Soviet and U.S. Approaches -- A Conference Report." *MEJ* 45, no. 4 (1991): 630-647.

 The summation of a joint conference between U.S. and Soviet scholars who specialize in affairs in the Middle East, South Asia, and Soviet Central Asia. The article examines the 'Orientalism' crisis of Soviet scholarship, the perceptions and misperceptions of scholars during the Cold War, representations of Islam in U.S. and Soviet scholarship as well as the role of Islam in Central Asia, Afghanistan, Iran and Pakistan.

0751 GAMMER, MOSHE. *Muslim Resistance to the Tsar: Shamil and the Conquest of Chechnia and Daghestan*. Portland, OR: Frank Cass, 1994.

This work examines the Muslim Murid movement and its leader Shamil who revolted against Tsarist Russian expansionism. Illustrates why Shamil is still considered a hero to this day.

0752 GRESH, ALAIN. "Continuity and Change in the Soviet Policy: The Gulf Crisis and the Islamic Dimension." *MERIP* 167 (1990): 4-10.
Looks at Soviet policy during the Gulf war and examines how the Soviets dealt with the Islamic issue.

0753 GROSS, JO-ANN, ed. *Muslims in Central Asia: Expressions of Identity and Change*, Durham and London: Duke University Press, 1992.
An edited volume of essays which originated from a conference discussing "approaches to the study of Islam in Central and Inner Asia," sponsored by the Middle East Institute at Columbia University. This work seeks to present the various approaches to the process of identity formation in Central Asia. The authors place their studies within the historical, political, and cultural context of each region. In addition, the essays illustrate the fluidity as well as the variety of identity concepts of Central Asia's Muslims. The work is divided into three sections, the first explores the multiplicity of identity formation in Central Asia in general and includes a study on Muslims of Northern Afghanistan. The second part focuses on the role of Islam as an ideology in Northwestern China and Eastern Turkistan and an analysis of the 19th century Islamic leader Shaykh Zaynullah Rasnulev in the Volga-Urals Region. The third section examines the *Jadid* modernist movement and the importance of literature in the social history of Central Asian Muslims.

0754 HAGHAYEGHI, MEHRDAD. "Islamic Revival in the Central Asian Republics." *CAS* 13, no. 2 (1994): 249-266.
Seeks to discover whether the role that Islam will play in Central Asia will be of a political nature as in Saudi Arabia and Iran or secular as in Turkey.

0755 HETMANEK, ALLEN. "Islamic Revolution and Jihad Comes to the Former Soviet Central Asia: The Case of Tajikistan." *CAS* 12, no. 3 (1993): 365-378.
Spells out why the Islamic revival in Central Asia in general and Tajikistan in particular was dismissed by area specialists. The article then moves on to discuss the revival's characteristics and the factors behind its rise.

0756 _____. "The Reawakening of Soviet Islam." *MEI* 7, no. 2 & 3 (1990): 34-40.
This article examines the reasons for discontent with the Soviet state in the Turko-Muslim Republics. The essay explores issues such as socio-economic deprivation, dissatisfaction with the local party and state bureaucracies and assesses the possibility of a turmoil-free future for the republics.

0757 HUNTER, SHIREEN T. "The Emergence of the Soviet Muslim: Impact on the Middle East." *MEI* 8, no. 5 (May 1992): 32-40.

Explores the possibility of economic and regional cooperation between the newly independent Muslim nations of the former Soviet Union and the Middle East region especially Iran, Turkey, Pakistan, and Afghanistan. The article also relays the factors which may lead to regional tension and conflict.

0758 ISRAELI, RAPHAEL. "Return to the Source: The Republics of Central Asia and the Middle East." *CAS* 13, no. 1 (1994): 19-31.

Examines the former Soviet republics of Central Asia to determine how they view the Middle East. Seeks to discover which country and model of government is likely to play the largest role in the development of these countries.

0759 KELLER, SHOSHANA. "Islam in Soviet Central Asia, 1917-1930: Soviet Policy and the Struggle for Control." *CAS* 11, no. 1 (1992): 25-50.

Looks at the Soviet attempts to stamp out Islamic identity in Central Asia in order to unite the people under their control.

0760 LAZZERINI, EDWARD J. "Beyond Renewal: The *Jadid* Response to Pressure for Change in the Modern Age." *Muslims in Central Asia: Expressions of Identity and Change*, 151-166. Ed. Jo-Ann Gross. Durham and London: Duke University Press, 1992.

Discusses the *Jadid* movement in 19th century Central Asia which sought to reconcile Islamic traditions with Western advancements.

0761 MAKHAMOV, MAVLON. "Islam and the Political Development of Tajikistan." *Central Asia: Its Strategic Importance and Future Prospects*, 195-210. Ed. Hafeez Malik. New York: St. Martin's Press, 1994.

Traces the relationship between Islam and nationalism in Tajikistan. Analyzes this relationship within the context of the economy, tribalism, and pressure from neighboring countries. The author concludes by suggesting that the best political model for Tajikistan would be the current Chinese model.

0762 MALASHENKO, ALEXI V. "Islam Versus Communism: The Experience of Coexistence." *Russia's Muslim Frontiers*, 67-78. Ed. Dale Eickelman. Bloomington: Indiana University Press, 1993.

The influence of communism on Muslim society within the former Soviet republics is examined in this chapter. The author traces the history of the relations between the Soviet state and Muslim communities and concludes that Islam was never compromised by communism.

0763 MALIK, HAFEEZ. "Tartarstan: A Kremlin of Islam in the Russian Federation." *JSAMES* 17, no. 1 (September 1993): 1-27.

Explores the question of why two Muslim Russian republics, Tartarstan and Bashkirtostan, have taken totally different political paths.

0764 MESBAHI, MOHIADDIN. "Gorbachev's New Thinking and Islamic Iran: From Containment to Reconciliation." *Iran: Political Culture in the Islamic Republic*, 260-296. Eds. Samih K. Farsoun, and Mehrdad Mashayekhi. London and New York: Routledge, 1992.

Traces Iranian-Soviet relations during the war between Iran and Iraq. The chapter also examines the impact Islamic revivalism in the Caucasus and Central Asia have had on relations between Tehran and Moscow.

0765 NABY, EDEN. "Ethnicity and Islam in Central Asia." *CAS* 12, no. 2 (1993): 151-167.

Surveys the religious and ethnic dynamics in Central Asia within the larger context of rural-urban conflict as well as the larger role of Islam in political opposition.

0766 NAUMKIN, VITALY. "Islam in the States of the Former USSR." *AAAPSS* 524 (November 1992): 131-42.

Written by the Director of the Institute of Oriental Studies of the Russian (formerly Soviet) Academy of Sciences, this article examines Islam in Central Asia under Soviet rule. Reports that while the Soviet government eliminated the intellectual life of Islam, the unsophisticated popular trend remained. Under *perestroika*, Islam became one of the many forms of political protest. The author suggests that unclear prospects remain for the success of the combination of political Islam and nationalism in Central Asia.

0767 OLCOTT, MARTHA BRILL. "Central Asia's Islamic Awakening." *CH* 93, no. 582 (April 1994): 150-154.

The author contends that while there is a resurgence in Muslim religious practices and a search for Islamic literalism in Central Asia, the notion that the people of Central Asia desire to create an Islamic state is exaggerated. She illustrates how the leaders of the newly independent states have sought to limit Islam and thereby have increased its appeal.

0768 _____. "Soviet Central Asia: Does Moscow Fear Iranian Influence." *The Iranian Revolution: Its Global Impact*, 203-230. Ed. John L. Esposito. Miami: Florida International University Press, 1990.

Seeks to discover whether the Iranian revolution accelerated existing Islamic revivalist trends in the Soviet Union.

0769   PANARIN, SERGEI. "Muslims of the Former USSR: Dynamics of Survival."
CAS 12, no. 2 (1993): 137-149.
Explores the dynamics of the "geopolitical, intra-confessional, linguistic, ethnic and settlement structures" of the Muslim population of the former Soviet Union.

0770   POLIAKOV, SERGEI P. *Everyday Islam: Religion and Tradition in Rural Central Asia.* Armonk, NY: M.E. Sharpe, Inc., 1992.
Written by a Russian ethnographer and based on thirty years of field research, this work argues that Central Asia's traditional religious customs and values are the cause for the current stagnation. The author states that only by breaking with the traditional past will the region of Central Asia become a modern society. Divided into five sections, the book begins with background information on traditionalism in Central Asia, the sources as well as the methodology utilized in the book. The second section examines the economic bases of traditionalism by looking at commercial engagements, employment and demographic statistics, and private business. The third section looks at the impact of traditionalism on the family and the development of the family structure. The fourth section explores the role that Islam plays in society by examining religious institutions and the religious leaders. The final section analyzes the dynamics between traditionalism and certain classes in society such as the working class, the intelligentsia and ensuing tensions.

0771   POWELL, DAVID E. "The Revival of Religion." *CH* 558 (1991): 328-32.
Discusses the enthusiasm generated among the people of the Soviet Union by the opening up of the country to religion. Also looks briefly at the Islamic revival in Central Asia.

0772   RASHID, AHMED. *The Resurgence of Central Asia: Islam or Nationalism?* Karachi: London and Atlantic Highlands, New Jersey: Oxford University Press: Zed Books, 1994.
Written by a journalist who has focused on Central Asian issues, this book traces the history and geography of the newly independent states of Kazakhstan, Uzbekistan, Tajikistan, Kyrgystan, and Turkmenistan. In addition, the work surveys the social and economic situation of each state under communist rule and the challenges that they face with independence. The book concentrates on the following issues: the status of woman, the role of Islam, the lasting effects of Soviet rule, nuclear proliferation, as well as economic and environmental problems. It examines the reaction of neighboring states to the emergence of the new Muslim countries. Offers an assessment of the future prospects for these states including the development of a viable political and economic system and the impact that Islam and nationalism will have on this development process.

0773 RO'I, YACCOV. "The Islamic Influence on Nationalism in Soviet Central Asia." *POC* (July 1990): 49-64.

An assessment of the impact of Soviet Central Asia's traditional religion on the development of local nationalism. It also looks at whether nationalists have adopted Islamic teachings to sway the population and whether Islam is the unifying component to bring different nationalists together.

0774 _____. "Iran's Islamic Revolution and the Soviet Muslims." *The Iranian Revolution and the Muslim World*, 261-269. Ed. David Menashri. Boulder, CO: Westview Press, 1990.

In light of recent openings in the Soviet political system, this article seeks to describe the influence of the Iranian revolution on Soviet Muslims and how it was expressed under Communist control.

0775 RORLICH AZADE-AYSE. "Islam and Atheism: Dynamic Tension in Soviet Central Asia." *Soviet Central Asia The Failed Transformation*, 186-218. Ed. William Fierman. Boulder, CO: Westview Press, 1991.

Explores the effects of the incorporation of the Muslims of Central Asia into the Russian empire. Shows how Muslims were cut off from the rest of the Islamic world and how this helped shape their own religious identity.

0776 ROY, OLIVIER. "Ethnic Identity and Political Expression in Northern Afghanistan." *Muslims in Central Asia: Expression of Identity and Change*, 73-86. Ed. Jo-Ann Gross. Durham and London: Duke University Press, 1992.

Examines the multiple levels of identity in northern Afghanistan. Discusses the fluidity of ethnic labels as well as the relevance of political and social components in the process of identity formation.

0777 RUMER, BORIS Z. *Soviet Central Asia: A Tragic Experiment*. Boston: Unwin Hyman, 1989.

Written by a research associate at the Russian Research Center of Harvard University, this book examines why the Muslims of Central Asia will cause problems for the Soviet Union. The author cites how Moscow's economic development plan has largely ignored the Muslims of Central Asia. The work concludes that because of Moscow's lack of concern for the economic, religious, and social needs of the Muslims of Central Asia, a large problem may be brewing on the horizon.

0778 RYWKIN, MICHAEL. *Moscow's Muslim Challenge: Soviet Central Asia*. Armonk, NY: M.E. Sharpe, 1990.

This revised edition traces Soviet policy toward its Muslim population in Central Asia. Describes how Moscow tried to forge a "new Soviet people" with the Russian ethnic group as its center. Moscow also encouraged the growth of

Muslim national republics as long as power was maintained in the hands of those in Moscow. Divided into four parts, the first three chapters are a historical overview. Chapters four and five deal with economic and demographic issues. Chapters six and seven are devoted to cultural themes including a discussion of Islam in Central Asia, language, and education. The next four chapters focus on political and ideological issues.

0779   SAIVETZ, CAROL R. "Islam and Gorbachev's Policy in the Middle East." *JIA* 42, no. 2 (March 1989): 435-456.
       Analyzes the changes in Soviet Middle East policy in general and the rise of Gorbachev in 1985, with particular emphasis on the role of Soviet perceptions of Islam in these changes.

0780   _____. "The Soviet Union and Iran: Changing Relations in the Gorbachev Era." *Iran at the Crossroads: Global Relations in a Turbulent Decade*, 181-198. Ed. Miron Rezun. Boulder, CO: Westview Press, 1990.
       This chapter examines Iranian-Soviet foreign policy relations and the new relationship that unfolded under Gorbachev's foreign policy.

0781   SAROYAN, MARK. "Authority and Community in Soviet Islam." *Accounting for Fundamentalisms: The Dynamic Character of Movements*, 513-530. Eds. Martin E. Marty, and R. Scott Appleby. Chicago and London: The University of Chicago Press, 1994.
       Focuses on the activity of the Muslim Religious Boards which were under the control of the *ulama* and acted as the sole Islamic arbiters in Soviet post-World War II period. Examines the organizational structure, social composition, ideology, as well as the fate of the Muslim Boards in the years of Soviet *perestroika* (restructuring) and *glasnost* (liberalization).

0782   SUBTELNY, MARIA EVA. "The Cult of Holy Places: Religious Practices Among Soviet Muslims." *MEJ* 43, no. 4 (1989): 593-604.
       An examination of the significance of the cult of holy places by Muslims in the Soviet Union. The author contends that these religious practices are a way of life and may have political significance in the near future.

0783   TOGAN, ISENBIKE. "Islam in a Changing Society: The Khojas of Eastern Turkistan." *Muslims in Central Asia: Expressions of Identity and Change*, 134-148. Ed. Jo-Ann Gross. Durham: Duke University Press, 1992.
       Examines the role of Islam in Eastern Turkistan between the 17th and late 18th centuries. The article seeks to evaluate the process of change in political rule, from one of steppe values to a system based on Islamic beliefs. In addition, the author analyzes the concepts of legitimacy, particularly the system

where legitimacy was given to the descendants of Ching-gas Khan and then shifts to the descendants of the Prophet Muhammed.

0784 VOLL, JOHN OBERT. "Central Asia as Part of the Modern Muslim World." *Central Asia in Historical Perspective*, 62-81. Ed. B. Manz. Boulder, CO: Westview Press, 1994.

Asserts that Central Asia was an integral part of the Islamic world until the 19th century and that Soviet rule has never really broken this tie.

1.   *China*

0785 DICKS, A. R. "New Lamps for Old: The Evolving Legal Position of Islam in China, With Special Reference to Family Law." *Islamic Family Law*, 347-385. Eds. Chibli Mallat, and Jane Conners. London: Graham & Trotman, 1990.

This essay explores the evolution of the accommodation between the Chinese and Islamic legal systems concerning family law matters.

0786 DILLON, MICHAEL. "Muslim Communities in Contemporary China: The Resurgence of Islam After the Cultural Revolution." *JIS* 5, no. 1 (1994): 70-101.

Discusses the size and distribution of the Muslim population in China. Provides a brief historical background of the Hui and Uighur Muslim communities as well an examination of their religious beliefs and practices.

0787 GLADNEY, DRU C. "The Hui, Islam, and the State: A Sufi Community in China's Northwest Corner." *Muslims in Central Asia: Expressions of Identity and Change*, 89-111. Ed. Jo-Ann Gross. Durham: Duke University Press, 1992.

Based on three years of fieldwork among the Sufi Hui community of northwest China, this article examines the bond between Hui ethnic identity and Islamic traditions.

0788 _____. *Muslim Chinese: Ethnic Nationalism in the People's Republic.* Cambridge, MA: Harvard University Press, 1991.

This work, drawn from years of field research in Muslim communities in China, examines the largest Muslim minority group, the Hui minority. The book provides insight into the identity of the Hui and the role that ethnic nationalism plays in Chinese society and national identity. The seven chapters explore various issues concerning the Hui community including: identity and diversity, the role that they play as a minority in Chinese politics, wide ranging Islamic and cultural traditions, and their relationship and interaction with the Chinese state.

0789 _____. "The Muslim Face of China." *CH* 92, no. 575 (September 1993): 275-280.
       An examination of the policy of the Chinese government toward its Muslim minority. The work also explains how this minority has an important influence on government foreign policy in the Middle East and Central Asia.

0790 _____. "Transnational Islam and Uighur National Identity: Salman Rushdie, Sino-Muslim Missile Deals, and the Trans-Eurasian Railway." *CAS* 11, no. 3 (1992): 1-21.
       Contends that through processes of transnationalization and Islamicization, which can be illustrated by certain events such as the Salman Rushdie protest and the Sino-Saudi missile deal, the Uighur Muslims have been used by the Chinese government to promote its foreign policy objectives in the Middle East.

0791 ISRAELI, RAPHAEL. "Muslim Plight Under Chinese Rule." *The Crescent in the East*, 227-243. Ed. Raphael Israeli. London: Curzon Press Ltd., 1989.
       This chapter examines the Chinese Muslim community and their relationship with the Communist government.

B.   South Asia

0792 AHMAD, MUMTAZ. "Islamic Fundamentalism in South Asia: The Jamaat-i-Islami and the Tablighi Jamaat." *Fundamentalisms Observed*, 457-530. Eds. Martin E. Marty, and R. Scott Appleby. Chicago and London: The University of Chicago Press, 1991.
       Offers a comparative analysis of the two most important Islamic movements in the South Asian subcontinent: the Jama'at-i-Islami and the Tablighi Jama'at. Illustrates how these two movements have chosen two fundamentally different paths to reach the same goal of the revival of pristine Islam. While the Jama'at-i-Islami has placed emphasis on the creation of an Islamic state based on the Qur'an and the Sunna of the Prophet Muhammed, the implementation of the *Shari'ah*, and the resacralization of political life, the Tablighi Jama'at seeks to provide a moral and religious uplifting for its believers whether an Islamic state exists or not.

0793 AHMED, RAFIUDDIN. "Redefining Muslim Identity in South Asia: The Transformation of the Jama'at-i-Islami." *Accounting for Fundamentalisms*, 669-705. Eds. Martin E. Marty, and R. Scott Appleby. Chicago and London: The University of Chicago Press, 1994.

Describes the ideological shift of the Jama'at-i-Islami movement away from its original aim as a builder of an Islamic society to a political pressure group that uses multiple tactics to achieve what it could not at the polls in South Asia.

0794 ARJOMAND, SAID AMIR. "Religion and Constitutionalism in Western History and in Modern Iran and Pakistan." *The Political Dimensions of Religion*, 69-100. Ed. Said Amir Arjomand. Albany: State University of New York Press, 1993.

Using Iran and Pakistan as models, this chapter provides a historical perspective of the birth of the "political tradition of constitutionalism" and examines how constitutionalism was appropriated into Islamic politics.

0795 GABORIEAU, MARC. "The Study of Muslim Communities in the European Conferences on Modern South Asian Studies." *IC* 63, no. 1-2 (January 1989): 133-148.

Examines by theme all the papers presented at the conference on Muslim communities in South Asia from 1966-1986. Appended to the article is a list of all the papers considered.

0796 HARDY, PETER. "Islam and Muslims in South Asia." *The Crescent in the East*, 36-61. Ed. Raphael Israeli. London: Curzon Press Ltd., 1989.

This chapter examines the multiple characteristics of the Muslim population of South Asia.

0797 METCALF, BARBARA D. "'Remaking Ourselves': Islamic Self-Fashioning in a Global Movement of Spiritual Renewal." *Accounting for Fundamentalisms*, 706-725. Eds. Martin E. Marty, and R. Scott Appleby. Chicago and London: The University of Chicago Press, 1994.

Examines the teachings and organization of the Tablighi Jama'at movement which the author says is active in Malaysia, several African nations, Europe and some cities in the United States. The article illustrates how the movement, which refrains from political activity, seeks only to transform individual lives and create faithful Muslims.

0798 YEGAR, MOSHE. "The Muslims of Burma." *The Crescent in the East*, 102-139. Ed. Raphael Israeli. London: Curzon Press Ltd., 1989.

This chapter provides census information about the Muslim population in Burma to help illustrate its historical development and discusses political unrest of the Muslim minority.

1.   *Afghanistan*

0799   CANFIELD, ROBERT L. "Afghanistan: The Trajectory of Internal Alignment." *MEJ* 43, no. 4 (1989): 635-48.
This article explores the major changes in Afghanistan in the last decade of the war with the Soviet Union.

0800   EDWARDS, DAVID B. "Summoning Muslims: Print, Politics, and Religious Ideology in Afghanistan." *JAS* 52, no. 3 (1993): 609-628.
Explores the evolution of the Hizb-i Islami, an Afghan campus study group, and shows how it developed into a powerful political party.

0801   HANAFI, M. JAMIL. "Islam in Contemporary Afghanistan." *The Crescent in the East*, 23-35. Ed. Raphael Israeli. London: Curzon Press Ltd., 1989.
This chapter surveys the history of Muslims in Afghanistan and their religious beliefs.

0802   EL HELBAWY, KAMAL. "The Future of Power-Sharing in Afghanistan." *Power-Sharing Islam?*, 145-158. Ed. Azzam Tamimi. London: Liberty for Muslim World Publications, 1993.
Provides a framework of the various Afghan factions involved in the current political struggle and notes the internal and external factors that contribute to continuity of the power struggle.

0803   KHALEZAD, ZALMAY. "Iranian Policy Toward Afghanistan Since the Revolution." *The Iranian Revolution and the Muslim World*, 235-241. Ed. David Menashri. Boulder, CO: Westview Press, 1990.
This article discusses four different influences on Iranian foreign policy toward Afghanistan: domestic factional policies, strategic considerations, ideology, and sectarianism.

0804   ROY, OLIVIER. "Afghanistan: An Islamic War of Resitance." *Fundamentalisms and the State: Remaking Polities, Economies, and Militance*, 491-510. Eds. Martin E. Marty, and R Scott Appleby. Chicago and London: The University of Chicago Press, 1991.
Provides an analysis of the Afghan Mujahidin and their struggle against the Soviet army. Declares this movement to be unique because the fight for liberation mobilized under the banner of Islam included the unlikely coalition between the traditional segment of Afghan society and the militant young educated and urban Islamist laymen.

0805 _____. "Ethnic Identity and Political Expression in Northern Afghanistan." *Muslims in Central Asia: Expression of Identity and Change*, 73-86. Ed. Jo-Ann Gross. Durham: Duke University Press, 1992.

Examines the multiple levels of identity in northern Afghanistan. Discusses the fluidity of ethnic labels as well as the relevance of political and social components in the process of identity formation.

0806 _____. "The *Mujahedin* and the Preservation of Afghan Culture." *Afghanistan and the Soviet Union: Collision and Transformation*, 40-47. Eds. Milan Hauner, and Robert L. Canfield. Boulder, CO: Westview Press, 1989.

Examines the attempts of the religious networks that sought to maintain their Islamic heritage during the Soviet occupation of Afghanistan.

0807 _____. "The Mujahidin and the Future of Afghanistan." *The Iranian Revolution: Its Global Impact*, 179-202. Ed. John L. Esposito. Miami: Florida International University Press, 1990.

Investigates why Iranian political ideology has had a minimal effect on the Mujahidin in Afghanistan.

0808 TARZI, SHAH M. "Politics of the Afghan Resistance Movement: Cleavages, Disunity, and Fragmentation." *AS* 31, no. 6 (June 1991): 479-495.

Analysis of the influence of traditional factions in the formation of the Islamic Afghan resistance movement.

0809 WAKIL, ABDUL. "Iran's Relations With Afghanistan After the Islamic Revolution." *Orient* 32, no. 1 (March 1991): 97-115.

This article analyzes Iran's seeming lack of support for the Afghan Mujahidin and the prospect for future Iran-Afghan relations.

0810 WEINBAUM, MARVIN G. "War and Peace in Afghanistan: The Pakistani Role." *MEJ* 45, no. 1 (December 1991): 71-85.

Focusing on the Pakistani objectives in Afghanistan, this article claims the Afghani resistance movement would have been rendered ineffective without the aid of Pakistan. Examines the role of the Pakistani military intelligence and external assistance in mobilizing resistance leaders.

2. Bangladesh

0811 AHAMED, EMAJUDDIN and D. R. J. A. NAZNEEN. "Islam in Bangladesh: Revivalism or Power Politics." *AS* 30, no. 8 (August 1990): 795-808.

Surveys the steps of Islamization taken in 1977 by the Bangladesh government and describes the rise in the number of religious organizations and activists.

0812 BANU, U. A. B. RAZIA AKTER. *Islam in Bangladesh*. Leiden: E.J. Brill, 1992.

Focuses on religion and the process of social change within a larger Weberian framework. It seeks to provide a sociological analysis of Islamic beliefs and practices in Bangladesh in addition to a portrayal of the influence of Islamic beliefs on political and socio-economic developments. The first two chapters are devoted to tracing the origins of Islam in Bengal in the 13th century and its transformation over the past seven centuries. The next seven chapters contain sample surveys conducted in May-July 1983 in various rural and urban Bangladeshi areas. They examine and illustrate the differing types of religious beliefs, practices and political culture of the people of Bangladesh. The final chapter is a summery of the author's research.

0813   GHOSH, PARTHA S. "Bangladesh at the Crossroads: Religion and Politics." *AS* 33, no. 7 (July 1993): 697-710.
    Offers an analysis of the influence of the destruction of the Babu Masjid in Ayodhya, India on Bangladesh politics within the wider context of whether Bangladesh should be an Islamic or secular state.

0814   KALIMULLAH, NAZMUL AHSAN and CAROLINE BARBARA FRASIER. "Islamic Non-governmental Organizations in Bangladesh with Reference to Three Case Studies." *IQ* 34, no. 2 (1990): 71-92.
    Based on the results of three case studies, this article traces the growth of Islamic developmental NGOs working in Bangladesh.

0815   RASHIDUZZAMAN M. "Islam, Muslim Identity and Nationalism in Bangladesh." *JASMES* 18, no. 1 (1994): 36-60.
    Examines the cultural and political dynamics of Islam and Muslim consciousness in Bangladesh and their confrontation with the secularists and the Bengali nationalists.

0816   RASHIDUZZAMAN, M. "The Liberals and the Religious Right in Bangladesh." *AS* 34, no. 11 (November 1994): 974-990.
    Examination of the factors in the confrontation between Bengali liberals and conservative Islamists.

0817   SHAMSUL ALAM, S. M. "Islam, Ideology, and the State in Bangladesh." *JAAS* 28, no. 1-2 (January 1993): 88-106.
    An analysis of the attempts of the state to create a cohesive political ideology in Bangladesh. The article is divided into three parts and deals with the special kind of Islam in Bangladesh, the attempt of the 'Awami League regime to create a secular ideology during its tenure in office in 1971-1975, and the Islamization process of the military regime between 1975-1990.

0818 WALKER, DENNIS. "Islam and Nationalism in Bangladesh." *HI* 14, no. 2 (June 1991): 35-63.

Discusses the role Islam played in Bangladesh as a means of differentiating Bangladeshis religiously and culturally from Hindus and India after separation from Pakistan in 1971.

3. India

0819 ANDERSON, MICHAEL. "Islamic Law and the Colonial Encounter in British India." *Islamic Family Law*, 205-224. Eds. Chibli Mallat, and Jane Conners. London: Graham & Trotman, 1990.

This article examines the role that Anglo-Muhammadan law in India had in influencing and mobilizing colonial power. Seeks to understand how the creation process of this law affected its content and how well the law met with Muslim understanding of their own identity and social order.

0820 DEKMEJIAN, R. HRAIR. "Comparative Study of Muslim Minorities: A Preliminary Framework." *AJISS* 8, no. 2 (1991): 307-315.

Using Indian Muslims as a model, this article offers an initial outline to be a basis for a research model in order to better undertake a comparative study of Muslim minorities.

0821 FANSELOW, FRANK S. "Muslim Society in Tamil Nadu (India): An Historical Perspective." *JIMMA* 10, no. 1 (January 1989): 264-289. This article surveys the development of the Muslim community in the southern state of Tamil Nadu.

0822 HUSSAIN, MONIRUL. "The Muslim in India." *JCA* 19, no. 3 (1989): 279-296.

The author examines the position of Muslims in India in the context of the divisions between India, Pakistan and Bangladesh. Argues that the left is the only political force today which can eradicate communalism.

0823 KHALIDI, OMAR. "The Shi'ahs of the Deccan: An Introduction." *HI* 15, no. 4 (December 1992): 31-52.

Analyzes the origin, emergence, and development of the Shi'a in South Central India from the fifteenth century to modern times.

0824 MAHMOOD, TAHIR. "Islamic Law and State Legislation on Religious Conversion in India." *Islam and Public Law: Classical and Contemporary Studies*, 159-192. Ed. Chibli Mallat. London, Dordrecht, and Boston: Graham & Trotman, 1993.

This chapter explores the legal status of Islam and Islamic law in India especially with regard to the Indian Constitution and other related Indian statutes.

0825 MARKOVÁ, DAGMAR. "On the Minority Position of Indian Muslims." *ArOr* 60, no. 4 (1992): 438-453.
Begins with a historical background of Islam in India and moves on to assess the position of Muslims as a minority in India.

0826 _____. "Various Responses of the Indian Muslim Community to Contemporary Modernization." *ArOr* 62, no. 2 (1994): 123-139.
Addresses three processes: Islamization, modernization, and Westernization in the Muslim community in India.

0827 MENSKI, WERNER F. "The Reform of Islamic Family Law and a Uniform Civil Code for India." *Islamic Family Law*, 253-294. Eds. Chibli Mallat, and Jane Conners. London: Graham & Trotman, 1990.
This article explores the degree to which Islamic family laws were changed in India and assesses the desirability of a uniform civil code.

0828 MONSHIPOURI, MAHMOOD. "Backlash to the Destruction at Ayodhya: A View From Pakistan." *AS* 33, no. 7 (July 1993): 711-721.
Provides an examination of the impact of the destruction of the Babu Masjid in Ayodhya India by Hindu militants and the ensuing riots on Pakistani-Indian relations.

0829 THAKUR, RAMESH. "Ayodhya and the Politics of Indian Secularism: A Double-Standards Discourse." *AS* 33, no. 7 (July 1993): 645-664.
Explores the causes behind the destruction of the Babu Masjid in Ayodhya, India and the ensuing riots.

4.   *Pakistan*

0830 AHMAD, MUMTAZ. "Islam and the State: The Case of Pakistan." *The Religious Challenge to the State*, 239-267. Eds. Matthew C. Moen, and Lowell S. Gustafson. Philadelphia: Temple University Press, 1992.
Traces the Islamization process in Pakistan over a 30-year period focusing on the differences between Field Marshall Ayub Khan, who ruled from 1958-1969, and the religious community. Asserts that this time period is important because it sets the stage for future struggles within the Islamization process.

0831 _____. "The Politics of War: Islamic Fundamentalism in Pakistan." *Islamic Fundamentalisms and the Gulf Crisis*, 155-185. Ed. James Piscatori. The United States of America: The American Academy of Arts and Science, 1991.

Illustrates how the Gulf war enabled the Pakistani Islamic movement to mobilize popular support for Iraq. The article provides a brief background of the three primary Pakistani Islamic parties and shows how these three diverse parties shared the same conviction that the war was another example of Western imperialism.

0832 BELONKRENITSKY, VYACHESLAV YA. "Islam and State in Pakistan." *Russia's Muslim Frontiers*, 149-159. Ed. Dale Eickelman. Bloomington: Indiana University Press, 1993.

Provides a succinct overview of the Islamic currents which have shaped the Pakistani state. The article also examines the social and political implications of Islamization after al-Haq's implementation of military rule.

0833 BINDRA, S. S. *Politics of Islamisation: With Special Reference to Pakistan.* New Delhi: Deep & Deep Publications, 1990.

This work discusses and analyzes the attempts in Pakistan to create an Islamic state based on the Qur'an and the Sunna. The book is divided into five chapters starting with the history of Islam. The second chapter looks at the process of Islamization between the years 1947-71 and the deliberations in the Constituent Assembly on the Objective Resolution--which served as the basis for the 1956, 1962, and 1973 Constitutions. The implementation process of Islamic provisions of all the constitutions is analyzed in chapter two and three. Chapter four examines the political goals of Zia ul-Haq which inspired his drive for Islamization. The final chapter offers the author's conclusions.

0834 CHOPRA, SURENDA. "Islamic Fundamentalism and Pakistan's Foreign Policy." *INQ* 49, no. 1-2 (1993): 1-36.

Illustrate the dominant role that Islam has played in Pakistan's foreign policy. It shows how Pakistani leadership has often played the "Islamic card" when it suited their needs.

0835 FULLER, GRAHAM E. *Islamic Fundamentalism in Pakistan.* Santa Monica, CA: Rand, 1991.

This survey was prepared for the U.S. Under Secretary of Defense for Policy and seeks to analyze the origins of Islamic fundamentalism in Pakistan, the impediments faced by Pakistani Islamic group, internal sectarian conflict, as well as foreign policy decisions. The author offers a brief analysis of the Islamic fundamentalist party and speculates on their possible policies should they assume power. The final section deals with the implications for U.S. policy and US interests.

0836 GILANI, RIAZUL HASAN. "A Note on Islamic Family Law and Islamization in Pakistan." *Islamic Family Law*, 339-347. Eds. Chibli Mallat, and Jane Conners. London: Graham & Trotman, 1990.

This article explores the transition from Anglo-Muhammadan law towards the Fundamental Islamic form in Pakistan.

0837 HUSSAIN, ASAF. "Islam and Political Integration in Pakistan." *The Crescent in the East*, 62-78. Ed. Raphael Israeli. London: Curzon Press Ltd., 1989.

This chapter explores the role of Islam in Pakistani politics and the charismatic leadership which helped to integrate Islam into the Pakistani state.

0838 IRFANI, SUROOSH. "Islamic Revival--Quest for Identity and Legitimacy: Implications for Pakistan." *SS* 13, no. 1 (1989): 35-52.

Explores the Islamic revival in the Arab world and assesses its impact on Pakistan.

0839 JEHLE, GEOFFREY A. "An Islamic Perspective on Inequality in Pakistan." *PDR* 31, no. 3 (1992): 295-316.

From an Islamic perspective, this article studies income distribution in Pakistan between 1984-1988.

0840 KENNEDY, CHARLES H. "Islamization and Legal Reform in Pakistan, 1979-89." *PA* 63, no. 1 (March 1990): 62-77.

States that contrary to prevailing interpretations, former President Zia-ul-Huq's "Islamic reforms" have had little impact on policy, despite their public profile. Even so, the article asserts that the reforms remain vital political issues. Also explores the institutional actors and their interests in Islamic law.

0841 _____. "Islamization of Real Estate: Pre-Emption and Land Reforms in Pakistan, 1978-1992." *JIS* 4, no. 1 (1993): 71-83.

Highlights the difficulties that Zulfiqar Bhutto's land reforms faced during the implementation phase because they were deemed Islamic.

0842 KHAN, FAZAL R. "Entertainment Video and the Process of Islamization in Pakistan: Theoretical Perspectives on a Policy Imperative." *AJISS* 8, no. 2 (1991): 289-306.

Examines the impact of entertainment video in Pakistan on the government's professed goal of Islamization.

0843 _____. "Youth Viewers of Pakistan Television (PTV) and the Enculturation Model of the Islamization Process: Towards Exploring Some Empirical Basics." *AJISS* 9, no. 1 (1992): 19-39.

Developing an outline of an enculturation paradigm, this article assesses the influence Pakistan television has on the Islamization process.

0844 KURIN, RICHARD. "Islamization in Pakistan: The Sayyid and the Dancer." *Russia's Muslim Frontiers*, 175-189. Ed. Dale Eickelman. Bloomington: Indiana University Press, 1993.
Examines how the Pakistani government's policy of Islamization has influenced the lives of two Pakistani citizens.

0845 No entry.

0846 MALIK, S. JAMAL. "Legitimizing Islamization -- The Case of the Council of Islamic Ideology in Pakistan, 1962-1981." *Orient* 30, no. 2 (June 1989): 251-268.
Examines the role of the Council of Islamic Ideology which the author asserts was a critical vehicle in the Islamization process, started before Zia-ul-Haq's regime, in Pakistan.

0847 NASR, SEYYED VALI REZA. "Islamic Opposition to the Islamic State: The Jama'at-i Islami." *IJMES* 25, no. 2 (May 1993): 261-283.
Through an examination of the Jama'at-i Islami, this article looks at the role of Islamic movements in the political sphere and in the democratization process.

0848 _____. "Mawdudi and the Jama'at-i Islami: The Origins, Theory and Practice of Islamic Revivalism." *Pioneers of Islamic Revival*, 98-124. Ed. Ali Rahnema. London: Zed Press, 1994.
This chapter provides a biography of the life of the Islamic revivalist Mawdudi and examines his ideology, his model of an Islamic state, and how his discourse and vision displays itself in the politics of the Jama'at-i Islami over the past fifty years.

0849 _____. "Pakistan: Islamic State, Ethnic Polity." *FFWA* 16, no. 2 (June 1992): 81-89.
Discusses the various characteristics which make up and shape the Pakistani state.

0850 _____. "Students, Islam, and Politics: Islami Jami'at-i Tulaba in Pakistan." *MEJ* 46, no. 1 (December 1992): 59-76.
Analyzes the important role played by the Pakistani Islamic student organization, Islami Jami'at-i Tulaba--a wing of the Jama'at-i-Islami, in Islamic revivalism. Examines the organization's historical development, organizational structure, social bases, and socio-political significance in Pakistani politics.

0851 _____. *The Vanguard of the Islamic Revolution: The Jama'at-i-Islami of Pakistan*. Berkeley: London: University of California Press: I.B. Tauris, 1994.

Illustrating that Islamic revivalism is nothing new, this work looks at the roots, evolution, and political agenda of one of the oldest Islamic movements, Pakistan's Jama'at-i-Islami. The author offers an analysis that centers on the movement's vision of the future and the tensions that this vision has created among its members as they try and transform Pakistan's society. In addition to the study of the Jama'at-i-Islami, this work also examines the contemporary Islamic resurgence in general.

0852 NOVOSSYOLOV, DIMITRI B. "The Islamization of Welfare in Pakistan." *Russia's Muslim Frontiers*, 160-174. Ed. Dale Eickelman. Bloomington, IN: Indiana University Press, 1993.

This chapter analyzes the implementation of Pakistani Islamic welfare legislation asserting that the government's institutionalization of zakat and *ushur*, which had previously been voluntary, has secularized the nature of these religious obligations.

0853 PAL, IZZUD-DIN. "Pakistan and the Question of Riba." *MES* 30, no. 1 (January 1994): 64-78.

Surveys four different theories of interest in Pakistan to illustrate that interest found in a capitalist society is not "incompatible with Islamic justice."

0854 PEARL, DAVID. "Three Decades of Executive, Legislative and Judicial Amendments to Islamic Family Law in Pakistan." *Islamic Family Law*, 321-338. Eds. Chibli Mallat, and Jane Conners. London: Graham & Trotman, 1990.

Examines the reasons behind the various amendments to Islamic family law in Pakistan over the past thirty years.

0855 RAIS, RASUL BAKHSH. "Pakistan: Hope Amidst Turmoil." *JOD* 5, no. 2 (April 1994): 132-143.

Through an examination of Pakistan's democratic efforts, this essay argues that Pakistan is an example of how secular parties may be victorious over Islamic parties in elections.

0856 SHAH, NASIM HASAN. "Islamic Concept of State and Its Effect of Islamization of Laws in Pakistan." *HI* 16, no. 1 (March 1993): 5-18.

Discusses the concept of an Islamic state and the implementation of Islamic law in Pakistan.

C.   Southeast Asia

0857   ABAZA, MONA. "Perceptions of Middle Eastern Islam in Southeast Asia and Islamic Revivalism." *Orient* 35, no. 1 (March 1990): 107-121.

This article surveys the impact of Middle Eastern Islam on the Muslims of Southeast Asia. The author concludes that the Middle East, especially Islamic revivalism, plays an important role in Southeast Asian politics.

0858   CHE MAN, W. K. "Problems of Minority Populations in Nation-Building: The Case of the Moros in the Philippines and the Malays in Thailand." *JIMMA* 13, no. 1 (January 1992): 59-70.

Examines the separatist movements of the Moros and Malays and the difficulties that the state has faced in integrating them into society.

0859   MAY, R. J. "The Religious Factor in the Three Minority Movements: The Moro of Philippines, the Malays of Thailand, and Indonesia's West Papuans." *CSA* 13, no. 4 (March 1992): 396-412.

Compares and contrasts three minority communities--two Muslim and one Christian-- regarding the role that religion plays in the identity formation process of each of these movements.

0860   NASH, MANNING. "Islamic Resurgence in Malaysia and Indonesia." *Fundamentalisms Observed*, 691-739. Eds. Martin E. Marty, and R. Scott Appleby. Chicago and London: The University of Chicago Press, 1991.

Offers a comparative analysis of the Islamic movements in Malaysia and Indonesia. The essay explores the ramifications of a global Islamic resurgence in their local manifestations and illustrates how differing colonial experiences influenced their development and growth.

0861   PROVENCHER, RONALD. "Islam in Malaysia and Thailand." *The Crescent in the East*, 140-156. Ed. Raphael Israeli. London: Curzon Press Ltd., 1989.

This chapter surveys the historical development of Islam and the role that Islam plays in the present-day states of Thailand and Malaysia.

0862   THOMAS, M. LADD. "The Thai Muslims." *The Crescent in the East*, 156-179. Ed. Raphael Israeli. London: Curzon Press Ltd., 1989.

This chapter explores the political and economic conditions of the Muslim minority living in Thailand.

0863   VON DER MEHDEN, FRED R. "Malaysian and Indonesian Islamic Movements and the Iranian Connection." *The Iranian Revolution: Its Global Impact*, 233-254. Ed. John L. Esposito. Miami: Florida International University Press, 1990.

Focusing on government relations, state attempts to contain the impact of the Islamic revolution on their respective societies, and the popular reaction to the revolution, this article assesses the impact of the revolution on Malaysia and Indonesia.

1.   Indonesia

0864   FEDERSPIEL, HOWARD M. "Muslim Intellectuals and Indonesia's National Development." *AS* 31, no. 3 (March 1991): 232-246.
This essay weighs the significance of the role that Muslim intellectuals play in the Indonesian political sphere.

0865   SOEBARDI, S. and C. P. WOODCROFT-LEE. "Islam in Indonesia." *The Crescent in the East*, 180-210. Ed. Raphael Israeli. London: Curzon Press Ltd., 1989.
This chapter discusses the socio-cultural and political forms of Islam in the most populous Muslim country in the world, Indonesia. Offers a historical survey of the spread of Islam to Indonesia.

0866   STEENBRINK, KAREL. "Indonesian Politics and a Muslim Theology of Religions: 1965-1990." *ICMR* 4, no. 2 (1993): 223-246.
Explores the issue of religion and the role that it plays in Indonesian society and politics.

2.   Malaysia

0867   ABU BAKAR, MOHAMAD. "External Influences on Contemporary Islamic Resurgence in Malaysia." *CSA* 13, no. 2 (September 1991): 220-228.
Analyzes international influences on the Islamic revival in Malaysia, while never losing sight of the domestic "re-education" forces at work in this trend.

0868   _____. "Islam in Malaysia's Foreign Policy." *HI* 13, no. 1 (March 1990): 3-13.
While stating that Malaysia's foreign policy was not completely devoid of Islamic coloring, the author contends that "Islam has never occupied a central position in Malaysia's foreign policy."

0869   ALI, MUSTAFA. "The Islamic Movement and the Malaysian Experience." *Power-Sharing Islam?*, 109-124. Ed. Azzam Tamimi. London: Liberty for Muslim World Publications, 1993.
Traces the historical development of Islam in Malaysia focusing on the involvement of the Islamic Party of Malaysia (PAS) in the political process over the past forty years.

0870 ANWAR, MUHAMMAD. "The Role of Islamic Financial Institutions in the Socio-economic Development in Malaysia." *PDR* 30, no. 4 (December 1991): 1131-1142.

Examines the role that Islamic financial institutions play in Malaysia's development.

0871 BANKS, DAVID J. "Resurgent Islam and Malay Rural Culture: Malay Novelist and the Intervention of Culture." *AE* 17, no. 3 (August 1990): 531-548.

This article examines the influence of Islamic revivalism in rural Malaysia through an analysis of four prominent Malay novels. The author argues that the novels reflect the perception among many Malaysians that Islam should play a larger role in the political realm.

0872 HARDING, ANDREW J. "Islam and Public Law in Malaysia: Some Reflections in the Aftermath of *Susie Teoh's* Case." *Islam and Public Law: Classical and Contemporary Studies*, 193-205. Ed. Chibli Mallat. London, Dordrecht, and Boston: Graham & Trotman, 1993.

This chapter discusses the conversion of minors to Islam in Malaysia. The article examines the legal case of a Chinese Malaysian girl, raised Buddhist, who converted to Islam and its repercussions in Malaysian society.

0873 HOROWITZ, DONALD L. "The Qur'an and the Common Law: Islamic Law Reform and the Theory of Legal Change (Part I)." *AJCL* 42, no. 2 (March 1994): 233-293.

This study, the first in a two-part series, notes the many changes in legal systems around the world and states that Islamic legal reforms are an integral part of this process. The author, using Malaysia as a case study, explains the extensive changes that have occurred in Malaysian Islamic law. Asserts that Malaysian jurists have borrowed from different legal systems as well as from British secular law.

0874 REGAN, DANIEL. "Islam as a New Religious Movement in Malaysia." *The Changing Face of Religion*, 124-146. Eds. James A. Beckford, and Thomas Luckmann. London: Sage Publications Ltd., 1989.

Seeks to discover how to distinguish the similarities and differences between certain "cult-like" groups of the Islamic movement in Malaysia and the American Hare Krishna movement.

3. Philippines

0875 GOWING, PETER G. "The Muslim Filipino Minority." *The Crescent in the East*, 211-226. Ed. Raphael Israeli. London: Curzon Press Ltd., 1989.

This essay discusses the Filipino Muslims, the only Muslim minority living in a Christian state in Asia.

0876 HORVATICH, PATRICIA. "Ways of Knowing Islam." *AE* 21, no. 4 (November 1994): 811-826.

An examination of the way in which the Sama of Southern Philippines are restructuring their understanding of Islam. The article also looks at the influential role that education has played in the development of their contemporary Islamic discourse.

0877 MAJUL, CESAR ADIB. "The Iranian Revolution and the Muslims in the Philippines." *The Iranian Revolution: Its Global Impact*, 255-280. Ed. John L. Esposito. Miami: Florida International University Press, 1990.

Details four major reasons why the Iranian revolution had political repercussions on the Philippines.

0878 MAY, R. J. "The Moro Movement in Southern Philippines." *Politics of the Future: The Role of Social Movements*, 321-339. Eds. Christine Jennett, and Randa G. Stewart. Melbourne, Australia: Macmillan, 1989.

This chapter describes the Filipino Muslim separatist movement. Shows how Islam has acted as a binding force, connecting Filipino Muslims to the larger Islamic community.

V.   EUROPE

0879 ABDULLAH, M. SALIM. "The Religion of Islam and its Presence in the Federal Republic of Germany." *JIMMA* 10, no. 2 (July 1989): 438-439.

This essay briefly surveys the contemporary Muslim community in Germany.

0880 AHMAD, WAQAR I. and CHARLES HUSBAND. "Religious Identity, Citizenship, and Welfare: The Case of Muslims in Britain." *AJISS* 10, no. 2 (1993): 217-233.

Describes the inequalities that Britain's Muslim community faces in what the author calls the "anti-Islamic racism currently prevalent in Britain.

0881 ANWAR, MUHAMMAD. "Muslims in Britain, Some Recent Developments." *JIMMA* 11, no. 2 (1990): 347-361.

Surveys the growing Muslim population in Britain and examines the challenges they face as Muslims in a Christian society.

0882 _____. "Muslims in Western Europe." *Religion and Citizenship in the Arab World and Europe*, 71-94. Ed. Jorgen S. Nielsen. London, England: Grey Seal Books, 1992.

This chapter assesses the demographic characteristics of Muslims in Western Europe as well as the challenges they face as a minority.

0883 ARONSFELD, C. C. "Muslim Holy War in Britain." *MS* 36, no. 8 (1990): 8-10.

Argues that many of the Muslims in Britain seek to engage in a holy war against "apostates" such as Salman Rushdie.

0884 BERKOVITS, BERNARD. "*Get* and *Talaq* in English Law: Reflections on Law and Policy." *Islamic Family Law*, 119-146. Eds. Chibli Mallat, and Jane Conners. London: Graham & Trotman, 1990.

This article addresses the question of how British law should treat Islamic and Jewish divorce cases in England and to what degree should English courts recognize Islamic and Jewish law concerning divorce.

0885 COTTLE, SIMON. "Reporting the Rushdie Affair: A Case Study in the Orchestration of Public Opinion." *RC* 32, no. 4 (April 1991): 45-57.

Provides a detailed analysis of a lead news story broadcast by one of the UK's independent television stations to show how the diversity of Muslim opinion in the UK over the Rushdie affair made Muslim opinion seem monolithic.

0886 ELSAS, CHR. "Turkish Islamic Ideals of Education: Their Possible Function for Islamic Identity and Integration in Europe." *The Integration of Islam and Hinduism in Western Europe*, 174-186. Eds. W.A.R. Shadid, and P.S. van Koningsveld. The Netherlands: Kok Pharos Publishing House, 1991.

Contends that the type of Islam that the Turkish population practices in Europe as well as their ideals of education are the most useful for Muslim integration into European society.

0887 FELLMAN, NINA. "Islam in Finnish Textbooks on Religious Education." *IQ* 35, no. 4 (1991): 244-254.

Critically examines the portrayal of Islam in religious textbooks in Finland.

0888 HOFFER, C.B.M. "The Practice of Islamic Healing." *Islam in Dutch Society: Current Developments and Future Prospects*, 40-53. Eds. W.A.R. Shadid, and P.S. van Koningsveld. Kampen, The Netherlands: Kok Pharos Publishing House, 1992.

Based on research conducted on Islamic healers and their clients in the Netherlands, this chapter analyzes the extent to which Islamic practices concerning healing were practiced in a Dutch environment.

0889 KASTORYANO, RIVA. "Muslim Migrants in France and Germany: Law and Policy in Family and Group Identity." *Islamic Family Law*, 167-180. Eds. Chibli Mallat, and Jane Conners. London: Graham & Trotman, 1990.
This article examines how the French and German legal systems have dealt with a large influx of Muslim immigrants.

0890 KEEBER, MICHAEL. "A Study of Islamic Preaching in France." *IMCR* 2, no. 2 (1991): 275-294.
Provides insight into the role that Friday Sermons in France's mosques play in the re-Islamization of France's Muslim community.

0891 LANDMAN N. "Sufi Orders in the Netherlands: Their Role in the Institutionalization of Islam." *Islam in Dutch Society: Current Developments and Future Prospects*, 26-39. Eds. W.A.R. Shadid, and P.S. van Koningsveld. Netherlands: Kok Pharos Publishing House, 1992.
Outlines the principle characteristics of Sufi Islam and focuses on the influence of Sufism on Muslims in the Netherlands.

0892 LANDMAN, NICO. "Muslims and Islamic Institutions in the Netherlands." *JIMMA* 12, no. 2 (1991): 410-433.
Based upon interviews conducted with Muslim leaders, this study surveys the institutionalization of Islam in the Netherlands.

0893 LAWLWESS, RICHARD I. "Religion and Politics Among Arab Seafarers in Britain in the Early Twentieth Century." *IMCR* 5, no. 1 (1994): 35-56.
Describes the international Islamic organizations that Arab seafarers were involved with in Britain during the first half of the 20th century.

0894 LEDERER, GYORGY. "Islam in Albania." *CAS* 13, no. 3 (1994): 331-359.
While claiming that Islam in Albania "is as the West would like it to be: non-political, moderate, loyal to the government and fully respecting the rules of European democracy," this article examines the role that Islam plays in Albania.

0895 LEVEAU, REMY. "Islam in France." *The Integration of Islam and Hinduism in Western Europe*, 122-133. Eds. W. A. R. Shadid, and P.S. van Koningsveld. The Netherlands: Kok Pharos Publishing House, 1991.

Drawing upon the results of a survey and public opinion polls of the French and Muslim population in France, this article looks at the often turbulent and discriminating experiences that Muslims face in French society.

0896 _____. "Maghrebi Immigration to Europe: Double Insertion or Double Exclusion?" *AAAPSS* 524 (November 1992): 170-180.
   This article examines the immigration of North Africans to Europe since 1970 and finds that the immigrants use Islam as a vehicle of collective negotiation. However, the author believes that the immigrants have conformed to European norms and that they need to respond as a community to actions taken against them by the policies of European governments.

0897 EL MANSSOURY, F. "Muslims in Europe: The Lost Tribes of Islam." *JIMMA* 10, no. 1 (1989): 63-84.
   Summation of three church research papers on Muslims in Europe which focus on issues raised by the growing presence of Muslims in Europe.

0898 NIELSON, J. S. "Muslim Organizations in Europe: Integration or Isolation?" *The Integration of Islam and Hinduism in Western Europe*, 43-59. Eds. W.A.R. Shadid, and P.S. van Koningsveld. The Netherlands: Kok Pharos Publishing House, 1991.
   Traces the steps taken to create Muslim organizations in Europe and assesses the extent to which these organizations have helped Muslims integrate into European society.

0899 O'BRIEN, PETER. "Islam vs. Liberalism in Europe." *AJISS* 10, no. 3 (September 1993): 367-381. Examines why the West has such rooted fears of Muslim countries.

0900 PARKER-JENKINS, MARIE. "An Examination of the Educational Needs of Muslim Children in Contemporary Britain." *AJISS* 9, no. 3 (1992): 351-369.
   Assesses the difficulties in providing adequate education for Muslim children in British public schools.

0901 PARSONS, ANTHONY. "Iran and Western Europe." *Iran's Revolution: The Search for Consensus*, 69-84. Ed. R. K. Ramazani. Bloomington and Indianapolis: Indiana University Press, 1990.
   This chapter discusses Iranian relations with Western industrial powers including Britain, France, West Germany, and Italy. Explains why most of these countries have maintained economic, and for the most part diplomatic relations with Iran since the revolution.

0902   POULTER, SEBASTIAN. "The Claim to a Separate Islamic System of Personal Law for British Muslims?" *Islamic Family Law*, 147-166. Eds. Chibli Mallat, and Jane Conners. London: Graham & Trotman, 1990.

This essay offers an analysis of the Union of Muslim Organization of UK and Eire resolution which seeks formal recognition of a separate Islamic family law for all British Muslims. The author examines why this resolution was unsuccessful and the issues it raised concerning human rights.

0903   _____. "The Muslim Community and English Law." *ICMR* 3, no. 2 (1992): 259-273.

Presents the major portions of English law that could pose problems for the Muslim community in Britain.

0904   RAZA, MOHAMMAD S. *Islam in Britain: Past, Present and Future.* Leicester, U.K.: Volcano Press Ltd., 1993.

Examines the Pakistani-Indian Muslim community in Britain and seeks to answer the question of how the community lives as Muslims in Britain's secular society. Surveys various aspects of their lives including class structure, sectarian divisions, Muslim organizations, political leaders, women's issues, Islamic literature, and the debates and dialogues between religions.

0905   REEBER, MICHAEL. "Islamic Preaching in France: Admonitory Addresses or a Political Platform?" *ICMR* 4, no. 2 (1993): 210-222.

Seeks to determine whether the mosques in France have become a platform for Islamic political activism.

0906   ROBERSTON, B. A. "Islam and Europe: An Enigma or a Myth?" *MEJ* 48, no. 2 (March 1994): 288-308.

Exploring Europe's relations with the Middle East and the concerns of the 'Islamic Threat,' this article reviews the historical relations between Europe and the Middle East in light of the Iranian revolution, expanding global economic integration and the growing immigrant communities in Europe.

0907   ROOIJACKERS, M. "Religious Identity and Subjective Well-Being Among Young Turkish Muslims." *Islam in Dutch Society: Current Developments and Future Prospects*, 66-74. Eds. W. A. R. Shadid, and P.S. van Koningsveld. Netherlands: Kok Pharos Publishing House, 1992.

Describes aspects of religious identity and cultural integration among second generation Muslims in the Netherlands.

0908   SAHARA, TETSUYA. "The Islamic World and the Bosnian Crisis." *CH* 93, no. 586 (November 1994): 386-389.

This essay relates the response of Muslim countries to the plight of Bosnian Muslims.

0909 SANDER, A. "The Road From Musalla to Mosque: The Process of Integration and Institutionalization of Islam in Sweden." *The Integration of Islam and Hinduism in Western Europe*, 62-88. Eds. W. A. R. Shadid, and P. S. van Koningsveld. The Netherlands: Kok Pharos Publishing House, 1991.

Traces the waves of Muslim immigration to Sweden during the last half of this decade and examines the problems and challenges Muslims face integrating in Swedish society.

0910 SHADID, W.A.R. and P.S. VAN KONINGSVELD. "Institutionalization and Integration of Islam in the Netherlands." *The Integration of Islam and Hinduism in Western Europe*, 89-121. Eds. W.A.R. Shadid, and P.S. van Koningsveld. Kampen, The Netherlands: Kok Pharos Publishing House, 1991.

Explores the differing Muslim organizations and communities and the stages of their institutionalization in Dutch society.

0911 _____. "Islamic Primary Schools." *Islam in Dutch Society: Current Developments and Future Prospects*, 107-122. Eds. W. A. R. Shadid, and P. S. van Koningsveld. Kampen, The Netherlands: Kok Pharos Publishing House, 1992.

Examines Islamic primary schools in the Netherlands and focuses on the reasons behind their establishment.

0912 _____. "Legal Adjustments for Religious Minorities: The Case of Ritual Slaughtering." *Islam in Dutch Society: Current Developments and Future Prospects*, 2-25. Eds. W. A. R. Shadid, and P. S. van Koningsveld. Kampen, The Netherlands: Kok Pharos Publishing House, 1992.

Describes some of the major developments that have occurred in Holland concerning ritual slaughtering of animals as practiced by Muslims and Jews.

0913 _____. "Blaming the System or Blaming the Victim? Structural Barriers Facing Muslims in Western Europe." *The Integration of Islam and Hinduism in Western Europe*, 2-21. Eds. W. A. R. Shadid, and P.S. van Koningsveld. Kampen, The Netherlands: Kok Pharos Publishing House, 1991.

Provides an analysis of the social and legal obstacles that Muslims in Western Europe face in terms of their religious practices.

0914 _____. Eds. *The Integration of Islam and Hinduism in Western Europe*, Kampen, The Netherlands: Kok Pharos Publishing House, 1991.

This collection of essays is the proceedings of a 1990 workshop entitled "Religion and Emancipation of Ethnic Minorities in Western Europe." Examines the integration of Muslims and Hindus into Western European society. Divided into four parts, the first part discusses the role of Muslims in associations in Europe. Part two looks at the process of integration and institutionalization of Muslims in European society. The third part explores Islamic education and the obstacles its development faces in Europe. The final part explores Hindus in Western Europe.

0915 _____, eds. *Islam in Dutch Society: Current Developments and Future Prospects*, Kampen, The Netherlands: Kok Pharos Publishing House, 1992.

This edited collection of articles is the second volume of the proceedings of a conference entitled "Religion and Emancipation of Ethnic Minorities in Western Europe." This work examines the issues raised about Muslim immigrants living in the Netherlands. Divided into three sections, the first part deals with "Islamic Faith and Rituals in the Netherlands." Contains articles on ritual slaughtering among Muslims, Sufi orders and the role they play in the institutionalization of Islam as well as the function of Islamic healers. The second section is comprised of five articles devoted to the study of the social and religious life of second generation Muslims in the Netherlands. The final section contains four articles that examine the historical background, development, and practices of Muslim organizations.

0916 EL-SOLH, CAMILLIA FAWZI. "Arab Communities in Britain: Cleavages and Commonalities." *ICMR* 3, no. 2 (1992): 236-258.

Explores the differences that separate the Arab communities in Britain and the similarities that bind them together.

0917 SUNIER, TH. "Islam and Ethnicity Among Turks: The Changing Role of Islam and Muslim Organizations." *Islam in Dutch Society: Current Developments and Future Prospects*, 144-162. Eds. W. A. R. Shadid, and P.S. van Koningsveld. Netherlands: Kok Pharos Publishing House, 1992.

Examines the role that Islam plays among young Turkish immigrants in the Netherlands and the influence that Muslim organizations have on this changing role.

0918 VAN BOMMEL, A. "The History of Muslim Umbrella Organizations." *Islam in Dutch Society: Current Developments and Future Prospects*, 124-143. Eds. W. A. R. Shadid, and P. S. van Koningsveld. Kampen, The Netherlands: Kok Pharos Publishing House, 1992.

Traces the historical development of Muslim organizations in the Netherlands.

0919 VAN DE WETERING, S. "The Arabic Language and Culture Teaching Program to Moroccan Children." *Islam in Dutch Society: Current Developments and Future Prospects*, 90-106. Eds. W. A. R. Shadid, and P. S. van Koningsveld. Kampen, The Netherlands: Kok Pharos Publishing House, 1992.

Based on field work, this chapter explores the controversy surrounding the mother language teaching program in the Netherlands. Discusses the differing aims between the Moroccan parents who supported the program and those of the Dutch community who had certain objections.

0920 VAN DER LANS, J. M. and M. ROOIJACKERS. "Types of Religious Belief and Unbelief among Second Generation Turkish Migrants." *Islam in Dutch Society: Current Developments and Future Prospects*, 56-63. Eds. W. A. R. Shadid, and P. S. van Koningsveld. Kampen, The Netherlands: Kok Pharos Publishing House, 1992.

Explores the attitudes of second generation Turkish Muslims towards Islamic norms and beliefs in the Netherlands.

0921 VAN OOIJEN, H. "Religion and Emancipation: A Study of the Development of Moroccan Islamic Organizations in a Dutch Town." *Islam in Dutch Society: Current Developments and Future Prospects*, 163-180. Eds. W. A. R. Shadid, and P. S. van Koningsveld. Kampen, The Netherlands: Kok Pharos Publishing House, 1992.

Through an examination of the development of religious beliefs among Moroccan Muslims living in the Netherlands, this chapter seeks to answer the following question: "To what extent are Islamic organizations promoting emancipation or isolation?"

0922 WAARDENBURG, J. D. J. "Muslim Associations and Official Bodies in Some European Countries." *The Integration of Islam and Hinduism in Western Europe*, 24-42. Eds. W. A. R. Shadid, and P. S. van Koningsveld. Kampen, The Netherlands: Kok Pharos Publishing House, 1991.

Explores the organizational structures set up to protect Muslim minority interests in Europe as well as the relationship between the state and these Muslim organizations.

0923 WAGTENDONK, K. "Islamic Schools and Islamic Education: A Comparison between Holland and other Western European Countries." *The Integration of Islam and Hinduism in Western Europe*, 154-173. Eds. W. A. R. Shadid, and P. S. van Koningsveld. Kampen, The Netherlands: Kok Pharos Publishing House, 1991.

Through a study of Islamic education in Europe, the author seeks to discover why Holland, with a smaller number of Muslims, has more Islamic schools than other European countries.

0924 ZIVOJINOVIC, DRAGOLJUB R. "Islam in the Balkans: Origins and Contemporary Implications." *MQ* 3, no. 4 (September 1992): 51-65.

Examines Islamic movements in Bosnia-Hercegovina and argues that Bosnia's leaders want to "make Sarajevo a European beachhead for the spread of the Islamic revival in Europe."

VI. MIDDLE EAST

0925 AKHAVI, SHAHROUGH. "The Impact of the Iranian Revolution on Egypt." *The Iranian Revolution: Its Global Impact*, 138-156. Ed. John L. Esposito. Miami: Florida International University Press, 1990.

Examines Iranian-Egyptian relations within the context of Sunni-Shi'a relations. Assesses the influence of Iranian Shi'a political ideology on Sunni religious thinkers in Egypt.

0926 BAKHASH, SHAUL. "Iran's Relations With Israel, Syria, and Lebanon." *Iran at the Crossroads: Global Relations in a Turbulent Decade*, 115-128. Ed. Miron Rezun. Boulder, CO: Westview Press, 1990.

This chapter assesses the changing shifts of Iranian foreign policy toward Israel, Syria, and Lebanon since the Iranian revolution. The author asserts that Iran does not play a major role in the Palestinian-Israeli conflict, a role it does play in the larger Arab-Israeli dispute.

0927 BOROVALI, FUAT. "Iran and Turkey: Permanent Revolution or Islamism in One Country?" *Iran at the Crossroads: Global Relations in a Turbulent Decade*, 81-93. Ed. Miron Rezun. Boulder, CO: Westview Press, 1990.

Offers a political comparison of Iran and Turkey and ascertains that while structural similarities do exist the Iranian revolution caused Iran to forge a different path than that taken by Turkey.

0928 DEEB, MARY-JANE. "Militant Islam and the Politics of Redemption." *AAAPSS* 524 (November 1992): 52-65.

This article investigates the conditions under which militant Islam emerges through an examination of Islamic movements in Algeria, Turkey, Libya, Lebanon, the West Bank and Gaza Strip. The author finds the conditions to include political stagnation, weakening of central authority, economic stagnation, a decline in the standard of living, deteriorating security, perverse influence of Western culture and leaders perceived as un-Islamic.

0929 DUNN, MICHAEL COLLINS. "Islamist Parties in Democratizing States: A Look at Jordan and Yemen." *MEP* 2, no. 2 (1993): 16-27.

Compares and contrasts the experiences of the Islamist parties in the democratization process in Jordan and Yemen. Seeks to illustrate that political Islam and democracy are not inherently incompatible and that each Islamic movement must be examined within the political context of its own country.

0930 GAUSE, F. GREGORY III. "Revolutionary Fevers and Regional Contagion: Domestic Structures and the Export of Revolution in the Middle East." *JSAMES* 14, no. 3 (1991): 1-23.

This article contends that the new political structures of the Arab regimes have enabled them to resist the "ideological pressure" of Iran's efforts to export the revolution.

0931 KARAWAN, IBRAHIM A. "Monarchs, Mullas, and Marshalls: Islamic Regimes?" *AAAPSS* 524 (November 1992): 103-119.

This article examines three types of regimes that the author asserts represent 'Islam in power'; the conservative dynasty of Saudi Arabia, the populist clerical rule in Iran, and the authoritarian military rule in Sudan and Pakistan. The author states that the interpretation of Islam reflects the interests and ideology of those who control the state machinery and points out that domestic opposition frequently challenges the regimes on religio-political grounds. Concludes that military regimes have the most difficulty with political opposition because of a lack of legitimacy and the ability to co-opt the opposition.

0932 MAYER, ANN ELIZABETH. "The Fundamentalist Impact on Law, Politics, and Constitutions in Iran, Pakistan, and the Sudan." *Fundamentalisms and the State: Remaking Polities, Economies, and Militance*, 110-151. Eds. E. Martin Marty, and R. Scott Appleby. Chicago and London: The University of Chicago Press, 1991.

Offers a comparative study that examines the philosophies which shaped the state Islamization programs in Iran, Pakistan, and Sudan in the post-1967 era.

0933 MESSICK, BRINKLEY. "Literacy and the Law: Documents and Document Specialists in Yemen." *Law and Islam in the Middle East*, 61-76. Ed. Daisy Hilse Dwyer. New York: Bergin & Garvey, 1990.

Concentrating on the law of evidence in Yemen, this article points to changes made by Muslim jurists concerning the validity of written documents as legal proof.

0934 OLMERT, YOSEF. "Iranian-Syrian Relations: Between Islam and Realpolitik." *The Iranian Revolution and the Muslim World*, 171-188. Ed. David Menashri. Boulder, CO: Westview Press, 1990.

Analyzes the development and pragmatic necessity that became the crux of strong Syrian-Iranian relations despite extremely different political ideologies.

0935 ÖZBUDUN, ERGUN. "Khomeinism--A Danger for Turkey?" *The Iranian Revolution and the Muslim World*, 242-249. Ed. David Menashri. Boulder, CO: Westview Press, 1990.

Discusses the influence of the Iranian revolution and Ayatollah Khomeini's political Islamic vision on Turkish Islamic groups and the political system in Turkey.

0936 PERRY, GLENN E. "The Islamic World: Egypt and Iran." *Politics and Religion in the Modern World*, 97-134. Ed. George Moyser. London and New York: Routledge, 1991.

Using Egypt and Iran as models who represent many of the Islamic trends in the Middle East, this article examines the role that Islam plays in the political sphere of these two countries.

0937 PICKART, GEORGE A. *The Battle Looms: Islam and Politics in the Middle East : A Report to the Committee on Foreign Relations, United States Senate*, U.S. Government Publishing Office, Washington, D.C., 1993.

A report given before the Senate's Committee on Foreign Relations about the different Islamic movements in Algeria, Tunisia, Egypt, and Jordan. Discusses the situation in each country and makes recommendations for the U.S. Senate based upon perceptions from the author's visits.

0938 REKHESS, ELIE. "The Iranian Impact on the Islamic Jihad Movement in the Gaza Strip." *The Iranian Revolution and the Muslim World*, 189-206. Ed. David Menashri. Boulder, CO: Westview Press, 1990.

Asserting that the Iranian revolution had a profound effect in galvanizing Islamic Jihad to action in the Gaza Strip, this article examines the extent to which the Khomeini's Islamic political vision has been internalized by that movement.

0939 SACHEDINA, ABDULAZIZ A. "Activist Shi'ism in Iran, Iraq, and Lebanon." *Fundamentalisms Observed*, 403-456. Eds. Martin E. Marty, and R. Scott Appleby. Chicago and London: The University of Chicago Press, 1991.

Analyzes how Shi'i political activists such as the Ayatollah Khomeini, the Ayatollah Baqir al-Sadr, and Imam Musa al-Sadr transformed traditionally quietist Shi'i political ideology into an activist ideology of rebellion and confrontation. This article provides a historical background of Shi'i theology and the roots of contemporary Shi'i political activism.

0940   SAEED, JAVAID. *Islam and Modernization -- A Comparative Analysis of Pakistan, Egypt, and Turkey.* Westport, CT: Praeger Publishers, 1994.
Through a comparative historical analysis of Islam's role in the modernization programs of Pakistan, Egypt, and Turkey, this work examines the "prevalent ideas about Islam and the so-called Islamic traditions which affect every aspect of life in a Muslim society." Chooses the Islamic religion as the key variable in the study of the attempts of these countries at modernization in order to gain a better understanding of "prevalent ideas and practices" in Muslim societies. Argues that in order for the modernization process to continue the "reformation of the existing religious thought," must take place.

0941   SAJEDI, AMIR. "Iran's Relations With Saudi Arabia." *InQ* 49, no. 1-2 (1993): 75-96.
Surveys the relations between Iran and Saudi Arabia which the author states have historically been antagonistic due to Sunni-Shi'i differences.

0942   SHARON, MOSHE. "The Islamic Factor in Middle East Politics." *MS* 40, no. 1 (January 1994): 7-10.
Briefly describes the reasons for the rise of Islamic political activism.

0943   VOLL, JOHN OBERT. "Fundamentalism in the Sunni Arab World: Egypt and the Sudan." *Fundamentalisms Observed*, 345-402. Eds. Martin E. Marty, and R. Scott Appleby. Chicago and London: The University of Chicago Press, 1991.
Seeking to define who Islamic fundamentalists are in the Sunni Arab world and to determine their objectives and goals, this article begins with a historical background of 18th- and 19th-century Islamic revivalism. The author then examines Islamic fundamentalism in Egypt and Sudan in the twentieth century. The essay includes information on the establishment of the Muslim Brotherhood, the impact of Sayyid Qutb during Nasser's era, the Sudanese Muslim Brotherhood, fundamentalism under Sadat and the Islamic movement under Mubarak.

A.   Egypt

0944   ABDALLA, AHMED. "Egypt's Islamists and the State: From Complicity to Confrontation." *MERIP* 183 (July 1993): 28-32.
This article examines the policies of the Egyptian government vis-à-vis the Islamists which have led to the recent crackdown on their organizations.

0945   ABDELNASSER, WALID MAHMOUD. *The Islamic Movement in Egypt: Perceptions of International Relations 1967-81.* London and New York: Kegan Paul International, 1994.

This work examines the international vision of the Egyptian Islamic movement between 1967-1981. Divided into four chapters and a conclusion, the first provides a historical overview of the traditional role of Islam in foreign policy, the development of the Muslim Brethren between 1928-1981, the growth of the Islamic associations in the universities, and the birth of secret Islamic organizations such as al-Jihad and Jama'at al-Muslimin. The second chapter surveys the differing attitudes and perceptions of the Islamic movement towards political events, such as the Iranian revolution, and developments in the rest of the Middle East. The third chapter assesses the positions that the Islamic movement adopted against perceived external threats such as the Arab-Israeli conflict, Western imperialism, and Soviet communism. Chapter four presents the elements which, according to the author, represent the Islamic movement's position on international relations as well as the opinions and prescriptions of the movement on the role of the "umma." The conclusion summarizes the writer's findings.

0946   ABU-LUGHOD, LILA. "Islam and Public Culture:.The Politics of Egyptian Television Serials." *MERIP* 180 (January 1993): 25-30.

Contending that state-controlled Egyptian television serials influence the population with political messages, this essay examines who controls these messages and assesses the influence of the Islamists on these serials.

0947   AUDA, GEHAD. "Egypt's Uneasy Party Politics." *JOD* 2, no. 2 (March 1991): 70-78.

Looks at the 1990 elections in Egypt and the strategies of the different parties including the Muslim Brotherhood.

0948   _____. "The 'Normalization' of the Islamic Movement in Egypt from the 1970s to the early 1990s." *Accounting for Fundamentalisms: The Dynamic Character of Movements,* 374-412. Eds. Martin E. Marty, and R. Scott Appleby. Chicago and London: The University of Chicago Press, 1994.

This article examines the Egyptian Islamic movement of the 1970s and 1980s and discusses their ideology, membership, and organization, as well as the movement's relation to the democratization process. Asserting that the Egyptian Islamic movement passed through two phases, the author analyzes how and why the movement became main-stream in the 1980s and normalized its relations with the regime of Husni Mubarak.

0949 _____. "An Uncertain Response: The Islamic Movement in Egypt." *Islamic Fundamentalisms and the Gulf Crisis*, 109-130. Ed. James Piscatori. Chicago, Illinois: The American Academy of Arts and Science, 1991.

Through an analysis of domestic and international variables, this article seeks to determine how the Egyptian Islamic movement dealt with the crisis caused by the Gulf war. Argues that the manner in which the Islamic movement responded to the Gulf crisis created deep ideological divisions among the various factions of the movement.

0950 BAKER, RAYMOND. "Afraid for Islam: Egypt's Muslim Centrists Between Pharaohs and Fundamentalists." *DA* 120, no. 3 (June 1991): 41-68.

Seeking to gain a clearer understanding of what Islam and politics in Egypt actually means, this article offers a narrative of Egypt's Muslim Brotherhood.

0951 BOTIVEAU, BERNARD. "Contemporary Reinterpretations of Islamic Law: The Case of Egypt." *Islam and Public Law: Classical and Contemporary Studies*, 261-277. Ed Chibli Mallat. London, Dordrecht, and Boston: Graham & Trotman, 1993.

This chapter argues that the inclusion in Article 2 of the Egyptian constitution amended in 1980 to read 'the Islamic *shari'ah* is the principle source of legislation' represents an institutionalization of legal Islamization in Egypt.

0952 CANTORI, LOUIS J. "The Islamic Revival as Conservatism and as Progress in Contemporary Egypt." *Religious Resurgence and Politics in the Modern World*, 183-194. Ed. Emile Sahliyeh. Albany: State University of New York Press, 1990.

Explores Islamic resurgence in Egypt through the conservative corporatist paradigm and asserts that mainstream Islamic revival in Egypt takes the shape of "reformist revitalization."

0953 COMMINS, DAVID. "Hasan al-Banna (1906-1949)." *Pioneers of Islamic Revival*, 125-153. Ed. Ali Rahnema. London: Zed Press, 1994.

This chapter explores the life of Hassan al-Banna and examines his ideology, his organizational skills, and the way in which he popularized his ideas that have had a profound impact on Islamic movements around the Arab world.

0954 DAJANI, ZAHIA RAGHEB. *Egypt and the Crisis of Islam*. New York: Peter Lang, 1990.

Surveys the response of three Egyptian authors--Taha Husayn, Muhammad Husayn Haykal, and Abbass Mahmud al 'Aqqad--to the religious crisis in Egypt. Contends that these authors should be considered "pioneers for a modern Islamic school of thought." Also outlines the "Islamic identity of Egypt."

0955   EDGE, IAN. "A Comparative Approach to the Treatment of Non-Muslim Minorities in the Middle East, with Special Reference to Egypt." *Islamic Family Law*, 31-54. Eds. Chibli Mallat, and Jane Conners. London: Graham & Trotman, 1990.
Using Egypt as a case study, this article examines the position of non-Muslim minorities in classical Islamic law and then analyzes the law in practice.

0956   AL ERIAN, ESSAM. "The Future of Power-Sharing in Egypt." *Power-Sharing Islam?*, 159-168. Ed. Azzam Tamimi. London: Liberty for Muslim World Publications, 1993.
Discusses the current Egyptian political system and traces the role that the Muslim Brotherhood plays in this arena.

0957   FANDY, MAMOUN. "Egypt's Islamic Group: Regional Revenge?" *MEJ* 48, no. 4 (1994): 607-625.
This article asserts that the southern character of the Egyptian Islamic group Al-Jama'a al-Islamiyya has been largely neglected. It provides an examination of the social and economic impact that the policies of the Nasser, Sadat, and Mubarak regimes have had on the southern provinces.

0958   _____. "The Tensions Behind the Violence in Egypt." *MEP* 2, no. 1 (1993): 25-34.
This article explores why Egyptian citizens do not support the government's attempts to crack down on Egyptian Islamists.

0959   FLORES, ALEXANDER. "Secularism, Integration and Political Islam: The Egyptian Debate." *MERIP* 183 (July 1993): 32-38.
This article examines the Egyptian debate between the proponents of the separation of religion and state and those who believe that Islam is inherently political.

0960   GAFFNEY, PATRICK D. "The Changing Voices of Islam: The Emergence of Professional Preachers in Contemporary Egypt." *MW* 81, no. 1 (1991): 27-47.
Surveys the changes that have helped forge the ulema as a group that could be compared to an official clergy.

0961   _____. *The Prophet's Pulpit: Islamic Preaching in Contemporary Egypt.* Berkeley: University of California Press, 1994.

Based on field research conducted in Egypt, this study presents an ethnography of Islamic preaching in Egypt. The work traces the transformation of the ulama in traditional form into a formalized structure not unlike a Christian clergy. Chapters examine their public rhetoric and the different type of advocates that they have become.

0962 GALLAGHER, NANCY E. "Islam v. Secularism in Cairo: An Account of the Dar al-Hikma Debate." *MES* 25, no. 2 (1989): 208-215.
Examines the debate in Egypt over whether to implement Islamic law.

0963 GOLDBERG, ELLIS. "Smashing Idols and the State: The Protestant Ethics and Egyptian Sunni Radicalism." *Comparing Muslim Societies: Knowledge and the State in a World Civilization*, 195-236. Ed. Juan R. I. Cole. Ann Arbor: The University of Michigan Press, 1992.
This chapter offers a comparative analysis of 16th-century Protestant reformers and contemporary Sunni Muslim activists in Egypt. The chapter examines Weber and a research agenda for religious change, the Protestant paradigm, the historical background of Muslim official consensus, contemporary Islamic discourse, and the social origins and personal attributes of the Jihad group.

0964 GORDON, JOEL. "Political Opposition in Egypt." *CH* 90, no. 544 (February 1990): 65-68, 79-80.
The problems the Egyptian state is encountering in its attempt at democratic reform is the central focus of this work. The article highlights three individuals who personify the confrontation: Interior Minister Zaki Badri who represents the extreme side of the regime; Umar Abd Rahman who represents the radical Islamic opposition; and Khalid Abdel Nasser who represents militant Nasserism.

0965 HADDAD, BASSAM SA. "The Assassination of Fuda." *ASJ* 1, no. 1 (1993): 16-19.
Examines the assassination of Farag Ali Fuda, an Egyptian secularist, who was killed by the Islamic organization Jihad. Looks at the reasons why Fuda's writings inflamed some Islamists.

0966 _____. "Islamic Liberals and Secularism." *ASJ* 1, no. 2 (September 1993): 26-31.
Recounts some of the arguments concerning the relationship between Islam and politics made by Islamic liberals in the Arab world in general and Egypt in particular.

0967   HILL, ENID. "Law and Courts in Egypt: Recent Issues and Events Concerning Islamic Law." *The Political Economy of Contemporary Egypt*, 240-264. Ed. Ibrahim M. Oweiss. Washington, D.C.: Center for Contemporary Arab Studies, Georgetown University, 1990.

This chapter examines Egypt's judicial system and looks at the differences between the prescriptions of the *shari'ah* and certain laws and codes. Special attention is given to the changes in the law that occurred in the 1970s and 1980s as the government tried to assert its Muslim piety.

0968   LESCH, ANN MOSELY. "The Muslim Brotherhood in Egypt: Reform or Revolution?" *The Religious Challenge to the State*, 182-208. Eds. Matthew C. Moen, and Lowell S. Gustafson. Philadelphia: Temple University Press, 1992.

Provides an analysis of the Muslim Brotherhood in Egypt including their origins and the changing role it has played under the regimes of Nasser, Sadat, and Mubarak.

0969   MAKRAM-EBEID, MONA. "Democratization in Egypt: The 'Algeria Complex.'" *MEP* 3, no. 3 (1994): 119-124.

Discusses the implications of the fear of Islamic extremists on the decisions of the leaders of Egyptian civil society.

0970   _____. "Political Opposition in Egypt; Democratic Myth or Reality." *MEJ* 43, no. 3 (1989): 423-36.

Written by a member of the High Executive Council of the New Wafd Party, this article examines the problems inherent in the transition to a competitive democracy. Catalogs the major Egyptian political parties including: the National Democratic Party, the New Wafd, the Socialist Labor Party, the National Unionist Progressive Party, the Liberal Party as well as the Muslim Brotherhood. Provides an overview of the 1987 parliamentary election campaign and its results as well as prescriptions for President Mubarak's dilemma in dealing with political instability.

0971   MENDEL, MILÓS. "The Concept of "at-takfir wa'l-hidjra" in Islamic Fundamentalism." *ArOr* 61, no. 2 (1993): 131-146.

Using Egypt of the 1970's as a case study, this article explores the historical development of the ideological concept of "at-takfir wa'l-hijra" or the "concept of exodus from a cursed society."

0972   MURPHY, CARYLE. "Egypt: An Uneasy Portent of Change." *CH* 93, no. 580 (February 1994): 78-82.

Using Egypt as an indicator of how the Arab-Israeli peace will affect the Arab world internally and externally, this article discusses the struggle between the Mubarak regime and Islamists and offers reasons for the rise of the Islamic movement.

0973 NAJJAR, FAUZI M. "The Application of Sharia Laws in Egypt." *MEP* 1, no. 3 (1992): 62-73.

An examination of the debate over the adoption of the *Shari'ah*, or aspects of the *Shari'ah* in Egypt as the constitution of the state.

0974 PELLETIERE, STEPHEN C. *Shari'a Law, Cult Violence and System Change in Egypt*. Carlisle, PA: Strategic Studies Institute, U.S. Army War College, 1994.

Examines the present day problems in Egypt which the author asserts stem from economic difficulties. Provides some background information on the Muslim Brotherhood as well as what the author defines as "religious cults" who demand the implementation of Islamic law. This work states that more problems could arise if the International Monetary Fund pushes Egypt to make difficult economic reforms. Looks at how the problem can be solved in Egypt in "ways that support the interests of the United States."

0975 PITTAWAY, JAMES. "A Benign Brotherhood?" *AM* (January 1989): 25-33.

Challenges the typical stereotypes of the Muslim Brethren in Egypt and the movement's vision for the future.

0976 RAMADAN, ABDEL AZIM. "Fundamentalist Influence in Egypt: The Strategies of the Muslim Brotherhood and the Takfir Groups." *Fundamentalism and the State: Remaking Polities, Economies, and Militance*, 152-183. Eds. E. Martin Marty, and R. Scott Appleby. Fundamentalism Project, 3. Chicago and London: The University of Chicago Press, 1991.

Examines what the author has defined as two forms of fundamentalism in Egypt; a radical fundamentalism and a moderate mainstream fundamentalism. Provides an analysis of the ideologies of the Takfir organizations--the Military Technical College organization, the Society of Muslims, the Jihad organization, Al-Jama'at al Islamiyya--and the New Muslim Brotherhood. Asserts that while both fundamentalist groupings sought to implement the *shari'ah* (Islamic law), the methods they chose to achieve this goal were very different.

0977 REED, S. "The Battle for Egypt." *FA* 72, no. 4 (1993): 49-62.

Analyzes the relations between Egypt's government and the Gama'a al-Islamiya (The Islamic Group). The article discusses the regime's economic performance, the organizational and mobilization skills of the Gama'a, the prospects for an Islamist takeover, recent responses by Husni Mubarak's government, and the impact of these events on U.S. policy towards Egypt and the Middle East.

0978 RUBIN, BARRY. *Islamic Fundamentalism in Egyptian Politics*. New York: St. Martin's Press, 1990.

The work seeks to identify and examine the different groups that constitute Islamic political activists of Egypt. An introduction explains the factors that have contributed to the rise of Islamic fundamentalism, the segments of society who oppose fundamentalism and the prospects for the future of the movement as a political force. The next four chapters assess the different Islamic political groupings. The Muslim Brotherhood is analyzed as the oldest Islamic group. The author then moves on to study the ideology, motives and revolutionary actions of the *jama'at*. The *jam'iyat*, the campus and community based militant groups are examined next. The fourth group, the pro-government religious establishment, is discussed including sections on their power as well as their debates with radical groups. The next two chapters examine the groups' attitudes toward critical political issues. The work assesses their views toward foreign policy issues such as the US, Israel, Iran and other Arab countries, attitudes toward internal methods of change and what the nature of an Islamic state or society should be. The final chapter summarizes the author's findings.

0979 RUGH, ANDREA B. "Reshaping Personal Relations in Egypt." *Fundamentalisms and Society: Reclaiming the Sciences, the Family, and Education*, 151-180. Eds. Martin E. Marty, and R. Scott Appleby. Chicago and London: The University of Chicago Press, 1991.

Examines how Egyptian Islamic revivalists have drawn upon an already pervasive phenomenon in Egypt--the expansion of primary kin-centered relationships--to steer Egyptian Muslim loyalty toward the broader-based Muslim community. Divided into three sections, this article outlines the historical and structural elements of modern-day personal relationships; surveys the ideological views of Islamic activists toward personal relationships; and a summary of the themes dealing with the influence of these activists on social relationships.

0980 SAGIV, DAVID. "Judge Ashmawi and Militant Islam in Egypt." *MES* 28, no. 3 (July 1992): 531-46.

Examines the Egyptian reaction to the book "Political Islam" written by Judge Ashmawi, the Chief Justice of the High Court of Appeals and the High Court for the Security of Egypt.

0981 EL-SAYED, MOUSTAPHA K. "The Islamic Movement in Egypt: Social and Political Implications." *The Political Economy of Contemporary Egypt*, 222-239. Ed. Ibrahim M. Oweiss. Washington, D.C.: Center for Contemporary Arab Studies, Georgetown University, 1990.

This chapter explores the development of the Islamic movement in Egypt. The author locates different characteristics within the movement and compares and contrasts its radical and mainstream manifestations.

0982 WALKER, DENNIS. "Pan-Islamism as a Modern Ideology in the Egyptian Independence Movement of Mustapha Kamil." *HI* 17, no. 1 (March 1994): 57-109.

Analyzes whether the Kamilist movement was Egypt-oriented or whether it brought out feelings of Pan-Islamism that overcame Egyptian nationalism and sought to re-shape Egypt within a larger Islamic state.

B.   The Gulf States

0983 AHRARI, M. E. "Iran, GCC and the Security Dimensions in the Persian Gulf." *Reconstruction and Regional Diplomacy in the Persian Gulf*, 193-212. Eds. H. and N. Entessar Amirahmadi. London and New York: Routledge Press, 1992.

Examines the relations between Iran and the countries of the Gulf Cooperation Council.

0984 AMIRAHMADI, HOOSHANG. "Iran and the Persian Gulf: Strategic Issues and Outlook." *Islam, Iran, and World Stability*, 97-134. Ed. Hamid Zangeneh. New York: St. Martin's Press, 1994.

Examines Iran's influence over Islamic movements throughout the world. Discusses the implications of the Islamic republic's support for these movements on its external relations.

0985 BALLANTYNE, WILLIAM. "A Reassertion of the Shari'ah: The Jurisprudence of the Gulf States." *Islamic Law and Jurisprudence*, 149-160. Ed. Nicholas Heer. Seattle and London: University of Washington Press, 1990.

This chapter explores current trends of reassertion of the Shari'ah in the legal systems of the Gulf states. The article examines the position of the Shari'ah as a source of legislation in Bahrain, Kuwait, Saudi Arabia, Qatar, and the United Arab Emirates and to what extent it applies in commercial matters.

0986 CHUBIN, SHAHRAM. "Iran and the Persian Gulf States." *The Iranian Revolution and the Muslim World*, 73-84. Ed. David Menashri. Boulder, CO: Westview Press, 1990.

Analyzes the impact of the Iran-Iraq war on Iran's foreign relations, especially with the Gulf countries.

0987 CIGAR, NORMAN. "Islam and the State in South Yemen: The Uneasy Coexistence." *MES* 26, no. 2 (April 1990): 185-203.

An examination of the religious policy of the People's Democratic Republic of Yemen and its impact on the country's political system and society.

0988 DEKMEJIAN, R. HRAIR. "The Rise of Political Islamism in Saudi Arabia." *MEJ* 48, no. 4 (1994): 627-643.

This article probes the new Islamic wave that has appeared in Saudi Arabia and examines the causal factors that led to its rise, its ideology, leaders, and social basis.

0989 EICKELMAN, DALE F. "National Identity and Religious Discourse in Contemporary Oman." *IJIAS* 6, no. 1 (1989): 1-20.

This article examines the changes in religious discourse in Oman and its effect upon national and regional politics due to the spread of literacy and mass media.

0990 EICKELMAN, DALE F. and MALCOLM DENNISON. "Arabizing the Omani Intelligence Services: Clash of Cultures?" *IJICI* 7, no. 1 (March 1994): 1-28.

Discusses the response of the Omani internal security service to Islamist movements.

0991 GOLDBERG, JACOB. "Saudi Arabia and the Iranian Revolution: The Religious Dimension." *The Iranian Revolution and the Muslim World*, 155-170. Ed. David Menashri. Boulder, CO: Westview Press, 1990.

Examines Saudi-Iranian relations as each nation struggled to be the leading Islamic state.

0992 KECHICHIAN, JOSEPH. "The Gulf Cooperation Council: Containing the Iranian Revolution." *JSAMES* 13, no. 1-2 (1989): 146-165.

Traces how the Islamic government in Iran threatened the Gulf monarchies and how they in turn dealt with this perceived threat.

0993 _____. "Islamic Revivalism and Change in Saudi Arabia." *MW* 80, no. 1 (January 1990): 1-16.

Focusing on the role Juhayman al-Utaybi and Muhammad Abdullah al-Rahtumi, this article examines the origins of Islamist opposition in Saudi Arabia. Provides a historical background of the movement, the takeover of the Grand Mosque in Mecca in 1979, and the Shi'i uprisings. Provides a bibliography of al-Utaybi's letters and investigations on political legitimacy and the role of the Mahdi.

0994 LONG, DAVID E. "The Impact of the Iranian Revolution on the Arabian Peninsula and the Gulf States." *The Iranian Revolution: Its Global Impact*, 100-115. Ed. John L. Esposito. Miami: Florida International University Press, 1990.

Assesses the intellectual and political ramifications of the Iranian revolution on the policies of the Arabian Peninsula and the Gulf States.

C.   Iraq

0995 BARAM, AMATZIA. "From Radicalism to Radical Pragmatism: The Shi'ite Fundamentalist Opposition Movements of Iraq." *Islamic Fundamentalisms and the Gulf Crisis*, 28-51. Ed. James Piscatori. The United States of America: The American Academy of Arts and Science, 1991.

Examines the difficulties faced and actions taken by the competing Iraqi Islamic organizations during the Gulf war. Illustrates the fine line they were compelled to walk. While they opposed the secular Ba'thist regime, they also could not be seen as inviting the disintegration or destruction of Iraq.

0996 _____. "The Impact of Khomeini's Revolution on the Radical Shi'i Movement of Iraq." *The Iranian Revolution and the Muslim World*, 131-151. Ed. David Menashri. Boulder, CO: Westview Press, 1990.

Examines the profound impact of the Iranian revolution among the Iraqi Shi'a. Illustrates the influence of the revolution in mobilizing huge portions of Iraq's Shi'a population which Saddam Hussein's regime saw as a direct threat to the nation's stability.

0997 _____. "The Radical Shi'ite Opposition Movement in Iraq." *Religious Radicalism & Politics in the Middle East*, 95-125. Eds. Emmanuel Sivan, and Menachem Freidman. Albany: State University of New York Press, 1990.

Utilizing the writings of the Ayatollah Muhammed Baqir al-Sadr, the author explores the political ideology of the Iraqi Shi'ite opposition groups since the late 1970s with special attention paid to the most significant, the Islamic Da'wa party.

0998 _____. "Two Roads to Revolutionary Shi'ite Fundamentalism in Iraq." *Accounting for Fundamentalisms: The Dynamic Character of Movements*, 531-588. Eds. Martin E. Marty, and R. Scott Appleby. Chicago and London: The University of Chicago Press, 1994.

This article compares and contrasts the two predominant Iraqi Islamic movements; the Islamic Call Party and the Supreme Assembly for the Islamic Revolution in Iraq (SAIRI). It examines their history, organizational structure, ideology as well as their relations to Syria, Saudi Arabia, the West, the influence of Iran and their notions of democracy.

0999   BENGIO, OFRA. "Iraq's Shi'a and Kurdish Communities: From Resentment to Revolt." *Iraq's Road to War*, 51-66. Eds. Amatzia Baram, and Barry Rubin. New York: St. Martin's Press, 1993.

Examines various aspects of the Shi'i and Kurdish uprisings following the Gulf war.

1000   AL-JABBAR, FALIH ABD. "Why the Uprisings Failed." *MERIP* 176 (May 1992): 2-14.

An analysis for the failure of the Kurdish and Shi'i uprisings in Iraq following the Gulf war.

1001   KUMARASAMY, P. R. "Islam and Israel: Saddam Hussein's Two Pillar Strategy in the Persian Gulf Crisis." *SA* 14, no. 8 (1991): 913-923.

Contends that Saddam Hussein attempted to broaden his support in the Gulf war by portraying the conflict as a religious war.

1002   MALLAT, CHIBLI. "Muhammad Baqer as-Sadr." *Pioneers of Islamic Revival*, 251-272. Ed. Ali Rahnema. London: Zed Press, 1994.

This chapter explores the life of Muhammad Baqir as-Sadr and the intellectual and political development of the Iraqi Islamic movement, illustrating why as-Sadr's Islamic discourse was important not only for the Iraqi Islamic movement but for Islamic revivalism as well.

1003   _____. *The Renewal of Islamic Law: Muhammad Baqer as-Sadr, Najaf and the Shi'i International*. New York: Cambridge University Press, 1993.

An excellent work on the innovative Iraqi Shi'i cleric Muhammad Baqir as-Sadr who was killed in 1980 by Saddam Hussein's regime. The author analyzes the works of as-Sadr within the context of the intellectual atmosphere of Najaf during the 1960s and 1970s. Provides a discussion of Baqer as-Sadr's ideas on constitutional government, law, economics, banking and private property. Also valuable information on the clerical establishment and the Shi'i curriculum in the Najaf seminaries is offered. Mallat argues that Baqer as-Sadr's ideas were the inspiration for the 1979 Iranian constitution comparing the striking similar language between the constitution and as-Sadr's work "Preliminary Legal Note on the Project of a Constitution for the Islamic Republic in Iran." A very useful work for the study of the Shi'i clergy in contemporary Iraq.

1004 ROBINS, PHILIP. "Iraq: Revolutionary Threats and Regime Responses." *The Iranian Revolution: Its Global Impact*, 83-99. Ed. John L. Esposito. Miami: Florida International University Press, 1990.

Examines the response of Iraq to the perceived threat of Iran following the revolution. Asserts that the revolution had a modest effect on the internal policies of Iraq.

1005 SLUGLETT, PETER and MARION FAROUK-SLUGLETT. "Sunnis and Shi'as Revisited: Sectarianism and Ethnicity Authoritarian Iraq." *Iraq: Power and Society*, eds. Derek Hopwood, Habib Ishow, and Thomas Koszinowski. Reading, England: Ithaca Press, 1993.

Examines the sectarian situation in Iraq to assess the changes that have occurred since the Gulf war.

1006 SOETERIK, ROBERT. *The Islamic Movement of Iraq, 1958-1980*. Amsterdam: Middle East Research Associates, 1992.

Concentrates on the leadership role that the Shi'a religious leaders played in the Iraqi Islamic movement and their struggle with the Ba'thi state.

1007 WILEY, JOYCE N. *The Islamic Movement of Iraqi Shi'as*. Boulder and London: Lynne Reinner Publishers, 1992.

Discusses the contemporary Iraqi Shi'i movement. It provides an overview of the history of Shi'ism until 1958 and then examines the history of Shi'i revivalism in Iraq until 1991. The writer offers a chronological account of the evolution of the Shi'i political party Da'wa, its social base, ideological views and the political agenda of its leaders. Wiley characterizes the Iraqi Shi'i Islamic movement as reformist in nature and examines the political ideology of its most influential leader Baqer as-Sadr. The author concludes with a section on the future of the movement within the context of a post-Saddam Iraq.

D.   Jordan

1008   ABU JABER, KAMEL S. and SCHIRIN H. FATHI. "The 1989 Jordanian Parliamentary Elections." *Orient* 31, no. 1 (March 1990): 67-86.

Analyzes the 1989 Jordanian Parliamentary elections and offers reasons for the success of the Islamists.

1009 AL AKAILAH, ABDALLAH. "The Experience of the Jordanian Islamic Movement." *Power-Sharing Islam?*, 93-101. Ed. Azzam Tamimi. London: Liberty for Muslim World Publications, 1993.

Traces the involvement of the Islamic movement in the Jordanian political process noting its achievements during the first few years in parliament.

1010   MILTON-EDWARDS, BEVERLEY. "A Temporary Alliance with the Crown: The Islamic Response in Jordan." *Islamic Fundamentalisms and the Gulf Crisis*, 88-108. Ed. James Piscatori. Chicago, IL: The American Academy of Arts and Science, 1991.

Provides background information on relations between King Hussein and the Jordanian Islamic movement, the Islamic movement's response in Parliament to the Gulf war, popular support for Iraq and Saddam Hussein, and an outlook for the future of the Jordanian Islamic movement.

1011   PIRO, TIMOTHY. "Parliament, Politics, and Pluralism in Jordan: Democratic Trends at a Difficult Time." *MEI* 8, no. 6 (July 1992): 39-44.

Discusses the 1989 Jordanian elections, Jordanian government relations with the Islamists as well as the Jordanian economy.

1012   RIEDAL, TIM H. "The 1993 Parliamentary Elections in Jordan." *Orient* 35, no. 1 (March 1990): 51-63.

This article analyzes the results as well as the events that shaped the 1993 Jordanian elections including the results of the Islamic Action Front.

1013   TAL, LAWRENCE. "Is Jordan Doomed?" *FA* 72, no. 5 (November 1993): 45-58.

Examines the stability of the Jordanian state and the role the Kingdom plays in the peace process. After a discussion of the history and identity of the country, the author weighs the possibility of a confederation between Jordan and the Palestinians.

1014   WEDEMAN, BEN. "Democracy in Jordan: Election Results Send Mixed Signals on Peace Process and Islamists." *MEI* 10, no. 1 (November 1993): 9-13.

Offers an analysis of the November 1993 Jordanian elections. Discusses the reasons for the Jordanian Islamic Front's poor showing in comparison with the movement's 1989 achievements. Also examines the results and what the Islamists say about the future of the peace process.

E.   Lebanon

1015   "'Give Islamists Their Right to Participate in the Political Process': An Interview with Ayatollah Sayyed Fadlallah." *MEI* 10, no. 6 (September 1994): 18-22.

Interview conducted by George A. Nader of Middle East Insight with Ayatollah Fadlallah, a prominent Lebanese Shi'a scholar. Fadlallah discusses such issues as extremist and moderate Islam, Iran and Hizballah, the travel ban imposed on Lebanon by the United States, and views regarding the peace process.

1016 ABUKHALIL, AS'AD. "Ideology and Practice of Hizballah in Lebanon: Islamization of Leninist Organizational Principles." *MES* 27, no. 3 (1991): 390-403.

Traces the evolution of the Hizballah and contends that the organization is an "Islamic adoption to the era of Leninist revolutionary organizations."

1017 FADL ALLAH, AL-SEYED MUHAMMED HUSSEIN. "The New World Order and the Middle East -- An Islamic Perspective by Ayatollah Al-Sayed Muhammed Hussein Fadl Allah." *MEI* 8, no. 1 (July 1991): 9-13.

This article is based on interviews conducted by George A. Nader, MEI editor. Fadl Allah, a noted Islamic scholar is the spiritual leader of the Shi'i community in Lebanon and of the Lebanese Islamic Resistance Forces. He shares his perspective on the 'New World Order' following the Gulf war affirming his belief that there is no such thing as a new world order and asserting that U.S. hegemony is alive and well. He notes that the Middle East will remain within the sphere of the U.S. through a 'security arrangement for U.S. interests through states under American influence and control.'

1018 FAKSH, MAHMUD A. "The Shi'a Community of Lebanon: A New Assertive Political Force." *JSAMES* 14, no. 3 (1991): 33-56.

Looks at the transformation of the Shi'a community in Lebanon from a deprived group to a prominent political force.

1019 HAMZEH, A. NIZAR. "Lebanon's Hizbullah: From Islamic Revolution to Parliamentary Accommodation." *TWQ* 14, no. 2 (1993): 321-337.

Discusses the new political phase that Hizbullah has passed through since 1989 and the role that it plays in Lebanon's political system.

1020 HAMZEH, A. NIZAR and R. HRAIR DEKMEJIAN. "The Islamic Spectrum of Lebanese Politics." *JSAMES* 16, no. 3 (1993): 25-42.

Drawing upon fieldwork conducted in Lebanon, this study explores the major Islamic parties and factions and their roles in Lebanese politics.

1021 JAHANPOUR, FARHANG. "The Roots of the Hostage Crisis." *WT* 48, no. 2 (February 1992): 33-36.

The involvement of Iran in the Western hostage crisis in Lebanon is the focus of this essay.

1022 KRAMER, MARTIN. "Hizbullah: The Calculus of Jihad." *Fundamentalisms and the State: Remaking Polities, Economies, and Militance*, eds. Martin E. Marty, and R. Scott Appleby. The Fundamentalism Project, 3. Chicago and London: The University of Chicago Press, 1991.

Seeks to analyze the reasons and circumstances behind the violent acts perpetrated by Lebanon's Hizbullah. Also offers an examination of the effects of the movement's militancy.

1023 _____. "The Moral Logic of Hizballah." *Origins of Terrorism: Psychologies, Ideologies, Theologies, States of Mind*, 131-157. Ed. Walter Reich. Cambridge: Cambridge University Press, 1990.

Provides an examination of the differing views of leaders of Hizballah including: Husayn al-Musawi, Shaykh Subhi al-Tufayli, Sayyid Abba al-Musawi, Sayyid Ibrahim al-Amin and Ayatollah Sayyid Muhammad Husayn Fadlallah, on the mission of the movement, especially concerning suicidal bomb attacks and the kidnaping of foreigners.

1024 _____. "Redeeming Jerusalem: The Pan-Islamic Premise of Hizballah." *The Iranian Revolution and the Muslim World*, 105-130. Ed. David Menashri. Boulder, CO: Westview Press, 1990.   This article deals with the repercussions of the Iranian revolution on the Lebanese Hizballah party. Seeks to illustrate how Iranian foreign policy was very instrumental in the success of Hizballah because of Lebanon's unique circumstances.

1025 NORTON, AUGUSTUS RICHARD. "A Countersensational Perspective on the Shi'a of Lebanon." *Reconstruction and Regional Diplomacy in the Persian Gulf*, 45-64. Eds. H. and N. Entessar Amirahmadi. London and New York: Routledge Press, 1992.

Analyzes the impact of the Iranian revolution in mobilizing the Shi'a community in Lebanon. Also discusses the western media's perception of the Shi'a as terrorists.

1026 _____. "Lebanon: The Internal Conflict and the Iranian Connection." *The Iranian Revolution: Its Global Impact*, 116-137. Ed. John L. Esposito. Miami: Florida International University Press, 1990.

While acknowledging the important influence of Iran in Lebanese politics, this article also discusses the challenges Lebanon has faced from Syria and some segments of Lebanese society including Sunnis, Druze, Maronites, and the Amal Shi'i movement.

1027 _____. "Musa al-Sadr." *Pioneers of Islamic Revival*, 184-207. Ed. Ali Rahnema. London: Zed Press, 1994.

This chapter explores the impact of Imam Musa Al-Sadr on Lebanese political life. The study offers an examination of how he politicized the story of the martyrdom of Imam Hussein to revitalize the Lebanese Shi'i community and provides an explanation of why his legacy still lives on after his disappearance.

1028 _____. "Religious Resurgence and Political Mobilization of the Shi'a of Lebanon." *Religious Resurgence and Politics in the Contemporary World,* 229-241. Ed. Emile Sahliyeh. Albany: State University of New York Press, 1990.

Examines the factors which led to the political mobilization of the Shi'a community in Lebanon.

1029 _____. "The Shi'ites and the MNF." *The Multinational Force in Beirut, 1982-1984,* 226-236. Eds. Kjell Skjelsbaek, and Anthony McDermott. Miami: Florida International University Press, 1991.

Focuses on the role that the Shi'a community in Lebanon played in the demise of the Multinational Force in the early 1980s.

1030 PISCATORI, JAMES. "The Shi'a of Lebanon and Hizbullah, the Party of God." *Politics of the Future: The Role of Social Movements,* 292-320. Eds. Christine Jennett, Randa, and G. Stewart. Melbourne, Australia: Macmillan, 1989.

This chapter provides an analysis of the Shi'a community of Lebanon and its politicization. Examines its evolution, organizational structure, leadership, financial support, and followers.

1031 EL SOLH, RAGHID. "Religious Identity and Citizenship: An Overview of Perspectives." *Peace for Lebanon: From War to Reconstruction,* 231-240. Ed. Deirdre Collings. Boulder & London: Lynne Rienner Publishers, 1994.

Presents an overview of the interplay between religion and citizenship in Lebanese politics. Seeks to provide insight into what this interplay reveals about conflict and peace in Lebanon and prospects for the future.

1032 VAZIRI, HALEH. "Iran's Involvement in Lebanon: Polarization and Radicalization of Militant Islamic Movements." *JSAMES* 16, no. 2 (1992): 1-16.

Explores the impact of Iran's support of different Islamic factions In Lebanon.

F.   Palestine

1033   "The Islamist Movements in the Occupied Territories: An Interview with Iyad Barghouti." *MERIP* 183 (July 1993): 9-12.

Lisa Hajjar conducts an interview with Iyad Barghouti, a sociology professor at al-Najah University in Nablus and author of several works on the Palestinian Islamic movement, who discusses the appeal of Hamas and other Islamic factions.

1034   "'This Peace Process is Moving Against the Will of the Palestinians': Interview with Hamas Spokesman Ibrahim Ghosheh." *MEI* 10, no. 6 (September 1994): 50.

Ben Wedeman, Middle East Insight's Amman correspondent, conducts an interview with Hamas' spokesperson Ibrahim Ghosheh in Amman. Offers a discussion of Hamas' views on the peace process.

1035   ABU-AMR, ZIAD. "Hamas: A Historical and Political Background." *J'S* 22, no. 4 (1993): 5-19.

This article explores the rise of the Muslim Brotherhood and the Islamic Resistance Movement (Hamas) in the West Bank and Gaza Strip. The essay provides a brief overview of Hamas' ideology, aims, strategies, activities, popularity, external relations, funding, and future prospects.

1036   _____. *Islamic Fundamentalism in the West Bank and Gaza: Muslim Brotherhood and Islamic Jihad*. Bloomington and Indianapolis: Indiana University Press, 1994.

Utilizing Arabic sources and extensive interviews with those concerned, this book examines the Islamic groups in the West Bank and Gaza Strip. The author analyzes the birth of each group, their political development, ideological similarities and differences, and their relationship with one another and with the PLO. The work provides information on the role of each group in the *intifada* and their position on the question of Palestine. The conclusion offers an assessment of the political power of the Islamic groups in comparison to that of the PLO as well as prospects for the future.

1037   AHMAD, HISHAM H. *Hamas: From Religious Salvation to Political Transformation: The Rise of Hamas in Palestinian Society*. Jerusalem: PASSIA Publication, 1994.

This study, based on field work conducted in the Occupied Territories including many interviews with Hamas leaders, activists, and supporters, surveys the evolution of the Hamas movement. Looks at the various historical, political, economic, and social factors which have contributed to the movement's rise. The work moves on to factor in the national, regional, and international conditions which affected the expansion of the movement. It also explores how Hamas attracts support, as well as its relationship to other political 'bodies' including Palestinian parties, the Israelis, other Arab nations, and the international community. In addition, this work provides insight into Hamas' reaction to the peace process.

1038 AMIRAHMADI, HOOSHANG. "The Islamic Republic and the Question of Palestine: A Look at one of the Key Issues of Conflict Between the US and Iran." *MEI* 10, no. 4\5 (May 1994): 50-54.

Examines the Iranian Islamic Government's policy towards the question of Palestine, the Islamization of Iranian foreign policy and changes made in the post-Khomeini era.

1039 BARGHOUTI, IYAD. "Palestinian Islamists and the Middle East Peace Conference." *InS* 28, no. 1 (1993): 61-73.

States that while the secular Palestinian groups were not in agreement about whether to attend the Madrid peace conference, the different Islamist groups--Hamas, the Islamic Liberation Party, "al-Tahrir," and the Islamic Jihad Movement--all opposed attending. Yet each of the Islamic groups had their own reasons that differed from one another.

1040 _____. "Religion and Politics Among the Students of Najah National University." *MES* 27, no. 2 (1991): 203-218.

Based upon a survey conducted at Najah University in the West Bank which the author believes is the most representative of Palestinian society, this article examines the religious and political leanings of the students.

1041 BRINNER, WILLIAM M. "Arabs and Muslims as Minorities: An Historical Overview." *AAS* 27, no. 2 (March 1993): 9-23.

First delivered at a conference entitled "The Arab Minority in Israel: Dilemmas of Political Orientation and Social Change," this article surveys Muslim minorities for the last 250 years in order to present a paradigm that might provide a better understanding of the actions of the Muslim minorities in Israel.

1042 COMMINS, DAVID. "Taqi al-Din al-Nabhani and the Islamic Liberation Party." *MW* 81, no. 3-4 (1991): 194-211.

This article looks at Taqi al-Din al-Nabhani, the chief ideologue of the Islamic Liberation Party founded in 1952 in Jerusalem. The article provides a biography of al-Nabhani and examines his writings on Palestine, Islamic ideology, Muslim history, and the Islamic state.

1043   GHANDOUR, ZEINA. "Religious Law in a Secular State: The Jurisdiction of the *Shari'a* Courts of Palestine and Israel." *ALQ* 5, no. 1 (1990): 25-48.
Examines the degree to which Islamic law has been applied under the Ottomans, the British, and Israelis in Palestine and Israel.

1044   ISRAELI, RAPHAEL. *Muslim Fundamentalism in Israel.* London: Brassey's, 1993.
This work, sponsored by the Harry S. Truman Research Institute for the Advancement of Peace, utilizes a paradigm set forth by Hava Lazarus-Yafeh that seeks to determine the characteristics of fundamentalist organizations in various political and cultural settings. Within this parameter, the writer studies three Muslim villages within Israel's borders to answer the following questions. What are the roots of Islamic fundamentalism among Israeli Arabs and to what extent are they likely to become militant? What are the Islamic activists' socio-economic bases, their ideology and their views toward Jews, Zionism and the Arab-Israeli conflict? What are the organizational structures and methods of the movement and how do the Israeli Arabs receive the religious message? Finally, what links exist between Islamic fundamentalists within Israel and those in the West Bank and other Islamic movements? The conclusion offers some comments on the implications of his research and what it means to Israel and the stability of the Middle East?

1045   AL JARBAWI, ALI. "The Position of Palestinian Islamists on the Palestine-Israel Accord." *MW* 83, no. 1-2 (January 1994): 127-154.
This article first outlines and then analyzes the position of Palestinian Islamists on the Palestine-Israel Accord. The groups include Hamas, Islamic Liberation Party, the Islamic Jihad Movement in Palestine, and the Islamic Jihad Movement. The article also discusses how these parties will react to developments derived from the implementation of the Oslo Accord.

1046   JUBRAN, MICHEL and LAURA DRAKE. "The Islamic Fundamentalist Movement in the West Bank and Gaza Strip." *MEP* 2, no. 2 (1993): 1-15.
Discusses the political history of the various Islamic fundamentalist groups including Islamic Jihad, the Muslim Brotherhood and Hamas in the West Bank and Gaza Strip. Highlights the competition between Hamas and the PLO.

1047   KJORLIEN, MICHELE L. "Hamas: In Theory and Practice." *ASJ* 1, no. 2 (September 1993): 4-7.
Examines the role of Hamas as an opposition party within the Palestinian political sphere.

1048   LAYISH, AHARON. "The Status of the Shari'a in a non-Muslim State: The Case of Israel." *JAAS* 27, no. 1&2 (March 1993): 171-187.

First delivered as a speech at a conference entitled "The Arab Minority in Israel: Dilemmas of Political Orientation and Social Change," this article assesses the status of the various *shari'ah* courts in Israel and concludes that "Islamic law is undergoing a slow but steady change gradually leading to a synthesis of sorts with Israeli law."

1049 LEGRAIN, JEAN-FRANÇOIS. "A Defining Moment: Palestinian Islamic Fundamentalism." *Islamic Fundamentalisms and the Gulf Crisis*, 70-87. Ed. James Piscatori. Chicago, IL: The American Academy of Arts and Science, 1991.

Focuses on the dilemma that the Islamic Resistance Movement (Hamas) faced during the Gulf crisis; a pro-Saddam constituency and a dependency on Gulf financing. Details how the movement's leaders took a pragmatic gamble and distanced themselves from supporting Saddam Hussein and were able to enhance their own legitimacy vis-a-vis the PLO.

1050 _____. "The Islamic Movement and the Intifada." *Intifada: Palestine at the Crossroads*, 175-189. Eds. Jamal R. Nasser, and Roger Heacock. New York: Praeger, 1990.

Examines the role that the Islamic movement has played in different stages of the Palestinian uprising and contrasts this to the Palestinian national movement.

1051 _____. "Palestinian Islamisms: Patriotism as a Condition of Their Expansion." *Accounting for Fundamentalisms: The Dynamic Character of Movements*, 413-427. Eds. Martin E. Marty, and R. Scott Appleby. Chicago and London: The University of Chicago Press, 1994.

This article identifies two forms of Islamisms in the Palestinian case; Islamic Jihad as a revolutionary movement that seeks to throw off Israeli occupation and the Muslim Brotherhood that desires to Islamicize Palestinian society. The essay compares the ideology, behavior, actors, and the organizational structures of the two trends of political Islam before and after the Intifada.

1052 LESCH, ANN MOSELY and MARK TESSLER. "The West Bank and Gaza: Political and Ideological Responses to the Occupation." *Israel, Egypt, and the Palestinians: From Camp David to Intifada*, Bloomington and Indianapolis: Indiana University Press, 1989.

Examines Palestinian ideological responses to Israeli occupation in the West Bank and Gaza Strip. Discusses the Islamic currents and shows how the Islamic response is a distinctive ideological orientation that is linked with Palestinian nationalist goals.

1053   MAYER, THOMAS. "Pro-Iranian Fundamentalism in Gaza." *Religious Radicalism & Politics in the Middle East*, 143-155. Eds. Emmanuel Sivan, and Menachem Freidman. Albany: State University of New York Press, 1990.

This chapter examines the career of Palestinian physician Fathi 'Abd al-'Aziz Shqaqi who was an ardent supporter of the call for the reunification of the Sunni and Shi'ite communities to create a united Islamic *umma* (community).

1054   MILTON-EDWARDS, BEVERLEY. "The Concept of *Jihad* and the Palestinian Islamic Movement: A Comparison of Ideas and Techniques." *BJMES* 19, no. 1 (1992): 48-53.
Elaborates on the ties between the concept of *jihad* (holy war) as a mobilizing force and the Palestinian Islamists within the context of the intifada.

1055   MISHAL, SHAUL. "'Paper War'--Words Behind Stones: The Intifada Leaflets." *JQ* , no. 51 (June 1989): 71-94.
Through an examination of the political leaflets used by various Palestinian factions during the intifada, this essay compares and contrasts their religious and secular ideology.

1056   PAZ, REUVEN. "The Islamic Movement in Israel and Municipal Elections of 1989." *JQ* , no. 53 (1990): 3-26.
Originally published in Hebrew, this article examines the influence of the Islamic movement with Israel's Palestinian population.

1057   RASHAD, AHMAD. *Hamas: Palestinian Politics With an Islamic Hue.* Annandale, VA: United Association for Studies and Research, Inc., 1993.
This paper examines the origins, development, structure, support and funding, military operations, and ideology of the Islamic Resistance Movement (Hamas). Also looks at Hamas' relationship with the PLO and the West as well as Hamas' prospects for the future.

1058   REKHESS, ELIE. "Resurgent Islam in Israel." *AAS* 27, no. 1&2 (March 1993): 189-206.
First delivered as a speech for a conference entitled "The Arab Minority in Israel: Dilemmas of Political Orientation and Social Change," this article assesses the rise of Islamic revivalism among the Palestinians living in Israel and discusses the factors that led to its rise.

1059   SATLOFF, ROBERT. "Islam in the Palestinian Uprising." *Orbis* (June 1989): 389-401.
This article analyzes the causal factors for the rise of political Islamic groups in the West Bank and Gaza Strip. The author also discusses the organizational

make-up, aims and goals, and the effect of the popularity of Islamic Jihad and Hamas on Fatah.

1060 SCHIFF, ZE'EV and EHUD YA'ARI. "The Islamic Resistance Movement." *Intifada: The Palestinian Uprising -- Israel's Third Front*, 220-239. New York: Simon & Schuster, 1989.

This chapter, written by two Israeli journalists, traces the rise of the Islamic Resistance Movement, Hamas, and documents how the Israeli government was instrumental in its development.

1061 STEINBERG, MATTI. "The PLO and Palestinian Islamic Fundamentalism." *JQ* 52 (1989): 37-54.

Examines the relationship between the PLO and the growing Palestinian movement.

1062 TAMARI, SALIM. "Left in Limbo: Leninist Heritage and Islamic Challenge." *MERIP* 179 (January 1992): 16-21.

Written by a Bir Zeit sociology professor, this report explores the ideological and organizational development of the Palestinian political left and the challenge posed by the Palestinian Islamic movement.

1063 TARAKI, LISA. "The Islamic Resistance Movement in the Palestinian Uprising." *MERIP* 156 (January 1989): 30-33.

Offers a historical overview of the emergence of the Islamic Resistance Movement (Hamas) and an assessment of the movement's political vision.

1064 USHER, GRAHAM. "The Islamist Movement and the Palestinian Authority: Graham Usher Speaks With Bassam Jarrar." *MERIP* 189 (July 1994): 28-29.

Provides an interview with Bassam Jarrar, a leading Islamist thinker in the Occupied Territories, conducted by Graham Usher. In this interview Jarrar details major problems in Palestinian politics that face all Palestinians in light of developments in the peace process.

G.   Sudan

1065 ABBAS, ABDULLA ALI. "The National Islamic Front and the Politics of Education." *MERIP* 172 (1991): 22-25.

This article analyzes the educational policies of the Sudanese National Islamic Front and assesses their impact on society.

1066 EL AFFENDI, ABDELWAHAB. "Discovering the South: Sudanese Dilemmas for Islam in Africa." *AA* 89, no. 356 (July 1990): 371-389.

Traces the emergence of the modern Islamic movement in Sudan and offers an analysis of the interaction between 'Africanism' and political Islam in Sudan.

1067 _____. "Studying My Movement: Social Science Without Cynicism." *IJMES* 23, no. 1 (February 1991): 84.

Elaborates on the challenges faced by a Muslim studying Islamic revivalism in Sudan in the West and drawing upon Western methodology.

1068 _____. *Turabi's Revolution: Islam and Power in Sudan*. London: Grey Seal Books, 1991.

Written by a seasoned journalist who draws upon his intimate knowledge of Sudanese politics as a diplomat in the Sudanese foreign service. It is a comprehensive account of the rise of Islamic revivalism in Sudan, the influence of militancy, and the leading role played by Hasan al-Turabi. The author first discusses the roots of the modern reformist Islamic movements that were the precursor to contemporary Islamic movements. He moves on to detail the early beginnings of the Sudanese Islamic movement, the emergence of Islamically-oriented political parties and the issues and debates of independence. Later chapters describe the goals of the movement as it tried to define itself in the early years and demonstrates how the movement developed into a full fledged political party. The final chapter is devoted to the ideas of Hasan al-Turabi as well as an analysis of the national policy and ideology of the organization.

1069 DALY, M. W. "Islam, Secularism, and Ethnic Identity in the Sudan." *Religion and Political Power*, 83-98. Eds. Gustavo and M. W. Daly Benavides. Albany: State University of New York Press, 1989.

An assessment of the relationship between the North and the South in Sudan. The current civil war is seen as grounded in significant differences between the two regions in terms of identity as well as their concept of history.

1070 FLUEHR-LOBBAN, CAROLYN. "Protracted Civil War in the Sudan: Its Future as a Multi-Religious, Multi-Ethnic State." *FFWA* 16, no. 2 (June 1992): 67-79.

Assesses the future of Sudan as a multi-religious and ethnic state given the longevity of the civil war.

1071 HOLY, LADISLAV. *Religion and Custom in a Muslim Society: The Berti of Sudan*. Cambridge: Cambridge University Press, 1991.

Drawn from three years of field research among the Muslim community in the Sudan called the Berti, this ethnographic study examines the various religious rituals practiced by this Muslim community. Demonstrates that the more formal religious rituals are performed by the males and the popular religious rituals by the females. Contends that contrary to a widely held belief that these customary rituals are pre-Islamic pagan rituals, the author shows how these observances are a part of the Berti's religious system. Illustrates that the two different types of rituals are connected to the Berti's gender relationship. In addition, the work also explores how information concerning Islam is dispersed throughout society and the role that the religious schools play in upholding the religious traditions.

1072 IBRAHIM, RIAD. "Factors Contributing to the Political Ascendancy of the Muslim Brethren in Sudan." *ASQ* 12, no. 3-4 (June 1990): 33-53.
Contends that "historical and structural factors, rather than nebulous psychological ones," help to explain the rise of the Sudanese Muslim Brethren. Also assesses the political significance of the movement in Sudanese politics.

1073 JAMAL, ABBASHAR. "Funding Fundamentalism: The Political Economy of an Islamist State." *MERIP* 172 (1991): 14-21.
This essay analyzes the success of the National Islamic Front, the political wing of the Sudanese Muslim Brethren, in order to assess the prospects of other Islamic movements in the Arab world.

1074 _____. "Funding Fundamentalism: Sudan." *ROAPE* 52 (1991): 103-109.
Explores the success of the National Islamic Front in Sudan as a prototype for other aspiring Islamic movements in the Middle East region.

1075 MAKINDA, SAMUEL M. "Iran, Sudan and Islam." *WT* 49, no. 6 (June 1993): 108-111.
This article discusses Sudan's Islamic base, the Iranian-Sudanese connection, and the impact of this relationship on Sudan's Christian population and neighbors.

1076 NIBLOCK, TIM. "The Nature of the Community in the Middle East: A Case Study of Sudan." *Nature of the Islamic Community*, 209-232. Eds. Toshio Kuroda, and Richard I. Lawless. Tokyo: Keiso Shobo Publishing Co., 1991.
Discusses the concept of communities in the Middle East, arguing that they must be analyzed within the context of the environment that surrounds them. Provides a case study of Sudanese society to illustrate the point.

1077 SIMONE, T. ABDOU MALIQALIM. *In Whose Image? Political Islam and Urban Practices in Sudan*. Chicago and London: The University of Chicago Press, 1994.
Seeks to analyze the path that Sudan has chosen, the role that Islam plays in a culturally diverse society and the problems it faces in trying to mold a viable social order. The author brings to his analysis two years of field work experience in Khartoum. The work is divided into three sections. The first part

contains essays on the Sudanese civil war, relations between Islam and the state, and the search for a political identity vis-a-vis the international community as well as the search for a distinct Sudanese identity. The second part deals with the issue of Islam and the transformation of the Sudanese state and is comprised of articles on the process of Islamization within the context of forming indigenous solutions to problems; the centrality of Khartoum to the Islamic movement; ideological tenets and organizational methods of the Sudanese Islamic movement; aspects of the cultural Islamic revival in the Sudan and the politics of race and religion. The final part of this book is devoted to a critique of the Sudanese Islamic movement from a South African viewpoint.

1078   VOLL, JOHN OBERT. "Islamization in the Sudan and the Iranian Revolution." *The Iranian Revolution: Its Global Impact*, 283-301. Ed. John L. Esposito. Miami: Florida International University Press, 1990.

Examining the connection between internal Sudanese circumstances and the broader Islamic resurgence, this article assesses the influence of the Iranian revolution on Sudanese politics.

1079   _____. "Political Crisis in Sudan." *CH* 89, no. 546 (April 1990): 153-156, 178-180.

Beginning with an overview of the first three civilian and military regimes in Sudan, the author discusses the roots of military rule and the difficulties that the Bashiri government faces.

1080   WENGER, MARTHA. "Sudan: Politics and Society." *MERIP* 172 (September 1991): 3-7.

This essay offers a brief overview of Sudanese politics and society. Includes background on Sudanese religious and ethnic make-up, causes for the civil wars, and an overview of the various political parties including the National Islamic Front.

H.   Syria

1081   LOBMEYER, HANS GÜNTER. "Islamic Ideology and Secular Discourse: The Islamists of Syria." *Orient* 32, no. 3 (September 1991): 395-418.

Analyzes the role that Islam plays in the conflict between the secular Ba'thist regime and Islamist activists in Syria. Also discusses other factors which figure into the conflict such as the Sunni-'Alawi rift.

1082   WEISMANN, ITZCHAK. "Sa'id Hawwa: The Making of a Radical Muslim Thinker in Modern Syria." *MEJ* 29, no. 4 (October 1993): 601-623.

This article examines the development of the personality of Sa'id Hawwa who is regarded as one of the chief ideologues of the Syrian Islamic movement.

I.   Iran

1083   ABRAHAMIAN, ERVAND. *The Iranian Mojahedin.* New Haven, CT and London: Yale University Press, 1989.

Traces the history of the People's Mojahedin of Iran. The author examines the organizational structure of the Mojahedin and its evolution as a movement in order to describe its rise and fall. He provides rich descriptive information on the social origins, education, age and ethnicity of the movement's members as well as an analysis of the Mojahedin's intellectual ideology, which he describes as a "highly unorthodox" reading of Islamic texts, mixed with a combination of Latin American guerilla strategies, Marxism-Leninism, and Fanonian Third Worldism, sprinkled with drastically changed Shi'i symbols. The writer also includes the writings of Ali Shari'ati and demonstrates how both Shari'ati and the Mojahedin sought to bring about an Islamic Reformation through the intelligentsia and not the *ulama.*

1084   _____. "Khomeini: A Fundamentalist?" *Fundamentalism in Comparative Perspective*, 109-125. Ed. Lawrence Kaplan. Amherst: The University of Massachusetts Press, 1992.

This article asserts that to label the Ayatollah Khomeini as a fundamentalist is "misleading, distorting, and confusing." The author states that while Khomeini may have had some characteristics of a fundamentalist, the label obscures the whole picture of a multidimensional person.

1085   _____. *Khomeinism: Essays on the Islamic Republic.* Berkeley: University of California Press, 1993.

Drawing upon Persian material, the author contends that Khomeinism is a form of Islamic populism which contains the potential for change and does not reject modernity. Abrahamian asserts that Khomeinism is not a rigid but a flexible political movement. The first chapter provides an illustration of how Khomeini transformed traditional quietist Shi'ism into a militant political ideology that seems to have more in common with Third World populism of Latin America than with traditional Shi'ism. The second chapter explores Khomeini's ideas concerning private property, society and the state. The third chapter provides an analysis explaining how the celebration of May Day in Iran has combined aspects of European socialism with populist Islamic themes. The fourth chapter looks at the manipulation of Iranian history by the Islamic Republic. The fifth chapter illustrates the political paranoia which exists across the political spectrum. The final epilogue is devoted to noting the changes within the political structure in the post-Khomeini era.

1086 AFRASIABI, KEVEH L. *After Khomeini: New Directions in Iran's Foreign Policy*. Boulder, CO: Westview Press, 1994.

Offers a theoretical analysis of Iran's foreign policy following the death of the Ayatollah Khomeini in 1989. Chapters discuss issues such as the origins and development of Iran's foreign policy; Iran's foreign policy during the Gulf war; the Republic's foreign policy relations with the countries of the Gulf Cooperation Council; Iran's foreign policy strategy towards Central Asia following the break up of the Soviet Union; and Iran's place in the 'new world order.' Also offers policy recommendations in order to "Avoid a new Cold War in the Middle East."

1087 AFSHARI, M. REZA. "The Historians of the Constitutional Movement and the Making of the Iranian Populist Tradition." *IJMES* 25, no. 3 (August 1993): 477-494.

Examines the three tendencies of the historians of the Iranian constitutional movement of 1906--the traditionalist, the populist, and the elitist. Seeks to illustrate that each strain expressed their own political views that collectively provide for the history of the Iranian oppositional movement.

1088 AJAMI, FOUAD. "Iran: The Impossible Revolution." *FA* 67 (Winter 1988\1989): 135-155.

Analyzes the transformation of the Iranian revolution from a powerful movement to one that maintains the status quo. Argues that the practicalities of governing have pushed revolutionary fervor aside.

1089 AKHAVI, SHAHROUGH. "Post-Khomeini Iran: Global and Regional Implications." *SAIS* 10, no. 1 (December 1990): 149-162.

Beginning with a brief overview of the decade of Khomeini's leadership, this article then examines the impact of Khomeini's death on U.S. foreign policy and international relations in the Middle East.

1090 _____. "Shi'ism, Corporatism, and Rentierism in the Iranian Revolution." *Comparing Muslim Societies: Knowledge and the State in a World Civilization*, 261-293. Ed. Juan R. I. Cole. Michigan: The University of Michigan Press, 1992.

This chapter offers an analysis of the role of the state, the economic foundation of that state, and the uses of Shi'i ideology by Iranians in pre- and post-revolutionary Iran. The author uses the rentier state model and corporatist theory to explain transformations.

1091 AMIRAHMADI, HOOSHANG. "Terrorist Nation or Scapegoat?: Taking a Close Look at Iran and the 'Islamic Threat.'" *MEI* 10, no. 6 (September 1994): 23-29.

Debates the accuracy of labeling Iran a terrorist nation in light of the recent bombing against Jewish sites in London and Buenos Aires. Also examines the relationship between Iran and Israel and Iranian influence on other Islamic movements in the Middle East.

1092 AMIRAHMADI, HOOSHANG, and N. ENTESSAR, ed. *Reconstruction and Regional Diplomacy in the Persian Gulf,* London and New York: Routledge Press, 1992.

The post-revolutionary period in Iran has significantly changed the nature of Iran's domestic policies as well as its external relations. This volume of essays demonstrates the complexities inherent in these changes and discusses the negative impact the revolution has had on both Iran's economic development and its relations with the international community. The work explores four issues: Islam and revolution, economic destruction and reconstruction, Iran's relations with the Arab world as well as Iran's relations with the superpowers.

1093 AMUZEGAR, JAHANGIR. *The Dynamics of the Iranian Revolution - The Pahlavis Triumph and Tragedy.* Albany, NY: The State University of New York Press, 1991.

Provides a concise examination of the political and social events that led to the collapse of the Pahlavi dynasty. The author begins his examination in 1906, a year that marked the beginning of Iran's drive for political liberalization and economic diversification. Attributes the failure of the Pahlavi regime to deep-rooted contradictions pervading all different aspects of Iranian society, politics, and economy.

1094 ARJOMAND, SAID AMIR. "Constitution-Making in Islamic Iran." *History and Power in the Study of Law,* 113-127. Eds. J. Collier, and J. Starr. Cornell University Press, 1989.

Examines the development process of the writing and ideas behind the 1979 constitution of the Islamic Republic of Iran.

1095 _____. "History, Structure and Revolution in Shi'ite Tradition in Contemporary Iran." *IPSR* 10, no. 2 (1989): 111-119.

Advocating a Weberian paradigm, this article contends that the Islamic revolution was a modernizing force for Shi'ism and a traditionalizing one for the Iranian state.

1096 _____. "Millennial Beliefs, Hierocratic Authority, and Revolution in Shi'ite Iran." *The Political Dimensions of Religion*, 219-239. Ed. Said Amir Arjomand. Albany: State University of New York Press, 1993.

Compares the Shi'i millinarianism of the 19th century Babi movement to the millennial message included in the revolutionary ideology of 20th century Iran.

1097 _____. "Religion and Constitutionalism in Western History and in Modern Iran and Pakistan." *The Political Dimensions of Religion*, 69-100. Ed. Said Amir Arjomand. Albany: State University of New York Press, 1993.

Using Iran and Pakistan as models, this chapter provides a historical perspective of the birth of the "political tradition of constitutionalism" and examines how constitutionalism was appropriated into Islamic politics.

. 1098 _____. "The Rule of God in Iran." *Social Compass* 36, no. 4 (1989): 539-548.

Addresses the transformation of the Shi'i political theory of authority during the Iranian revolution.

1099 _____ "Shi'ite Jurisprudence and Constitution Making in the Islamic Republic of Iran." *Fundamentalisms and the State: Remaking Polities, Economies, and Militance*, 88-108. Eds. E. Martin Marty, and R. Scott Appleby. The Fundamentalism Project, 3. Chicago and London: The University of Chicago Press, 1991.

Examines the Iranian clerics' continuing attempts to reconcile Iranian state law with Shi'a jurisprudence on the basis of Ayatollah Ruhollah Khomeini's ideology of a theocratic Islamic government during the 1980s and early 1990s.

1100 _____ "A Victory for the Pragmatists: The Islamic Fundamentalist Reaction in Iran." *Islamic Fundamentalisms and the Gulf Crisis*, 52-69. Ed. James Piscatori. The United States of America: The American Academy of Arts and Science, 1991.

Describes how the pragmatists consolidated control of the Iranian political elite and were able to capitalize on the defeat of Saddam Hussein in the Gulf war.

1101 ATLAS, YEDIDYA. "Iran -- An Islamic Threat." *MS* 37, no. 7 (1992): 2-7.

A brief discussion of why the author believes Iran to be a threat to regional stability.

1102 AL AZM, SADIK J. "Is the Fatwa a Fatwa." *MERIP* 183 (July 1993): 27-28.

An examination of whether the *fatwa* issued by the Ayatollah Khomeini against Salman Rushdie for his writing of *Satanic Verses* should be considered a true *fatwa*.

1103 AZODANLOO, HEIDAR G. "Characteristics of Ayatullah Khomeini's Discourse and the Iraq-Iran War." *Orient* 34, no. 3 (September 1993): 403-420.

Through an analysis of Khomeini's religious and political discourse, the author illustrates how it was used to mobilize Iranians to fight against Iraq.

1104 _____. "Formalization of Friday Sermons and Consolidation of the Islamic Republic of Iran." *C* 1 (September 1992): 12-24.

This article focuses on the speech used by the religious and political figures of the Islamic Republic in their sermons during Friday services.

1105 BAKHASH, SHAUL. "After the Gulf War: Iran's Home Front." *WT* 45, no. 3 (March 1989): 46-48.

Seeks to answer whether the overthrow of the Pahlavi regime was in fact a true revolution and to discover the subsequent revolutionary changes. The author also offers prospects for the Islamic Republic after Khomeini.

1106 _____. "The Politics of Land, Law, and Social Justice in Iran." *Iran's Revolution: The Search for Consensus*, 27-47. Ed. R. K. Ramazani. Bloomington and Indianapolis and Washington, DC: Indiana University Press and Middle East Institute, 1990.

This chapter examines the application of Islamic law to public policy in post-revolutionary Iran. The article looks at matters that were problems for the leaders including: land reform, social justice, and the delineation of power in the upper echelons of the Islamic government.

1107 BANUAZIZI, ALI. "Iran's Revolutionary Impasse: Political Factionalism and Societal Resistance." *MERIP* 191 (November 1994): 2-8.

Examines the political situation in the Iranian Islamic Republic from two perspectives: that of state and society. Discusses the factionalism within the ruling political elite between the radicals and the conservatives as they vie for power. Also analyzes the resilience of various spheres of society in resisting officially sanctioned norms.

1108 BEEMAN, WILLIAM O. "Double Demons: Cultural Impedance in U.S.-Iranian Understanding." *Iran at the Crossroads: Global Relations in a Turbulent Decade*, 165-179. Ed. Miron Rezun. Boulder, CO: Westview Press, 1990.

Utilizing an anthropological and psychological perspective, this essay explores U.S.-Iranian relations and offers reasons for the great misunderstanding both countries demonstrate toward each other.

1109 BEHROOZ, MAZIAR. "Factionalism in Iran under Khomeini." *MES* 27, no. 4 (1991): 597-614.
Contends that during most of the Iran-Iraq war, foreign policy decisions in Iran were free of factionalism. With the cease-fire, factionalism reappeared with the introduction of a new third faction.

1110 BILL, JAMES A. "The United States and Iran: Mutual Mythologies." *MEP* 2, no. 3 (1993): 98-106.
Offers eight myths and counter-myths about perceptions of Iran today. The article provides an analysis of what is deemed as the reality of the situation.

1111 BINA, CYRUS. "Farewell to the Pax Americana: Iran, Political Islam, and the Passing of the Old Order." *Islam, Iran, and World Stability*, 41-74. Ed. Hamid Zangeneh. New York: St. Martin's Press, 1994.
Discusses the trend toward economic and political integration that has resulted from the end of the cold war. Author contends that Iran must be willing to become part of the global system if it is to survive as a state.

1112 BORGHEI, MOHAMMAD. "Iran's Religious Establishment: The Dialectics of Politicization." *Iran: Political Culture in the Islamic Republic*, 57-81. Eds. Samih K. Farsoun, and Mehrdad Mashayekhi. London and New York: Routledge, 1992.
Discusses the emergence of political Islam in Iran. The article focuses on activities at the Qom seminary in 1961-1963, affirming that the political nature of the seminary under Ayatollahs Shari'atmadari and Khomeini paved the way for the 1979 revolution.

1113 BOROUJERDI, MEHRZAD. "*Gharbzadegi*: The Dominant Intellectual Discourse of Pre- and Post-Revolutionary Iran." *Iran: Political Culture in the Islamic Republic*, 30-56. Eds. Samih K. Farsoun, and Mehrdad Mashayekhi. London and New York: Routledge, 1992.
Compares pre- and post-revolutionary discourse in Iran.

1114 CALABRESE, JOHN. "Iran II: The Damascus Connection." *WT* 46, no. 10 (October 1990): 188-190.
Second in a two-part series on Iran, this essay discusses the reasons for the Damascus-Tehran strategic relationship.

1115 CHEHABI, H. E. *Iranian Politics and Religious Modernism: The Liberation Movement of Iran Under the Shah and Khomeini*. Ithaca, NY: Cornell University Press, 1990.
This study demonstrates that the Liberation Movement of Iran led by Premier Bazargan was one of the most important historical factors which helped

facilitate the rise of an Iranian Islamic state. The author examines the ideological roots and the political activities of this modernist Islamic movement. Section one explores Iranian politics and the ideology of Iranian Islamic modernism. Sections two and three deal with the development and the political activities of the Liberation Movement of Iran.

1116 _____. "Religion and Politics in Iran: How Theocratic Is the Islamic Republic?" *DA* 120, no. 3 (June 1991): 69-91.
Offers a historical overview of the role of Islam and politics in the Pahlavi period and analyzes Iran's post-revolutionary attempts to create an Islamic state.

1117 CHELKOWSKI, PETER J. "In Ritual and Revolution: The Image in the Transformation of Iranian Culture." *Views* 10, no. 3 (March 1989): 7-11.
This article links Iranian photography--in the form of bank notes and stamps-- with Iranian culture as well as an examination of the use of photography in Iranian history.

1118 _____. "Khomeini's Iran as Seen Though Bank Notes." *The Iranian Revolution and the Muslim World*, 85-101. Ed. David Menashri. Boulder, CO: Westview Press, 1990.
Through a comparative analysis of the designs on Iranian bank notes in the Pahlavi and the Islamic Republic eras, this article seeks to illustrate how bank notes were used to propagate the new political ideology.

1119 CHUBIN, SHAHRAM. "Iran and the Gulf Crisis." *MEI* 7, no. 4 (December 1990): 30-35.
This article assesses how and in what areas Iran benefitted by the Gulf war and the destruction of Iraq.

1120 _____. "Iran and the War: From Stalemate to Cease-fire." *Iran at the Crossroads: Global Relations in a Turbulent Decade*, 131-145. Ed. Miron Rezun. Boulder, CO: Westview Press, 1990.
This chapter assesses the internal reasons that brought about an end to the nearly eight-year-old Iran-Iraq war.

1121 CLAWSON, PATRICK. "Iran after Khomeini: Weakened and Weary." *Orbis* 34, no. 2 (March 1990): 241-246.
First in a two-part series on Iran, the author discusses his perceptions of a weakened Islamic Republic after his visit to Iran.

1122   COTTAM, RICHARD. "Inside Revolutionary Iran." *Iran's Revolution: The Search for Consensus*, 3-26. Ed. R. K. Ramazani. Bloomington and Indianapolis: Indiana University Press, 1990.

This chapter examines the first decade following the Iranian Revolution and offers explanations for its success and failures.

1123   COTTAM, RICHARD W. "Charting Iran's New Course." *CH* 90, no. 552 (January 1991): 21-24, 36-37.

An exploration of the changes in economic policies and cultural attitudes of the first year of post-Khomeini Iran.

1124   DABASHI, HAMID. *Theology of Discontent: The Ideological Foundation of the Islamic Revolution in Iran*. New York: New York University Press, 1993.

A monumental monograph based on original sources analyzing the ideological foundation of the Iranian Islamic Revolution. The work examines eight Iranian intellectuals--four clerics and four laymen--in order to depict the wide spectrum of political dissent in Iran. Through the author's analysis of Iranian thinkers such as Jalal Al-e-Ahmad, Ali Shari'ati, Morteza Motahari and Ruhollah Khomeini the reader is able to gain an understanding of the diverse impulses which converged to overthrow the Pahlavi regime.

1125   DORRAJ, MANOCHEHR. "Populism and Corporatism in Post-Revolutionary Iranian Political Culture." *Iran: Political Culture in the Islamic Republic*, 214-233. Eds. Samih K. Farsoun, and Mehrdad Mashayekhi. London and New York: Routledge, 1992.

Assesses the role of populism and corporatism in Iranian political culture. The author states that the ruling clergy has tried to reign in populist fervor by synthesizing populism and Islamic corporatism.

1126   ENTESSAR, NADER. "Realpolitik and Transformation of Iran's Foreign Policy: Coping with the 'Iran Syndrome.'" *Islam, Iran, and World Stability*, 145-166. Ed. Hamid Zangeneh. New York: St. Martin's Press, 1994.

Discusses changes in Iran's foreign policy decisions since the death of the Ayatollah Khomeini. Due to Iran's conciliatory measures, argues for a more cooperative relations with the United States instead of the current "dual containment policy."

1127   ESPOSITO, JOHN L. "The Iranian Revolution: A Ten-Year Perspective." *The Iranian Revolution: Its Global Impact*, 17-39. Ed. John L. Esposito. Miami: Florida International University Press, 1990.

To gain a better understanding of the Iranian Islamic Republic, the implications of the Iranian revolution, political ideology, leadership, government institutions and domestic and foreign policy, this article offers a historical analysis of Iranian politics and society.

1128 _____. *The Iranian Revolution: Its Global Impact.* Miami: Florida International University Press, 1990.

The proceedings of an international conference on the global impact of the Iranian Revolution, seeks to offer insight into the following questions: Has the Revolution in Iran had an impact on other Islamic movements and if so to what extent? Why has Iran failed in its attempt to export its revolution? How deep has the Iranian revolution influenced political, economic and social conditions of other countries? The work is divided into five parts which deal with these questions in different regions. The first section is devoted to Iran and the implications of the Revolution. The second part deals with the countries of the Middle East and provides articles which analyze the impact of the Iranian Revolution on Iraq, the Arabian Peninsula and the Gulf States, Lebanon, Egypt, and Tunisia and Libya. Moving on to Southwest and Central Asia, this part is devoted to Afghanistan and Soviet Central Asia. Malaysia, Indonesia and the Philippines are discussed in the next section and the final portion of the book contains articles on the Sudan and Nigeria. The final chapter offers a review of the global impact of the Iranian revolution and a policy perspective.

1129 ESPOSITO, JOHN L. and JAMES P. PISCATORI. "The Global Impact of the Iranian Revolution: A Policy Perspective." *The Iranian Revolution: Its Global Impact*, 317-328. Ed. John L. Esposito. Miami: Florida International University Press, 1990.

Elaborates how fear of the export of the revolution has become the cornerstone of the West's foreign policy towards Iran. This has led to four major misconceptions of Iran in general and the Iranian revolution in particular. Also offers new perspectives for Western policy makers concerning Iran in light of new Iranian leadership.

1130 FARSOUN, SAMIH K. and MEHRDAD MASHAYEKHI. "Introduction: Iran's Political Culture." *Iran: Political Culture in the Islamic Republic*, 1-29. Eds. Samih K. Farsoun, and Mehrdad Mashayekhi. London and New York: Routledge, 1992.

This article describes what is meant by "political culture" and explains how it relates to the Islamic Republic of Iran.

1131 FARSOUN, SAMIH K. and MEHRDAD MASHAYEKHI, eds. *Iran: Political Culture in the Islamic Republic*, London and New York: Routledge, 1992.

A collection of articles which seek to understand how the Islamic Republic of Iran has managed to mobilize mass support, break down the political and social order of the Shah and create a new order. A group of social scientists offer studies which examine important aspects of the political culture of post-revolutionary Iran. This includes articles on the intellectual discourse before and after the revolution; the Iranian religious establishment; nationalism and political culture in Iran; the Islamic Constitution and issues of popular sovereignty and the separation of religion and state; the Islamization of Iranian film; populism and corporatism in Iranian political culture and Iranian-US relations.

1132 FISCHER, MICHAEL and MEHDI ABEDI. "Iranian Revolutionary Posters." *MERIP* 159 (July 1989): 29-32.
   This essay explores the representations of the Islamic Republic through their revolutionary posters.

1133 FISCHER, MICHAEL M. J. "Legal Postulates in Flux: Justice, Wit, and Hierarchy in Iran." *Law and Islam in the Middle East*, 115-142. Ed. Daisy Hilse Dwyer. New York: Bergin & Garvey, 1990.
   Offers a historical, sociological and philosophical analysis of the competing legal reform measures between secularists and religious clerics in Iran over the past century. This essay provides eight case studies of conflict resolution under the Pahlavi regime.

1134 FISCHER, MICHAEL M. J. and MEHDI ABEDI. *Debating Muslims: Cultural Dialogues in Postmodernity and Tradition*. Madison: University of Wisconsin Press, 1990.
   A collection of seven essays by two anthropologists about Islam in general and Shi'ism in particular using recent scholarship on Islamic societies. In order to bring verbal articulations of Muslims to the reader, the authors have drawn on insights from feminism, post-structuralism, Marxism, and post-modernism to deconstruct stereotypical Orientalist ideas. In the essays the anthropologists acquaint the reader with Islamic argumentation, an intercultural dialogue between Shi'ism, Baha'ism and Zoroastrianism, the varying traditions of Qur'anic exegesis, and the contemporary Islamist ideology of Khomeini and his followers. In addition the work seeks to locate Shi'ism territorially to allow the readers to hear the voices of those who are politically marginalized in Iran and the United States.

1135 FORAN, JOHN. "The Iranian Revolution and the Study of Discourses: A Comment on Moaddel." *C* 4 (1994): 51-60.
   Offers a critique of Mansoor Moaddel's book *Class, Politics, and Ideology in the Iranian Revolution*.

1136 FULLER, GRAHAM E. "War and Revolution in Iran." *CH* 88, no. 535 (February 1989): 81-84, 99-100.

An examination of Iran's future following the Iran-Iraq war and the impact of accepting the cease-fire on the Islamic revolution.

1137 GERAMI, SHAHIN. "Religious Fundamentalism as a Response to Foreign Dependency: The Case of the Iranian Revolution." *SC* 36, no. 4 (1989): 451-467.

This essay surveys the historical integration of Iran into the international market system and the development of the revolutionary movement.

1138 GREEN, JERROLD D. "Ideology and Pragmatism in Iranian Foreign Policy." *JSAMES* 17, no. 1 (1993): 57-75.

Contends that Iran's foreign policy decisions were often influenced by a mix of Islamic ideology and pure pragmatism--"an essence of politics."

1139 _____. "Iran's Foreign Policy: Between Enmity and Conciliation." *CH* 92, no. 570 (January 1993): 12-16.

This article explores Iran's foreign policy, noting the Islamic Republic's concerns as well as delineating its two-pronged policies in dealing with its neighbors.

1140 GURDON, CHARLES. "Iran and the West: Who's Threatening Who?" *JIMEE* 21 (1993): 67-79.

Analyzes whether Iran is truly a threat to the West or if it is a victim of Western "double standards."

1141 HAGHAYEGHI, MEHRDAD. "Politics and Ideology in the Islamic Republic of Iran." *MES* 29, no. 1 (1993): 36-52.

An exploration of the process of political and ideological Islamization in post-revolutionary Iran is the focus of this article. The author discusses three components of this process: education policies, the media, and institutional policies.

1142 HALLIDAY, FRED. "The Revolution's First Decade." *MERIP* 156 (January 1989): 19-21.

Discusses the direction Iran took ten years after the revolution.

1143 HARNEY, DESMOND. "The Iranian Revolution Tens Years On." *AA* 20, no. 2 (1989): 153-164.

Notes that the Iranian revolution, albeit a true revolution, has failed to have a major impact on the rest of the world that the French and Russian revolution did.

1144 HIRO, DILIP. "Iran in the 1990's." *MEI* 7, no. 2&3 (1990): 44-46.

This essay examines Iran's domestic policies and its relations with its neighbors under the leadership of President Rafsanjani. Also looks at Iran's future short-term prospects.

1145 HOOGLAND, ERIC. "The Islamic Republic at War and Peace." *MERIP* 156 (January 1989): 4-12.

This article examines Iran's objectives and actions during the Iran-Iraq war; reasons for its acceptance of the cease-fire; and the reconstruction efforts that followed.

1146 HOSSEINI, HAMID. "The Change of Economic and Industrial Policy in Iran: President Rafsanjani's Perestroika." *Islam, Iran, and World Stability*, 167-186. Ed. Hamid Zangeneh. New York: St. Martin's Press, 1994.

Analyzes changes in the Iranian economic structure following the 1979 revolution which include the nationalization of private industries and banks and a ban of foreign investment. The author contends that this structure was created out of political expediency and was not an attempt to adhere to Islamic economic principles.

1147 HUNTER, SHIREEN T. *Iran after Khomeini*. New York: Praeger, 1992.

This work examines the fate of the Iranian Revolution following the death of the Ayatollah Khomeini in 1989. The author begins by discussing the Iranian constitution first written in 1979 and subsequently revised following Khomeini's death. The second chapter offers information on the size and nature of the military. The work then provides an overview of the Iranian economy in the 1980's and the problems it faces in the 1990's and Iranian foreign policy in the post-Khomeini era. The author concludes by asserting that due to the pressing problems in the political system, the economy and foreign relations, the Islamic Republic has no choice other than to reform itself and head down a more pragmatic path. This process, the writer believes, has already begun and will continue under the more moderate wing lead by President Rafsanjani.

1148 _____. "Iran and the Arab World." *Iran at the Crossroads: Global Relations in a Turbulent Decade*, 97-114. Ed. Miron Rezun. Boulder, CO: Westview Press, 1990.

The author analyzes Iran's relations with various Arab regimes throughout the Iran-Iraq war and contends that interaction between Iran and her Arab neighbors has remained remarkably the same.

1149 _____. "Iran and the Soviets: The Chill Is Gone." *MEI* 7, no. 1 (January 1990): 17-23.

This essay assesses Iranian-Soviet relations in light of domestic factors and strategic interests of both nations.

1150 _____. *Iran and the World: Continuity in a Revolutionary Decade.* Bloomington and Indianapolis: Indiana University Press, 1990.

Examines Iran's foreign policy of the first decade since the revolution. Seeks to discover whether the Islamic Republic's foreign policy has been shaped purely by Islamic ideology or whether other international, regional, domestic, and historical variables have contributed to foreign policy decisions. Chapters provide a historical background on Iranian pre-revolutionary diplomacy as well as an analysis of Iran's Islamic worldview and its influence on the Republic's foreign policy. The work then offers studies of Iran's relation with its neighbors, the Arab world, Iraq, the United States, the Soviet Union, and other Third World countries.

1151 _____. "Iran, the Middle East, and the New World Order." *Iran, the Middle East, and the Decade of the 1990's*, 13-21. Montclair State College: Upper Montclair, New Jersey, 25 October 1991.

Proceedings of a one-day conference sponsored by the Department of Economic and Finance School of Business Administration. This paper seeks to define the buzzword "New World Order," the new emerging order, impact of recent changes on the international system and the implications for Iran and the Middle East.

1152 _____. "Post-Khomeini Iran." *FA* 68, no. 5 (December 1989): 133-149.

With the death of Khomeini, the article argues improvements in U.S.-Iranian relations will depend on the current domestic trends in Iran under Rafsanjani. Reassesses the premises of U.S. policy towards the Islamic Republic.

1153 _____. "Soviet-Iranian Relations in the Post-Revolution Period." *Iran's Revolution: The Search for Consensus*, 85-103. Ed. R. K. Ramazani. Bloomington and Indianapolis; Washington, DC: Indiana University Press; Middle East Institute, 1990.

This chapter relates how Iran's relations with the superpowers was said to be characterized by the slogan "Neither East Nor West," yet Iran seemed to challenge the West more than the East. The article asserts that, apart from the United States, Iran did not let the challenge harm its economic relations with the West. The author explains how Soviet-Iranian relations have been much closer and were driven by a unique relationship, geographical proximity, and a much stronger and vastly overwhelming Soviet military superiority.

1154 IWAI, HIDEKO. "Wilayah and State: In the Case of the Islamic Republic of Iran." *Nature of the Islamic Community*, 167-189. Eds. Toshio Kuroda, and Richard I. Lawless. Tokyo: Keiso Shobo Publishing Co., 1993.

Attempts to analyze the concept of *wilayat al-faqih* (the guardianship of the jurisconsult) from an Islamic perspective and discusses its significance to the people of Iran.

1155. No entry.

1156 JAHANPOUR, FARHANG. "Iran after Khomeini." *WT* 45, no. 8-9 (August 1989): 150-152.
    This essay discusses the impact of Khomeini on Iran and the difficult transition period after he died.

1157 _____. "Iran I: Wars Among the Heirs." *WT* 46, no. 10 (October 1990): 183-187.
    The first in a two-part series on Iran, this article relates the power struggle that occurred in Iran directly following the death of Ayatollah Khomeini. Also discusses the Iran-Iraq peace talks after the Iraqi invasion of Kuwait, Iran's role in securing the release of Western hostages in Lebanon and the repercussions of the Rushdie affair in Iran's relations with Britain.

1158 _____. "The Roots of the Hostage Crisis." *WT* 48, no. 2 (February 1992): 33-36.
    The involvement of Iran in the Western hostage crisis in Lebanon is the focus of this essay.

1159 KAPUR, ASHOK. "Relations With Pakistan and India." *Iran at the Crossroads: Global Relations in a Turbulent Decade*, 71-80. Ed. Miron Rezun. Boulder, CO: Westview Press, 1990.
    This chapter assesses Iran's foreign policy relations with Pakistan and India in light of the impact of the Iranian revolution as well as regional and global influences.

1160 KATZMAN, KENNETH. *The Warriors of Islam: Iran's Revolutionary Guard*. Boulder, CO: Westview Press, 1993.
    This book examines the role of the Islamic Revolutionary Guard Corps in Iranian society. Created after the 1979 revolution to support the clergy's consolidation of power, the revolutionary guard has developed into a powerful player in Iranian society and politics. The revolutionary guard has assumed the role of guardian of the revolution. As such, it has developed into an organized military; a monitor of the implementation of Islamic law; and a tool for exporting the Iranian revolution. The author argues that although the guard has become institutionalized in Iranian society, it has maintained its ideological radicalism.

1161 KAVOOSSI, MASOUD. "Labor Relations in Iran: The Islamic challenge." *MEI* 7, no. 2 & 3 (1990): 71-75.

This essay explores the Iranian state's relations with its industrial labor workers and shows the dilemma the government faces as it tries to Islamicize the system while increasing productivity.

1162 KAZEMI, FARHAD. "Religious Factionalism and Politics in Iran and Its Impacts in the Region." *Iran, the Middle East, and the Decade of the 1990's*, 7-11. Montclair State College: Upper Montclair, New Jersey, 1991.

The proceedings of a one-day conference sponsored by the Department of Economics and Finance School of Business Administration at Montclair State College. Categorizes the four different versions of Islamic politics that emerged during the revolution as the radical Islam of Ali Shari'ati, the militant Islam of Ayatollah Khomeini, the liberal Islam of Mehdi Bazargan, and the traditional Islam of the majority of the *ulama*. Briefly examines their perspectives on political Islam, the economy, and foreign policy dimensions.

1163 KAZEMI, FARHAD and JO-ANNE HART. "The Shi'i Praxis: Domestic Politics and Foreign Policy in Iran." *The Iranian Revolution and the Muslim World*, 58-72. Ed. David Menashri. Boulder, CO: Westview Press, 1990.

Examines the interplay between foreign policy concerns, such as the export of the revolution and domestic constraints.

1164 KEDDIE, NIKKI. "Reflections on the Influence of the Iranian Revolution." *Iran, the Middle East, and the Decade of the 1990's*, 33-37. Montclair State College: Upper Montclair, New Jersey, 1991.

Briefly outlines some of the major influences of the Iranian Revolution including the different degrees of influence between Sunni and Shi'i Muslims.

1165 KEDDIE, NIKKI R. "Why Iran Has Been Revolutionary." *Reconstruction and Regional Diplomacy in the Persian Gulf*, 19-32. Eds. Hooshang and N. Entessar Amirahmadi. London and New York: Routledge Press, 1992.

This article analyzes the Iranian revolution from a historical perspective, arguing that the 1979 revolution was not a unique situation but a continuation of revolts against foreign domination.

1166 KEDDIE, NIKKI R. and FARAH MONIAN. "Militancy and Religion in Contemporary Iran." *Fundamentalisms and the State: Remaking Polities, Economies, and Militance*, 511-538. Eds. Martin E. Marty, and R. Scott Appleby. Chicago and London: The University of Chicago Press, 1991.

Examines militant Shi'i Islamism in modern Iran. Discusses the role of the Fida'iyan-i Islam in post-World War II Iran, the Mujahidin-i Khalq, Khomeini, the formation of modern revolutionary discourse, militant actions exhibited during the revolution, the post-revolutionary period, and the movement towards accommodation by Iranian leadership.

1167 KHARRAZI, KAMAL. "Iran and Islamic Revivalism." *MEI* 9, no. 4 (May 1993): 17-19.

A special address presented at a symposium convened by *Middle East Insight* magazine by Iran's permanent representative to the United Nations. Discusses the relationship between Islamic resurgence and the Iranian Islamic Republic based on the premise that the Iranian revolution was part of, as well as an impetus for, the ongoing global Islamic revival.

1168 KIMMEL, MICHAEL. "'New Prophets' and 'Old Ideals': Charisma and Tradition in the Iranian Revolution." *SC* 36, no. 4 (1989): 491-510.

Through a Weberian paradigm of charisma, this essay explores Ayatollah Khomeini's charisma and its influence and impact on his followers in Iran.

1169 _____. "Religion and Revolution in Iran." *SC* 36, no. 4 (1989): 411-413.

Notes the role that religion played in the Iranian revolution, argues that this lent the revolution a very different character than that of previous revolutions.

1170 KNYSH, ALEXANDER. "Irfan Revisited: Khomeini and the Legacy of Islamic Mystical Philosophy." *MEJ* 46 #4, no. Autumn (1992): 631-653.

This essay traces the religious studies of the Ayatollah Khomeini and examines his views on Islamic mysticism. The author contends that Khomeini's views on *irfan* (gnosis) were strongly influenced by Ibn Arabi.

1171 KRAMER, MARTIN. "Khomeini's Messengers: The Disputed Pilgrimage of Islam." *Religious Radicalism & Politics in the Middle East*, 177-194. Eds. Emmanuel Sivan, and Menachem Freidman. Albany: State University of New York Press, 1990.

Through an examination of the Muslim pilgrimage to Mecca and the riots that occurred in 1987, this chapter explores the conflict between the Sunnis and the Shi'a as well as current politics that both Saudis and Iranians bring to the pilgrimage.

1172 KUPCHAN, CHARLES A. "And Ready to Talk." *Orbis* 34, no. 2 (March 1990): 256-251.

Second in a two-part series on Iran, this article discusses Iran's attempts to reach out to the international community based on the author's trip to the country.

1173 LINABURY, GEORGE. "Ayatollah Khomeini's Islamic Legacy." *Reconstruction and Regional Diplomacy in the Persian Gulf*, 33-44. Eds. Hooshang and N. Entessar Amirahmadi. London and New York: Routledge Press, 1992.

This article examines Ayatollah Khomeini's legacy both in Iran and throughout the Muslim world. Internally, Khomeini has succeeded in re-institutionalizing Islam, while externally Khomeini had restored pride among Muslims.

1174 MALEK, M. "The Impact of Iran's Islamic Revolution on Health Personnel Policy." *WD* 19, no. 8 (August 1991):

The author attempts to pinpoint the number of health professionals who left Iran following the Revolution. Analyzing the regime's reaction to the "brain drain" in this sector, the work finds that the policies adopted have had a limited influence in "Islamizing" trends.

1175 MALEK, MOHAMMED H. "Elite Factionalism in the Post-Revolutionary Iran." *JCA* 19, no. 4 (1989): 435-460.

Sheds light on the development of the state in Iran since the revolution focusing on different stages of elite conflict and the class and religious roots of this competition.

1176 MARTIN, VANESSA. *Islam and Modernism: The Iranian Revolution of 1906.* London: I.B. Tauris, 1989.

A detailed chronological study of the role of the ulama in Tehran from the late 1890's to the summer of 1909 when a new constitutional order was established. Drawing upon a wide mixture of sources--newspapers, British diplomatic reports, European and Iranian histories of the constitutional revolution, memoirs and pamphlets--the author analyzes the goals, ideology and political affiliations of the leading Iranian ulama of the time. In this detailing, the author places the ulama within their wider class structure as well as examining the wide range of political debates between the clerics as they influenced the revolutionary process.

1177 _____. "Religion and State in Khumaini's *Kashf al-asrar.*" *BSOAS* 55, no. 1 (1993): 34-45.

Examines Khomeini's first major political work "The Revealing of Secrets" published in 1943 to discern some of Khomeini's early concepts concerning the role of religion in political matters.

1178 MASHAYEKHI, MEHRDAD. "The Politics of Nationalism and Political Culture." *Iran: Political Culture in the Islamic Republic*, 82-115. Eds. Samih K. Farsoun, and Mehrdad Mashayekhi. London and New York: Routledge, 1992.

Argues that immediately following the revolution the socialists and the Islamists both vied for political hegemony. The article focuses on the political shortcomings of the Iranian socialist movement, which paved the way for the rule of the clergy.

1179   MENASHRI, DAVID. "The Domestic Power Struggle and the Fourth Iranian Majlis Elections." *Orient* 33, no. 3 (September 1992): 387-407.

Through an analysis of the Fourth Majlis elections in Iran, this study explores the political rivalries within Iran and political challenges facing the ruling elite.

1180   _____. *Education and the Making of Modern Iran*. New York and London: Cornell University Press, 1992.

Examines Iranian education and the role it has played in social, economic and political change in the past two centuries. Focuses primarily on higher education although it does pay attention to primary and secondary schooling. The work is divided into three sections; the first analyzes education under the Qajars. This is followed with a study of the educational process during the Pahlavi era, and the final portion discusses educational development since the Islamic revolution. The author examines the tensions between those promoting secular education and the religious establishment.

1181   _____. *Iran: A Decade of War and Revolution*. New York and London: Holmes & Meier Publishers, 1990.

This work contains articles that were formerly published in the *Middle East Contemporary Survey* which offers an annual analysis of the political, economic, military and foreign policy developments in Iran. The author provides an overview of the Islamic republic beginning with the years 1977-1978 in which the roots of discontent are explored. A yearly update of the situation is provided focusing on such issues as the seizure of power; the consolidation of power; internal factionalism and popular discontent; the domestic impact of the Iran-Iraq war; Islamization of the administration; foreign policy decisions and implications. The last two chapters evaluate the changes in the post-Khomeini years and a postscript on the first ten years of the Islamic revolution.

1182   _____. "Khomeini's Vision: Nationalism or World Order?" *The Iranian Revolution and the Muslim World*, 40-57. Ed. David Menashri. Boulder, CO: Westview Press, 1990.

Provides an analysis of the reasons for change from an Iranian nationalist outlook to an Islamic vision and eventually the return once again to an Iranian patriotic national policy.

1183   MESBAHI, MOHIADDIN. "Gorbachev's New Thinking and Islamic Iran: From Containment to Reconciliation." *Iran: Political Culture in the Islamic*

Republic, 260-296. Eds. Samih K. Farsoun, and Mehrdad Mashayekhi. London and New York: Routledge, 1992.

Traces Iranian-Soviet relations during the war between Iran and Iraq. The chapter also examines the impact Islamic revivalism in the Caucasus and Central Asia have had on relations between Tehran and Moscow.

1184 MILANI, MOHSEN. "The Ascendence of Shi'i Fundamentalism in Revolutionary Iran." *JSAMES* 13, no. 1-2 (1989): 5-28.

Explains how the fundamentalists in Iran defeated their opponents in six stages and created a theocratic state.

1185 MILANI, MOHSEN M. "The Evolution of the Iranian Presidency: From Bani Sadr to Rafsanjani." *BJMES* 20, no. 1 (1993): 83-97.

Traces the changes that have taken place in the office of the Iranian presidency since the revolution to better understand Iran's factional politics.

1186 _____. *The Making of Iran's Islamic Revolution: From Monarchy to Islamic Republic*. Boulder, CO: Westview Press, 1994.

This expanded and fully revised second edition provides insight into the Islamic revolution and the ensuing happenings. Drawing upon interviews with Iranian officials and unreleased documents, the author offers a detailed analysis of the internal factionalism in the Islamic Republic. Looks at the events leading up to the American hostage taking; Khomeini's life and work; Rafsanjani's political activism during the Shah's reign and recent reforms. Also deals with Iran's foreign policy relations following the collapse of the Soviet Union.

1187 _____. "Shi'ism and the State in the Constitution of the Islamic Republic of Iran." *Iran: Political Culture in the Islamic Republic*, 133-159. Eds. Samih K. Farsoun, and Mehrdad Mashayekhi. London and New York: Routledge, 1992.

Compares the Islamic Constitution of 1979 with the 1906-7 Iranian Constitution, examining the relationship between religion and state. Argues that the 1979 constitution has permanently ended the conflict between civil and Islamic law by formally subordinating the state to Shi'i law.

1188 _____. "The Transformation of the Valayat-e Faqih Institution: From Khomeini to Khameini." *MW* 82, no. 3-4 (1992): 175-190.

Examines the changes in the concept of the Guardianship of the Jurisconsult in Iran.

1189 _____. "US Foreign Policy and the Islamic Revolution." *Reconstruction and Regional Diplomacy in the Persian Gulf*, 237-259. Eds. H. and N. Entessar Amirahmadi. London and New York: Routledge Press, 1992.

Following the overthrow of the Shah and the taking of American hostages, U.S.-Iranian relations had reached an all time low. This chapter contends that Washington's hard-line stance against Khomeini served to strengthen the hand of Iranian radicals while weakening the position of the moderates.

1190 MOHADDESSIN, MOHAMMAD. *Islamic Fundamentalism: The New Global Threat*. Washington D.C.: Seven Locks Press, 1993.

Written by a ranking member of the People's Mojahedin of Iran, *Islamic Fundamentalism* seeks to explore the Ayatollah Khomeini's form of Islamic fundamentalism. The work offers an account of the history of fundamentalism along with explanations for its appeal. The author then discusses the theory of *velayat-e-faqih* (the guardianship of the jurisconsult), the Iranian constitution, and the post-Khomeinin regime. Other chapters include essays on Iranian foreign policy and Iran's export of the Revolution as well as a comparative look at the goals and ideology of the Mojahedin and the Islamic Republic.

1191 MOHSENI, NAVID. "Towards an Understanding of Intellectuals." *C* 1 (September 1992): 38-53.

This article applies an analytical framework to understanding the role of Iranian intellectuals on various levels of political and social change.

1192 NAFICY, HAMID. "Islamizing Film Culture in Iran." *Iran: Political Culture in the Islamic Republic*, 178-213. Eds. Samih K. Farsoun, and Mehrdad Mashayekhi. London and New York: Routledge, 1992.

Analyzes the process of Islamizing the film industry in Iran after the creation of the Islamic Republic. This process included restricting the importation of foreign films, censorship, and the creation of studios to produce Islamic films.

1193 NAFISI, RASOOL. "Education and the Culture of Politics in the Islamic Republic of Iran." *Iran: Political Culture in the Islamic Republic*, 160-177. Eds. Samih K. Farsoun, and Mehrdad Mashayekhi. London and New York: Routledge, 1992.

Compares the Iranian education system under the Pahlavi regime to that introduced by the Islamic Republic. Discusses why the Islamization of curriculum and the emphasis on Islamic values was a primary goal of the new regime.

1194 NETZER, AMNON. "Islam in Iran: Search for Identity." *The Crescent in the East*, 5-22. Ed. Raphael Israeli. London: Curzon Press Ltd., 1989.

This article outlines the significance of the Iranian Islamic Republic.

1195 NOORBAKSH, MEHDI. "The Middle East, Islam and the United States: The Special Case of Iran." *MEP* 2, no. 3 (1993): 78-97.

Using Iran as a case study, the article asserts that the U.S. government has preoccupied itself with the threat of Islamic fundamentalism and in turn has been blinded to the diversity in Islam and those Islamic movements which have encouraged moderation, reform, and legitimate change of existing political structures.

1196 OMID, HOMA. *Islam and the Post-Revolutionary State in Iran*. London: St. Martin's Press, 1994.

The author contends in this work that the Iranian revolution has failed to live up to the ideals of the Shi'i revolutionaries and Shi'i religious beliefs. As a result, Iran has been left with an inefficient administration, a long eight-year war in which many Iranians were killed, a less educated, poorer, and growing population and women in a more oppressed position than in previous times. From this viewpoint, the writer analyzes issues such as the *ulama*, the bureaucracy, the political theory of *Valayat-e-faqih*, internal opposition, the Iran-Iraq war, culture and education, women and the economy in post-revolutionary Iran.

1197 PARSA, MISAGH. *Social Origins of the Iranian Revolution*. New Brunswick, NJ: Rutgers University Press, 1989.

This work provides a detailed explanation of the social origins of the Iranian revolution. The author begins the book by introducing a theory of the cause and effects of revolutions and then proceeds to analyze the 1979 Iranian revolution within the context of this theory. Focus on the role various Iranian social groups and classes played before, during, and after the revolution. The author places particular emphasis on the ability of these groups to mobilize. The first chapter is a critique of different explanations of the causes for the revolution and the introduction of his own theory. Chapter two traces political conflicts in modern Iranian history. The third chapter analyzes the economic policies of the Pahlavi regime. Chapters four through seven discuss how different Iranian groups confronted the state. Chapter eight describes the final days of the conflict and the final two chapters analyze the political outcome of the revolution.

1198 PARVIN, MANOUCHER and MOSTAFA VAZIRI. "Islamic Man and Society in the Islamic Republic." *Iran: Political Culture in the Islamic Republic*, 116-132. Eds. Samih K. Farsoun, and Mehrdad Mashayekhi. London and New York: Routledge, 1992.

An assessment of the ideology of the Islamic Republic with respect to three aspects: the restoration of economic justice; the implementation of divine rule; and the creation of an Islamic society.

1199　PIPES, DANIEL. "The Ayatollah, the Novelist, and the West." *Com* 87, no. 6 (June 1989): 9-17.
　　　Explores the implications of the Salman Rushdie affair.

1200　PIPES, DANIEL and PATRICK CLAWSON. "Ambitious Iran, Troubled Neighbors." *FA* 72, no. 1 (1992): 124-41.
　　　Discusses the growing role of Iran in the region once its neighbor Iraq had been weakened by the Gulf war.

1201　POYA, MARYAM. "The Gulf War and Ideology: the Double-edged Sword of Islam." *The Gulf War and the New World Order*, 91-103. Eds. Haim Bresheeth, and Nira Yuval-Davis. London and New Jersey: Zed Books Ltd, 1991.
　　　Looks at how Iran maneuvered during the Gulf war by "adopting a pragmatic approach to encourage foreign capital."

1202　RAHNEMA, ALI and FARHAD NOMANI. *The Secular Miracle: Religion, Politics and Economic Policy in Iran*. London: Zed Books, 1990.
　　　This book provides a detailed account of political factionalism within Iran following the 1979 revolution and the role that Islam played in this struggle. The authors contend that different factions interpreted Shi'i Islam in a way that would best serve their political interests. The authors also show how underlying rivalries within the country influenced economic, political, and foreign policies.

1203　RAJAEE, FARHANG. "Iranian Ideology and Worldview: The Cultural Export of the Revolution." *The Iranian Revolution: Its Global Impact*, 63-80. Ed. John L. Esposito. Miami: Florida International University Press, 1990.
　　　Examines the characteristics of Iran's policy of 'export of the revolution.' Looks at how this ideology is and has been influenced by domestic realities and assesses whether goals have been met.

1204　_____. "Islam and Modernity: The Reconstruction of an Alternate Shi'ite Worldview in Iran." *Fundamentalisms and Society: Reclaiming the Sciences, the Family, and Education*, 103-128. Eds. Martin E. Marty, and R. Scott Appleby. The Fundamentalist Project, 2. Chicago and London: The University of Chicago Press, 1991.
　　　Examines the way in which Iranian Shi'ite activists seek to preserve their Muslim identity in an increasingly global world that has influenced all areas of society including science and technology. Discussing the interaction between modernity and Shi'ite ideology as well as the modification and adjustments resulting from the realities of everyday life. Offers an analysis of the perspectives of Iranian thinkers on science, technology and industry.

1205 _____. "The Political Relevance of the Intellectual Debates in Post-Revolutionary Iran." *Orient* 35, no. 2 (June 1994): 289-302.

This article examines intellectual debates in Iranian politics, their primary issues and goals, and how domestic and international events have shaped them.

1206 RAM, HAGGAY. "Crushing the Opposition: Adversaries of the Islamic Republic of Iran." *MEJ* 46, no. 3 (June 1992): 426-439.

Through an examination of the political "rhetoric" of the Iranian government in the Friday sermons, this article looks at how the leadership justified using a "scorched-earth" policy to silence its opposition in the first decade following the revolution.

1207 _____. "Islamic 'Newspeak': Language and Change in Revolutionary Iran." *MES* 29, no. 2 (April 1993): 198-219.

An exploration of the use of Islamic terms in political rhetoric in order to enhance the legitimacy of the Islamic Republic is the focus of this article.

1208 RAMAZANI, R. K. "Iran's Foreign Policy: Both North and South." *MEJ* 46, no. 3 (June 1992): 393-412.

The author focuses on the change in Iran's foreign policy theme "Neither East, nor West," to what the author terms "Both North and South."

1209 _____, ed. *Iran's Revolution: The Search for Consensus*, Bloomington and Indianapolis: Indiana University Press, 1990.

This edited volume of essays, the majority of which appeared in the 1989 issue of Middle East Journal, examines Iran's Islamic revolution and the implications for the region.

1210 _____. "Iran's Export of the Revolution: Politics, Ends, and Means." *The Iranian Revolution: Its Global Impact*, 40-62. Ed. John L. Esposito. Miami: Florida International University Press, 1990.

Probes the various aspects of the term 'export of the revolution' in Iranian foreign policy. Includes an examination of the political atmosphere in which the term emerged, the desired outcome of the export of the revolution including an analysis of Ayatollah Khomeini's political philosophy and the impact of Iranian-Islamic political tradition, and methods used by the Islamic Republic to achieve this goal.

1211 _____. "Iran's Foreign Policy: Contending Orientations." *The Search for Consensus*, 48-68. Ed. R. K. Ramazani. Bloomington and Indianapolis: Indiana University Press, 1990.

Explores Iran's foreign policy and demonstrates how it has been shaped by the interaction between domestic realities and the external environment.

1212 REZUN, MIRON. "The Internal Struggle, the Rushdie Affair, and the Prospects for the Future." *Iran at the Crossroads: Global Relations in a Turbulent Decade*, 201-218. Ed. Miron Rezun. Boulder, CO: Westview Press, 1990.

Examines the role that the Rushdie Affair plays in any assessment of Iranian foreign and domestic policy.

1213 _____, ed. *Iran at the Crossroads: Global Relations in a Turbulent Decade*. Boulder, CO: Westview Press, 1990.

This edited volume of articles is concerned with Iran's foreign policy since the Iranian Revolution. The first two chapters offer differing perspectives on Iranian foreign policy. Chapter three deals with Iran's relationship with Pakistan and India. A political comparison of Iran and Turkey is given in the fourth chapter. The next article details the considerable changes in the relationships between the Islamic Republic and Arab States. Chapter six explores Iran's relations with Israel, Lebanon and Syria. Causal factors of Iran-Iraq war as well as the Iranian leadership during the war is discussed. Chapter eight offers a historiographical survey of some of the better works written on the Iran-Iraq war. The next two articles discuss Iranian-US and Iranian-Soviet relations. The final chapter examines internal fighting and the Rushdie affair as well as Iran's prospects for the future.

1214 _____. "The 'Pariah' Syndrome: The Complexities of the Iranian Predicament." *Iran at the Crossroads: Global Relations in a Turbulent Decade*, 9-34. Ed. Miron Rezun. Boulder, CO: Westview Press, 1990.

This essay looks at the reasons behind Iran's foreign policy and discusses the role that Western and regional powers had in influencing Iranian foreign policy considerations.

1215 RICKS, THOMAS. "Power Politics and Political Culture: US-Iran Relations." *Iran: Political Culture in the Islamic Republic*, 234-261. Eds. Samih K. Farsoun, and Mehrdad Mashayekhi. London and New York: Routledge, 1992.

Analyzes the strains that led to the severing of U.S.-Iran relations.

1216 RIESEBRODT, MARTIN. *Pious Passion: The Emergence of Modern Fundamentalism in the United States and Iran*. Berkeley: University of California Press, 1993.

Provides comparative research on the fundamentalist movements in the United States and Iran. Includes a chapter on the origins, causes, and ideology of Shi'i fundamentalism in Iran.

1217 ROSE, GREGORY F. "Shi'i Islam: Bonyadgiri or Fundamentalism." *Religious Resurgence and Politics in the Modern World*, 219-228. Ed. Emile Sahliyeh. Albany, NY: State University of New York Press, 1990.

Discusses Islamic revivalism in Iran and asserts that Shi'i Islam is an excellent vehicle for political mobilization and can act as a force for modernization.

1218 SAFFARI, SAID. "The Legitimation of the Clergy's Right to Rule in the Iranian Constitution of 1979." *BJMES* 20, no. 1 (1993): 64-82.

Illustrates how the theory of the guardianship of the jurisconsult of the Ayatollah Khomeini became institutionalized in the early days of the revolution.

1219 SAIKAL, AMIN. "The West and Post-Khomeini Iran." *WT* 49, no. 10 (October 1993): 197-200.

An examination of U.S. foreign policy decisions influenced by a fear of an Islamic fundamentalist threat is the thesis of this essay.

1220 SARABI, FARZIN. "The Post-Khomeini Era in Iran: The Elections of the Fourth Islamic Majlis." *MEJ* 48, no. 1 (December 1994): 89-107.

Describes the 1992 fourth Islamic majlis elections in Iran. Examines the political structure of the Majlis and its post-Khomeini organization. Provides a summary of the relations between President Rafsanjani and the third term majlis. Details 'weapons of disqualification,' a number of electoral laws and the resulting victory of Rafsanjani supporters.

1221 SAVORY, ROGER M. "The Export of Ithna Ashari Shi'ism: Historical and Ideological Background." *The Iranian Revolution and the Muslim World*, 13-39. Ed. David Menashri. Boulder, CO: Westview Press, 1990.

Looking at the case of the Iranian revolution, this article seeks to discover whether the Ithna Ashari Shi'i tradition is inherently militant or quietist in nature. It explores the political question of whether Ithna Ashari Shi'ism rejects earthly power or is subjugated to it. The author also examines the play between Iranian nationalism and Shi'i Islamic history.

1222 _____. "Islam and Democracy: The Case of the Islamic Republic of Iran." *The Islamic World: From Classical to Modern Times*, 821-843. Eds. C. E. Bosworth, Charles Issawi, Roger Savory, and A.L.Udovitch. Princeton, NJ: The Darwin Press, Inc., 1989.

Through a case study of the Islamic Republic of Iran, this chapter addresses the topic of the compatibility of Islam and democracy.

1223 _____. "Religious Dogma and the Economic and Political Imperatives of Iranian Foreign Policy." *Iran at the Crossroads: Global Relations in a*

Turbulent Decade, 35-67. Ed. Miron Rezun. Boulder, CO: Westview Press, 1990.

This article examines Iranian foreign policy and asserts that it is based on unrealistic policies and is an antithesis to international policies.

1224 SCHAHGALDIAN, NIKOLA B. "Iran after Khomeini." *CH* 89 (1990): 61-64, 36-37.

An assessment of post-Khomeini Iran and the stability of the new government is the central focus of this article.

1225 SHOJAI, SIAMACK. "Iran in Global Perspective." *Islam, Iran, and World Stability*, 135-144. Ed. Hamid Zangeneh. New York: St. Martin's Press, 1994.

This article examines Iran's place in the new global order through an analysis of its policy decisions.

1226 SIAVOSHI, SUSSAN. "Factionalism and Iranian Politics: The Post-Khomeini Experience." *IrSt* 25, no. 3-4 (1992): 27-49.

Argues that viewing the Iranian political scene as only divided into two camps is misleading and describes the different factions that currently exist in the Iranian Islamic Republic.

1227 SICK, GARY. "Trial by Error: Reflections on the Iran-Iraq War." *MEJ* 43, no. 2 (March 1989): 230-245.

Examines several key turning points in the Iran-Iraq war and notes the major misjudgements that were made by nearly all parties involved.

1228 SYNDER, ROBERT. "Explaining the Iranian Revolution's Hostility to the United States." *JSAMES* 17, no. 3 (1994): 19-31.

Explores the reasons behind the Islamic Republic's antagonism towards the United States through a historical survey of the U.S. role in pre-revolutionary Iran.

1229 TEHRANIAN, MAJID. "Islamic Fundamentalism in Iran and the Discourse of Development." *Fundamentalisms and Society: Reclaiming the Sciences, the Family, and Education*, 341- 373. Eds. Martin E. Marty, and R. Scott Appleby. Chicago and London: The University of Chicago Press, 1991.

Examines the influence of Islamic discourse and its subsequent implementation on Iranian media and educational systems in post-revolutionary Iran. Also, looks at the role of the media and educational systems in creating and disseminating information about the Iranian Islamic movement before the revolution.

1230 TERMOURIAN, HAZHIR. "Iran's 15 Years of Islam." *WT* 50, no. 4 (1994): 67-70.

This essay comments on the religious, economic, and political problems facing Iran as well as outlining reasons why the author believes the revolution has failed.

1231 TOPRAK, BINNAZ. "The Reception of the Iranian Revolution by the Muslim Press in Turkey." *The Iranian Revolution and the Muslim World*, 250-260. Ed. David Menashri. Boulder, CO: Westview Press, 1990.

Through an examination of the Muslim press in Turkey, this article summarizes the various reactions of Muslim Turks to the Iranian revolution.

1232 TUCKER, ROBERT E. "Trench in Post Revolutionary Iranian Education." *JCA* 21, no. 4 (1991): 455-468.

Examines the impact of renewed religious values on official education. Argues that traditional Western literature on development and education is weak for a case like Iran.

1233 WEINRAUCH, JAMES. "Iran's Response to U.N. Resolution 598: The Role of Factionalism in the Negotiation Process." *AAA* 31 (December 1989): 15-28.

Through an examination of political factionalism in Iran, the author provides insight into Iran's willingness to submit to enter into formal negotiations to end the Iran-Iraq war.

1234 WRIGHT, ROBIN. *In the Name of God: The Khomeini Decade*. New York: Simon & Schuster, 1989.

A straight forward report written by a journalist whose main thesis is that Iran's strategic location and its oil wealth make Iran "too important to be ignored." The work begins with a historical survey of Iran up to the Iranian Revolution, and then discusses the jockeying for power after the revolution as well as the Ayatollah Khomeini's attempts to mediate between them. The author devotes a large portion of the book to Iran's war with Iraq including an analysis of its origin, Iran's defeats and victories, the role of the army, Revolutionary Guards, and the martyr children. The book concludes with an analysis of short-term prospects for Iran in light of the Ayatollah's death and relatively smooth transition of power.

1235 ZANGENEH, HAMID, ed. *Islam, Iran, and World Stability*, New York: St. Martin's Press, 1994.

An edited volume of essays providing analysis on the past, present, and future of Iran. The nine articles included in this work deal with a variety of issues including Iranian foreign policy; the role of Islam in the new world order; Iran's relations with Islamic resistance movements; and changes in Iran's economic policies.

1236   ZANGENEH, HAMID and JANICE M. MOORE. "Economic Development and Growth in Iran." *Islam, Iran, and World Stability*, 201-215. Ed. Hamid Zangeneh. New York: St. Martin's Press, 1994.

Comparison of pre- and post-revolutionary economic policies in Iran. Contends that immediately after the revolution, the government pursued policies that severely weakened the economy. These policies were pursued in an attempt to create and maintain political support.

1237   ZIBAKALAM, SADEGH. "The Genesis of the Islamic Revolution in Iran." *IC* 44, no. 2-3 (1990): 59-74.

Asserting that post-revolutionary political upheavals have commanded most of the academic attention, this essay explores the evolution of the Iranian revolution.

J.   Turkey

1238   AHMAD, FEROZ. "Politics and Islam in Modern Turkey." *MES* 27, no. 1 (1991): 3-21.

Notes the struggles that the Islamists have had in Turkey in achieving some kind of a "political breakthrough."

1239   BISHKU, MICHAEL B. "Ataturk's Legacy Versus Religious Reassertion: Secularism and Islam in Modern Turkey." *MQ* 3, no. 4 (September 1992): 75-93.

Addresses issues relating to Kemal Ataturk's nation-building in Turkey and the reassertion of Islam.

1240   HEPER, METIN. "The State, Religion and Pluralism: The Turkish Case in Comparative Perspective." *BJMES* 18, no. 1 (1991): 38-51.

Explores the relationship between the state and religion in Turkey which the author contends has been very different from that of other Muslim countries and has improved political pluralism in that country.

1241   MARDIN, SERIF. "The Nakshibendi Order of Turkey." *Fundamentalisms and The State: Remaking Polities, Economies, and Militance*, 204-232. Eds. E. Martin Marty, and R. Scott Appleby. Chicago and London: The University of Chicago Press, 1991.

Explores the Turkish Nakshibendi Sufi order in relation to specific important points of time in Islamic history. Gives an overview of the group's image in modern-day Turkey, its history, identity models, ideology and political impact in past and present.

1242 ÖZBUDUN, ERGUN. "Khomeinism--A Danger for Turkey?" *The Iranian Revolution and the Muslim World*, 242-249. Ed. David Menashri. Boulder, CO: Westview Press, 1990.

Discusses the influence of the Iranian revolution and Ayatollah Khomeini's political Islamic vision on Turkish Islamic groups and the political system in Turkey.

1243 SAYARI, SABRI. "Islam and International Relations in Turkey." *Cultural Transitions in the Middle East*, 214-224. Ed. Serif Mardin. Leiden: E.J. Brill, 1994.

Through an examination of a Turkish publication with a prominent Islamist editor, this chapter looks at Muslim attitudes concerning Turkey's foreign policy, particularly Turkey's relations with the West.

1244 STARR, JUNE. "Islam and the Struggle over State Law in Turkey." *Law and Islam in the Middle East*, 77-98. Ed. Daisy Hilse Dwyer. New York: Bergin & Garvey, 1990.

Based on sixteen months of empirical research in southwestern Turkey between 1966-1968, this article presents the extent to which national secular law is followed in a remote and rural area. The author asserts that differing types of legal systems, village and national, provide greater freedom for litigants to seek out a more advantageous outcome for their own particular case.

1245 _____. *Law as Metaphor: From Islamic Courts to the Palace of Justice.* Albany: State University of New York Press, 1992.

Explores the question of how the political elites in Turkey managed to replace Islamic law with secular codes given the pervasiveness of Islam in Ottoman and Turkish societies. Divided into three parts, the first examines how the Ottoman reformers of the 19th century had begun to shift away from Islamic law to secular law in order to preserve the empire. The second assesses the transformation of land law and administration in the 19th century as well as the impact of the Turkish Civil Code of 1926. The third section focuses on various aspects of the process of conflict resolution.

1246 TINAZ, NURI. "Religion, Politics and Social Change in Modern Turkey." *HI* 14, no. 4 (December 1991): 67-104.

Analyzes the minimalization of Islam in political affairs during the period in which Kemal Ataturk's secular reforms took place in Turkey. Also looks at the role Islam has played in the political sphere since that time.

Author Index

RABOOY, M., 0249
RAGOONATH, BISHNU, 0699
RAHMATULLAH, 0262
RAHNEMA, ALI, 0188, 0189,
  1202
RAIS, RASUL BAKHSH, 0855
RAJAEE, FARHANG, 1203, 1204,
  1205
RAM, HAGGAY, 1206, 1207
RAMADAN, ABDEL AZIM, 0976
RAMAZANI, NESTA, 0448
RAMAZANI, R. K., 1208, 1209,
  1210, 1211
RAPPORT, DAVID C., 0190
RASHAD, AHMAD, 1057
RASHID, AHMED, 0772
RASHID, SAMORY, 0700
RASHIDUZZAMAN, M., 0815,
  0816
RASSAM, AMAL, 0449
RAZA, MOHAMMAD S., 0904
RAZAVI, SHAHRASHOUB, 0450
RAZI, HOSSEIN G., 0191
REEBER, MICHAEL, 0905
REED, S., 0977
REEVES, MINOU, 0451
REGAN, DANIEL, 0874
REKHESS, ELIE, 1058
REZUN, MIRON, 1212, 1213,
  1214
RIEDAL, TIM H., 1012
REKHESS, ELIE, 0938
REZUN, MIRON, 0734
RICKS, THOMAS, 1215
RIESEBRODT, MARTIN, 1216
ROBERSTON, B. A., 0906
ROBERTS, HUGH, 0586, 0587,
  0588, 0589, 0590
ROBINS, PHILIP, 1004
RO'I, YACCOV, 0773, 0774
ROOIJACKERS, M., 0907, 0920
RORLICH, AZADE-AYSE, 0775
ROSE, GREGORY F., 1217

ROSS-SHERIF, FARIYAL, 0701,
  0702
ROY, DELIVIN A., 0263
ROY, OLIVIER, 0192, 0776, 0804,
  0805, 0806, 0807
RUBIN, BARRY, 0978
RUEDY, JOHN, 0562, 0591
RUGH, ANDREA B., 0979
RUMER, BORIS Z., 0777
RUSSELL, MONA L., 0452
RYWKIN, MICHAEL, 0778

EL SAADAWI, NAWAL, 0453
SABAGH, GEORGE, 0704
SABBAGH, SUHA, 0454, 0455
SACHEDINA, ABDULAZIZ A.,
  0193, 0705, 0939
SADOWOSKI, YAHYA, 0526
SAEED, JAVAID, 0940
SAFFARI, SAID, 1218
SAFI, LOUAY M., 0194
SAGIV, DAVID, 0980
SAHARA, TETSUYA, 0908
SAID, ABDUL AZIZ, 0195
SAIF, WALID, 0196
SAIKAL, AMIN, 1219
SAIVETZ, CAROL R., 0779, 0780
SAJEDI, AMIR, 0941
SALAME, GHASSAN, 0197
SALEH, NABIL, 0264
SALEM, NEHAD, 0456
SALEM, PAUL, 0198
SAMMUT, DENNIS, 0600
SANAD, JAMAL, 0457
SANASARIAN, ELIZ, 0458
SANDER, A., 0909
SANNEH, LAMIN, 0542
SARABI, FARZIN, 1220
SARMA, JONATHAN D., 0706
SAROYAN, MARK, 0781
SATLOFF, ROBERT, 1059
SAVORY, ROGER M., 0527,
  1221, 1222, 1223

Title Index

"Attitudes of Immigrant Women and Men in the Dearborn Area Toward Women's Employment and Welfare," 0298

"Attitudes to Female Empowerment in Four Middle Eastern Countries," 0442

"Authority and Community in Soviet Islam," 0781

"The Authority of the Past: Current Paradigms for an Islamic Future," 0090

"An Autobiographical Voice: Forugh Farrokhzad," 0370

"Ayatollah Khomeini's Islamic Legacy," 1173

"The Ayatollah, the Novelist, and the West," 1199

"Ayodhya and the Politics of Indian Secularism: A Double-Standards Discourse," 0829

"Backlash to the Destruction at Ayodhya: A View from Pakistan," 0828

"Bangladesh at the Crossroads: Religion and Politics," 0813

"Banking and Credit Rationing Under the Islamic Republic of Iran," 0266

"The Battle for Egypt," 0977

The Battle Looms: Islam and Politics in the Middle East: A Report to the Committee on Foreign Relations, United States Senate, 0937

"Behind the Veil Debate," 0375

"Bektashi Tekke and the Sunni Mosque of Albanian Muslims in America," 0716

"Benazir Bhutto and Future of Women in Pakistan," 0488

"A Benign Brotherhood?," 0975

Between Qur'an and Crown: The Challenges of Political Legitimacy in the Arab World, 0209

"Beyond Renewal: The *Jadid* Response to Pressure for Changing in the Modern Age," 0760

"Binding Religion: Moroccan and Turkish Runaway Girls," 0313

"Biography and Women's History: On Interpreting Doria Shafik," 0439

The Black Muslims in America, 0685

"Blaming the System or Blaming the Victim? Structural Barriers Facing Muslims in Western Europe," 0913

"The Body as Evil," 0333

"Brother/Sister Relationships: Connectivity, Love and Power in the Reproduction of Arab Patriarchy," 0379

"The Case for Muslim Constitutional Interpretive Activity in the United States," 0690

"Central Asia As Part of the Modern Muslim World," 0784

"Central Asian Islam: Fundamentalist Threat or Communist Bogeyman," 0748

"Central Asia's Islamic Awakening," 0767

"Certain Knowledge, Contestable Authority: Power and Practice on the Islamic Periphery," 0548

"Chadli's Perestroika," 0594

"The Challenge of Muslim 'Minorityness': The American Experience," 0661

"Continuities and Discontinuities in the Algerian Confrontation with Europe," 0591

"Continuity and Change in the Soviet Policy: The Gulf Crisis and the Islamic Dimension," 0752

"Controlled or Autonomous: Identity and the Experience of the Network, Women Living under Muslim Laws," 0460

"The Convenience of Subservience in Women and the State of Pakistan," 0377

"Convergence and Divergence in an Emergent Community: A Study of Challenges Facing U.S. Muslims," 0696

"Conversations Among Iranian Political Exiles on Women's Rights: Implications for the Community-Self Debate in Feminism," 0308

"A Countersensational Perspective on the Shi'a of Lebanon," 1025

The Crescent in the East: Islam in Asia Major, 0729

"The Crisis of Authoritarianism in North Africa: The Case of Algeria," 0573

"A Critique of Modernist Synthesis in Islamic Thought: Special Reference to Political Economy," 0054

"Crushing the Opposition: Adversaries of the Islamic Republic of Iran," 1206

Culinary Cultures of the Middle East, 0232

"The Cult of Holy Places: Religious Practices Among Soviet Muslims," 0782

"Cultural Relations Between the West and the World of Islam: Meeting Points and Possibilities of Co-operation in the Academic Level," 0227

"Da'wah in the West," 0697

"Death in Algiers," 0576

Debating Muslims: Cultural Dialogues in Postmodernity and Tradition, 0081

"The Decline of Islamic Fundamentalism," 0014

"A Defining Moment: Palestinian Islamic Fundamentalism," 1049

The Demise of Egyptian State Feminism and the Politics of Transition (1980-1991), 0362

"Democracy and Islam: The Cultural Dialectic," 0535

"Democracy and the Crisis of Governability in Pakistan," 0523

"Democracy Derailed," 0511

"Democracy in Islam," 0524

"Democracy in Jordan," 0498

"Democracy in Jordan: Election Results Send Mixed Signals on Peace Process and Islamists," 1014

"Democracy in the Middle East: The American Connection," 0499

"Democratization and Changing Gender Roles in Egypt," 0473

"Democratization and Islam," 0509

"Democratization in Egypt: The 'Algeria Complex,'" 0969

The Development of Arab-American Identity, 0687

"The Development of Islamic Banking and the Money Multiplier Process," 0241

"The Development of the Thought of Sayyid Qutb," 0201

"Development Studies and Women in the Middle East: The Dilemmas of Research and Development," 0280

"Devises and Desires: Population Policy and Gender Roles in the Islamic Republic," 0371

"A Different Voice: Taj os-Saltaneh," 0435

"Discourse, Power and Ideology in Modern Islamic Revivalist Thought: The Case of Sayyid Qutb," 0008

"Discovering the South: Sudanese Dilemmas for Islam in Africa," 1066

"Diversity in Rochester's Islamic Community," 0712

"Divorce in Contemporary Iran: A Male Prerogative in Self-Will," 0352

"Doctrinaire Economics and Political Opportunism in the Strategy of Algerian Islamism," 0588

"The Domestic Power Struggle and the Fourth Iranian Majlis Elections," 1179

"Double Demons: Cultural Impedance in U.S.-Iranian Understanding," 1108

Dreams of Trespass: Tales of a Harem, 0414

"The Druze in the United States," 0664

The Dynamics of the Iranian Revolution - The Pahlavis Triumph and Tragedy, 1093

"The Dynamics of Women's Sphere of Action in Rural Iran," 0342

"The Early Arab Immigrant Experience," 0693

"Early Islam and the Position of Women: The Problem of Interpretation," 0286

"Economic Development and Growth in Iran," 1236

"The Economic Impact of Islamic Fundamentalism," 0251

"Economic Morality in Islam," 0261

"Education and the Culture of Politics in the Islamic Republic of Iran," 1193

Education and the Making of Modern Iran, 1180

"Egalitarian Islam and Misogynist Islamic Tradition: A Critique of the Feminist Reinterpretation of Islamic History and Heritage," 0283

"Egypt: An Uneasy Portent of Change," 0972

Egypt and the Crisis of Islam, 0954

"The Egyptian and Iranian Ulama at the Threshold of Modern Social Change: What Does and What Does Not Account for the Difference?," 0163

"Egyptian Discourses on Gender and Political Liberalization: Do Secularist and Islamist Views Really Differ?," 0364

"Egypt's Islamic Group: Regional Revenge?," 0957

"Egypt's Islamists and the State: From Complicity to Confrontation," 0944

"Egypt's Uneasy Party Politics," 0947

"Elderly Muslim Immigrants: Needs and Challenges," 0701

"Elite Factionalism in the Post-Revolutionary Iran," 1175

"Elite Strategies for State Building: Women, Family, Religion and State in Iraq and Lebanon," 0381

"Muslims in Botswana," 0541

"Muslims in Britain, Some Recent Developments," 0881

Muslims in Central Asia: Expressions of Identity and Change, 0753

"Muslims in Europe: The Lost Tribes of Islam," 0897

"Muslims in Los Angeles," 0680

"Muslims in Montreal," 0688

"Muslims in North America: Mate Selection as an Indicator of Change," 0644

"Muslims in Prison: Claims to Constitutional Protection of Religious Liberty,"
    0692

"The Muslims in San Diego," 0671

"Muslims in Seattle," 0635

"Muslims in Western Europe," 0882

"Muslims in the United States: History, Religion, Politics and Ethnicity," 0637

"Muslims, Islam and the West Today," 0056

The Muslims of America, 0663

"The Muslims of Burma," 0798

"The Muslims of Indianapolis," 0676

"Muslims of the Former USSR: Dynamics of Survival," 0769

The Nakshibendi Order of Turkey," 1241

"National and International Aspects of Feminist Movements: The Examples of the
    Iranian Revolution of 1978-79," 0462

"National Development and Political Protest: Islamists in the Maghreb Countries,"
    0560

"National Identity and Religious Discourse in Contemporary Oman," 0989

"National Identity: Fundamentalism and the Women's Movement in Bangladesh,"
    0465

"The National Islamic Front and the Politics of Education," 1065

"National Mobility, War Conditions, and Gender Consciousness," 0392

"Nationalism and Feminism: Palestinian Women and the *Intifada* - No Going
    Back?," 0271

"Nationalism and Islamic Resurgence in Uzbekistan," 0747

"Nationalism and Nation Building in Islam," 0627

"Nationalism, Islamic Revival and the Need for a New Political Discourse in the
    Middle East: A Response for Hisham Sharabi," 0060

"The Nature of Islamic Resurgence in Near and Middle Eastern Muslim Societies,"
    0134

"The Nature of the Community in the Middle East: A Case Study of Sudan," 1076

Nature of the Islamic Community, 0137

"Net Working Capital Versus Net Owner's Equity Approaches to Computing
    Zakatable Amount: A Conceptual Comparison and Application," 0239

"The Next Disorderly Half Century: Some Proposed Remedies," 0175

"Women's Issues in Modern Islamic Thought," 0469

"Women's Resistance in the Arab World and in Egypt," 0453

"Women's Rights in the Arab Nation," 0456

Women's Rights in the Arab World, 0483

"Women's Struggles and Strategies in the Rise of Fundamentalism in the Muslim
   World: From Entryism to Internationalism," 0367

"Women's Subordination in Turkey: Is Islam Really the Villain?," 0384

"Workman's Bonus: *Shari'ah* Arguments For and Against," 0268

A World of Difference: Islam and Gender Hierarchy in Turkey, 0408

"The Worldview of Sunni Arab Fundamentalists: Attitudes Toward Modern
   Science and Technology," 0217

"Yemeni and Lebanese Muslim Immigrant Women in Southeast Dearborn,
   Michigan," 0299

"The Yemenis of Delano: A Profile of a Rural Islamic Community," 0657

"Youth Viewers of Pakistan Television (PTV) and the Enculturation Model of the
   Islamization Process: Towards Exploring Some Empirical Basics," 0843

Subject Index

Sanusiya, 0135
Satanic Verses, 0022, 0040, 0159,
0181, 0184, 1102 (*also see*
Salman Rushdie)
Saudi Arabia, 0038, 0101, 0754,
0985
-Islamic opposition in, 0993
-relations with Iran, 0941, 0991,
1128, 1171
-Shi'a, uprising in, 0993
scriptural essentialism, 0052
sects, 0039, 0047, 0130
sectarianism, 0212
secular leaders, 0024
secularism, 0150, 0215, 0216, 0562
secularization, 0012, 0090, 0096,
0150, 0209, 0560, 0563
security issues, 0149
sedition, 0113
Senegal, 0537
science, 0151, 0217
Shafik, Doria, 0439
Shaltut, Mahmud, 0228, 0229
Shamil, 0751
Sharabi, Hisham, 0060
Shar'iah, 0024, 0028, 0030, 0113,
0115-0117, 0157, 0215, 0216,
0253, 0264, 0269, 0792, 0967,
0973, 0976, 0985 (*also see*
Islamic law)
Shari'ati, Ali, 0167, 0188, 0189,
0208, 0477, 1083, 1124, 1162
Shari'atmadari, Ayatollah, 1112
Shi'a, 0028, 0067, 0081, 0086,
0107, 0130, 0152, 0193, 0197,
0220, 1006, 1007, 1134
-Ithna 'Ashari, 1221
-Sunni-Shi'a relations, 0925,
1005, 1053, 1164, 1171
Shi'i
-clergy, 1003
-fundamentalism, 1216
-ideology, 1090

-jurisprudence, 1099
-modernism, 0174
-political activism in
India, 0822
Iran, 0141, 0153, 0939
Iraq, 0153, 0939
Lebanon, 0153, 0939, 1015,
1016, 1025, 1027-1030
-political activists, 0939
-political thought, 0039, 0138,
0141, 0155, 0193, 0198,
0212, 0925, 0939, 1098
-radicalism, 0205
-symbols, 1083
Shi'ism (*see* Shi'a)
shrines, 0062
shura, 0246, 0497
Shqaqi, Fathi 'Abd al-'Aziz, 1053
Sivan, Emmanuel, 0118
slavery, 0415
socialism, 0243
Somalia, 0546
South Africa, 0539, 0540, 0544,
0545,
South Asia, 0749, 0750, 0792-
0798
-Muslim communities, 0795,
0796
Southeast Asia, 0857-0863
-Iranian Revolution, 0863
-Islam, 0857
Soviet Union, 0139, 0741-0744,
0748, 0751, 0762, 0763, 0777
(*also see* Cold War)
-Islam in the, 0745-0747,
0757-0759, 0766
-Muslim holy places, 0782
-Muslims in, 0774
-relations with
Afghanistan, 0799, 0804
Iran, 0764, 0780
Soviet
-foreign policy, 0749, 0752

About the Authors

YVONNE YAZBECK HADDAD is Professor of History of Islam and Christian-Muslim Relations at Georgetown University. Her earlier publications include *Contemporary Islam and the Challenge of History, Christian-Muslim Encounters, Muslims of America,* and *Contemporary Islamic Revival* (with John L. Esposito and John Voll, Greenwood, 1991).

JOHN L. ESPOSITO is Professor of Religion and International Affairs and Director of the Center for Muslim-Christian Understanding: History and International Affairs at the Edmund A. Walsh School of Foreign Service, Georgetown University. He is Editor-in-Chief of *The Oxford Encyclopedia of the Modern Islamic World* and author of *The Islamic Threat: Myth or Reality?* as well as several other books on Islam, including *Contemporary Islamic Revival* (with Yvonne Yazbeck Haddad and John Voll, Greenwood, 1991).

ELIZABETH HIEL was a research assistant at Georgetown University's Center for Muslim-Christian Understanding and has a master's degree from the Arab Studies Program at Georgetown. For several years, she worked as Director of Publications at the U.S.-Arab Chamber of Commerce in Washington, D.C., and she is currently a reporter for the *Blade* in Toledo, Ohio.

HIBBA ABUGIDEIRI is a doctoral candidate in history at Georgetown University and a research assistant at its Center for Muslim-Christian Understanding. Her research interest is focused on issues of gender and Islam about which she has published several articles and lectured both nationally and internationally.

ISBN 0-313-30480-7

HARDCOVER BAR CODE